PASSPORT'S GUIDES

ETHNIC

NEW ORLEANS

*A Complete Guide
to the Many Faces
& Cultures of
New Orleans*

MARTIN HINTZ

Printed on recyclable paper

PASSPORT BOOKS
a division of *NTC Publishing Group*
Lincolnwood, Illinois USA

To Sandy, for the next journey

Library of Congress Cataloging-in-Publication Data

Hintz, Martin.
    Passport's guide to ethnic New Orleans : a complete guide to the
many faces & cultures of New Orleans / Martin Hintz.
       p.   cm.
    Includes bibliographical references and index.
    ISBN 0-8442-9529-9 : $14.95
    1. New Orleans (La.)—Guidebooks. 2. Ethnology—Louisiana—New
Orleans. I. Title. II. Title: Ethnic New Orleans.
F379.N53H55   1995
917.63⊖50463—dc20   94-44397
                                                                       CIP

Cover Photos: Courtesy of Greater New Orleans Trade
& Convention Commission

Published by Passport Books, a division of NTC Publishing Group.
© 1995 by Martin Hintz

5 6 7 8 9 ML 0 9 8 7 6 5 4 3 2 1

Contents

Acknowledgments v

Introduction vii

1. The Crescent City 1
2. Creole/Cajun New Orleans 48
3. Irish New Orleans 63
4. German New Orleans 82
5. Italian New Orleans 94
6. Jewish New Orleans 113
7. African-American New Orleans 123
8. Hispanic/Caribbean New Orleans 157
9. Asian New Orleans 189
10. Other Communities

 Australian/New Zealand New Orleans 219

 Greek New Orleans 220

 Croatian New Orleans 222

 Middle Eastern New Orleans 224

 Suggested Readings 225

Maps

 Greater New Orleans iv
 The St. Charles Avenue District 6
 The Faubourg Marigny District 53
 The Irish Channel District 69
 The Canal Street District 89
 The Warehouse District 104
 The Lower Garden District 135
 The Lafayette Square District 165

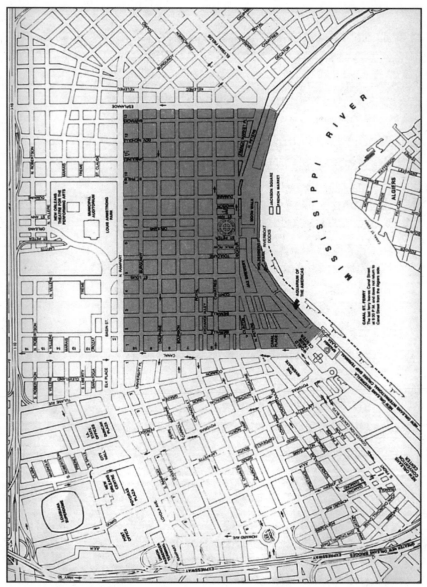

Greater New Orleans

Acknowledgments

The author would like to thank the citizens of New Orleans, of all nationalities, for their input, assistance, and friendliness. It is risky to mention names for fear of leaving out someone important, but there are many individuals to whom credit is due. Among them are Beverly Gianna and her staff at the Greater New Orleans Tourist and Convention Bureau; Mary Andrey at the Urban League of Greater New Orleans; Joseph Maselli, President of the American Italian Museum and Research Library; Syed B. Ali, President of the Pakistani Community Association; Kiem Do, President of the Asia Pacific American Society; Dan Lincove of Touro Synagogue; Robert Brandstator of the Jewish Federation of New Orleans; Dr. Rodney Jung and Henry Scanlon of the Irish Cultural Society of New Orleans; Hibernian Al Hennessy; Wayne Coleman, archivist at the Amistad Research Center; Caletha Powell and Deborah A. Sells of the Greater New Orleans Black Tourism Network; Attorney Richard Kuntz and Charles Hadley of the Deutsches-Haus; and Sandra Dartus, Executive Director of the French Quarter Festivals.

Among many media friends are food reviewer Linda Serio; editors Linda Powers and Louise McKinney of *Where: New Orleans* magazine; Jan Ramsey, Editor of *Offbeat* magazine; Ernesto Schweikert III, President and General Manager of KGLA-AM; and Bette Cadwell, Editor of the *Italian American Digest.* At the *Times Picayune* newspaper is ethnic reporter and columnist Tina Soong, as well as other staffers who provided many helpful leads and suggestions.

Regarding transportation and tours, thanks to Carrie Byron, Public Relations Coordinator for the New Orleans International Airport; Peggy Mahoney, Public Relations Director of Continental Airlines; Inez Douglas of Tours by Inez; and Gray Line of New Orleans. Thanks to the National Park Service's Jim Miculka, Chief of Interpretation, and anthropologist

Allison Pena. Special regards to the gang at the Hotel LaSalle on Canal and Rampart Streets. They keep a tidy, inexpensive house.

What would we be without history and backgrounders? Thank you, librarians at the Jefferson Parish Library; historians Mel Leavitt and Evans Casso; and Tulane University anthropologist Munro Edmundson. Among the many books I read about New Orleans to prepare for this guide, *Beautiful Crescent: A History of New Orleans* by authors Joan B. Garvey and Mary Lou Widmer, is a delightful resource.

Thanks also go to the Latin American Library at Tulane University and the Center for Pacific Area Studies at the University of New Orleans for all their extra help.

Apologies for anyone I've missed by name, and there are certainly many of them. So thanks to all the chefs, late-night sax players, bump-and-grind ladies, top-hatted doormen, fast-patter hustlers, earringed art students, tuxedoed bartenders, attentive waitresses, clergy, festival soundmen, hard-driving businesswomen, nightclub managers, savvy bus drivers, social workers, knowledgeable guides, shopkeepers, chatty radio deejays, beefy bouncers, concerned desk clerks, scholars, and plain ol' street folks who offered insights on what makes their town so wonderfully terrific.

Introduction

New Orleans: the city that never sleeps, the city where both the saints and sinners come marching in. The Big Easy. The Crescent City. Convention-ville. A city born in the swampy, gator-mud, now with its head in the sky. Eight different national flags have flown over this city's rooftops over the last dozen generations, their bright colors proclaiming fleur-de-lis French, monarchist Spanish, Bonaparte French, rough-and-tumble American, Independent Louisianian, Confederate, and the energetic Stars and Stripes once more.

This is a not a shoulder-shoving town like brawny New York or a town pushy with Chicago brashness, nor is it Caribbean-turgid like Miami or health-faddish like Los Angeles. New Orleans is its own Creole-cautious self in the steamy heat, where high-powered business deals and passionate dalliances are confirmed in the restaurant courtyards of Conte Street, the mansion gardens along St. Charles Avenue, or the glittering office towers on Poydras in the CBD (that's the Central Business District, y'all).

New Orleans, an Oz city bigger than ordinary life, is a creature equal parts fable and fact. With its reputation made in movies, books, and song, the city is its own public relations agent—a Barnum with a Southern drawl. One part holy, one part profane, even New Orleans's statues are of patrons made from a mold beyond the ordinary. Fiery young Joan of Arc, the Maid of Orleans, carries her banner high on a pedestal at Rivergate, outside the Tower of Mammon, the World Trade Center which backs up against the commercial bustle of the Mississippi River. Not far away, on the tiny Hilton Hotel lawn, is a bronze rendition of bulldoggy Winston Churchill holding up a hand in the *V* sign for victory (wags say he's just ordering two more absinthes from the bar). Confederate Robert E. Lee perches Zeuslike atop his 60-foot-high Doric column in Lee Circle. In Jackson Square, Old Hickory, General Andrew Jackson, has been astride his delicately balanced rearing horse since 1856 (sculptor Clark Mills interchanged heads on similar statues and peddled them to various Latin American dictators for placement in their plazas). At Basin and Iberville is a monument to the Vietnamese and American vets of the horrific Vietnam War.

New Orleans is a city of wonderful contrasts, of sloe-eyed comparisons between imagination and reality. The outbound spirit of a *Streetcar Named Desire* carries visitors deep into hushed summer dawns, returning in shadowed nights with wraiths redolent in white linen suits and panama hats. This is a town where "thank you, ma'ams" hang like fringe on silken umbrellas. Morning along the French Quarter's nightclub row evokes the scent of a naughty street fair stricken with a day-old hangover, while the avenues in the Garden District at dawn have a hint of mint julep in their perfumed air.

The evenings and autumns can be cool and fair, touched by the headiness of magnolia and bay leaf. The twilight lullaby is tempered by the sweet sounds of jazz—the soul-searing stuff of back-bedroom heat and on-stage explosion, a music that has indelibly marked New Orleans as The Scene.

A web of ethnic history entwines this city. Ghosts of light-fingered gamblers prowl the landings, chocolate-skinned dandies lurk beneath moss-draped dueling oaks; quadroon balls burst with magnificent décolletage. Night rhythms echo through the heart; twirling crimson parasols lead "second line" revelers away from cemeteries aptly but eerily tagged "Cities of the Dead."

And, yes, the dead live in New Orleans' underworld, which is the Voodoo Capital of America. Here belief in the beyond is easy to come by, and it is not unusual to have a picnic in a cemetery to celebrate the next level of existence. Death has always been a way of life in New Orleans. Witness the cruel epidemics of yellow fever, the dreaded Yellow Jack that made summers in the city a feared place to be. Or the cholera, the wars, the hunger of the early days.

This is a city that has a raw, dangerous edge, where poverty is just as severe as in any major urban area in the country. The *Times Picayune* newspaper keeps a daily box score on murders and military medics in training use local hospitals as on-the-spot proving grounds. So having fun as a traveler entails being smart, sticking to the well-traveled roads when appropriate, and accepting New Orleans for what it is: a thesaurus of bawdy, brash, feline, slick, snarling, wild, smooth, upbeat, delicious, and down-home. This original Painted Lady is a love-it or hate-it town. And New Orleans doesn't care what any outsiders think. It remains the city's nature to let all its clean and dirty wash hang out on the same line.

In New Orleans, fiction is sometimes—but not always—separated from fact, just as opposite sides of the street are not parted by boulevards but by the colloquial "neutral grounds," where brash Yankees warily talked business with Creoles in the early days after the Louisiana Purchase. Finding one's own measure of truth about New Orleans necessitates a visit, not just reading a pamphlet or viewing a prancing Elvis in the movie *King Creole*.

Rough and tough it might be, but the city is not invulnerable. New Orleans is protected from the Mississippi River and the sluggish waters of Lake Pontchartrain by a wedding ring of massive levees and water gates, with seventeen pumping stations to keep the floods at bay. Yet the Father of Waters continues to nibble the toes of this child its fertility has spawned. The shoulder-shoving Ol' Man River just keeps rollin' along through its half-mile-wide channel off the docks of Jackson Square, 110 miles north of the Gulf of Mexico (ninety miles as the crow flies). The river carries hundreds of thousands of gallons of mud-chocolate water past dikes that today's New Orleanian hopes will keep the waters at bay. Usually the system works well, but sometimes a hurricane tosses a two-three punch toward the hunkered citizens.

"Nature don't stop at the city's stoop," grin the toothless old men along Dumaine Street. This underbelly of frailty keeps everyone honest, if not humble.

It's a city where the Mardi Gras cries of "Throw me something, mister" earn a handful of speakeasy Carnival doubloons and baubles, valueless except to the collector. Here almost anything is allowed behind the gift-shop-grinning masks of plaster and feathers, at least on brassy Bourbon Street—*the* place to sample the tacky, tawdry, and tempting. Now that the celebrated red lights of Storyville have been snuffed, you can still find a wild time at places like the Cat's Meow.

But there are many islands of quiet in this otherwise raucous town. Six hundred and fifty churches help. The Audubon Park Zoo, expansive City Park, or levee-side benches along the French Quarter's Moon Walk are other respites So if the tourist rush turns to sore-foot sorrow, there are places to curl away for a few minutes or hours to watch the passing color. Ethnic New Orleans is a gumbo of skin tones, accents, and heritages. There are no *barrios,* no enclaves of the Diaspora, no block on block of only Irish green or Chinatown firecrackers. New Orleans has created its own magnificent, marbled mélange of faces from a vast cultural rainbow of émigrés. Mixed neighborhoods, yes. But compact ghettos, no. Of all the magnificent culture in New Orleans, the African-American influence is the strongest, accounting for 65 percent of the population. However, the melding of cultural personalities makes New Orleans one of the most delightfully vibrant urban areas in America.

Witness the Scottish-Slav lunch counter operator named Callan Sinclair in McRory's department store at 1001 Canal Street, who makes the most wonderful, and least expensive, jambalaya in town (under three bucks for a heaping plate). And there's no reason to question that the best beer taps are carefully poured by Joe Balthazar, who for the past thirty years has presented a proper Teutonic elegance in Kolb's German restaurant. With nary a drop of Bavarian blood, Balthazar can trace his heritage through a wonderfully assorted mixture of Spanish, French, Native American, and African-American.

Is New Orleans totally French? Not really. Savvy East Indian tycoons now have a corner on the Spanish-style real estate of the French Quarter, a neighborhood that was primarily Sicilian for almost half a century. Korean shopkeepers sell Mardi Gras masks. Vietnamese choirs fill the churches. Pierre Maspero's slave market at the corner of St. Louis and Chartres streets is now an upscale restaurant.

So if you're looking for ethnic variety, you've come to the right place. Tolerant? Generally. Virtuous? Hardly. But that's New Orleans, where the sun rises on the West Bank of the Mississippi River and sets on the East Bank. Somehow, it all makes sense to throw away a compass and a clock when coming here, because in New Orleans the twain do meet.

Editor's note: As is true for many American cities, New Orleans' ethnic neighborhoods are no longer clearly delineated. The maps that accompany the text are intended to show areas that are identified historically with different ethnic groups. We would like to thank the New Orleans Historic District Landmarks Commission for its help in the preparation of these maps.

chapter one

The Crescent City

History and Settlement

Cypress tangles, alligators, disease, insects, humidity, water, water, and more water. And they built a city here?

Of course.

The Crescent City, the City That Care Forgot, the Do-Whop City, America's Paris, Partyville U.S.A. By whatever name, New Orleans evolved from its rough-and-tumble past with an exuberant love of life. The city was shaped by a rainbow collection of nationalities who brought a wonderful mix of customs and traditions, creating a cultural gumbo perhaps more extravagantly diverse than any other urban society in North America. The Spanish, African, French, Irish, German, and Latin all played a part in creating today's exciting metroplex atop all that swampy muck. Lucky for contemporary conventioneers that they did.

But long before the Europeans arrived, clanking around the swamps with their surveying tapes and rods, the Native Americans lived off the land. The Choctaw, the Biloxi, the Mongoulacha, the Bayogoula, and others were hunters and gatherers who coexisted with nature, turning it to their own advantage without destroying it. Numerous native societies lived throughout the lower Mississippi Valley. They understood the importance of the narrow waterways that linked them with the world beyond their bayous. The secret routes connected the rushing muddy waters of the Great River and the relatively calm expanse of Lake Pontchartrain, which, at twenty-five miles wide and forty miles long, seems formidable at first glance. Over the centuries, Native Americans had perfected their portage and paddle connections all along the coast and upriver into Arkansas and supposedly as far north as Minnesota. They traded with indigenous people in Mexico, as well as deep in Latin America and even in the Caribbean islands. These extensive cultural exchanges were profitable. The tribes dealt in shells, furs, cotton blankets, turquoise, smoked fish, copper, baskets, and pottery. Pearls and quartz were often used as currency.

Despite the bugs and the sticky weather, the suctionlike mud, and the hungry 'gators, the first explorers took their clue from the Native Americans. When they saw the hummocks and other tufts of high ground, they imagined forts and ports where others might have seen only inhospitable land.

The Mississippi River has another 110 miles to go along its crooked way before finding the Gulf of Mexico. But the strategic location of lakes and riverways in the vicinity of what would become New Orleans were apparent, along with economic potential. After all, that was what exploration and colonization were all about—money.

As early as 1543, Spanish conquistadors had sloshed their way through the area, stirring up the egrets, discarding their litter, and moving on. Nobody else paid much attention until the late seventeenth century. In 1682, French explorer Robert Cavelier, Sieur de La Salle, cautiously edged his way out of Canada to explore the Mississippi River basin. Eventually reaching the Gulf of Mexico after months of struggle, he claimed the entire area drained by the river for foppish Louis the Great. Louie number fourteen, to be exact, was also known as the Sun King. La Salle, ever aware of his benefactor's expected largesse, called the area *Louisane* in honor of the bewigged king.

La Salle received permission by Louis to settle the new colony, but he was unable to find the mouth of the river on his return trip and somehow wound up in Texas. There he was murdered by his own exhausted and disgruntled men, on March 20, 1687.

For another decade, the French ignored their possessions in the Gulf. Only when the British began nosing around did Louis XIV order Pierre Le Moyne, Sieur d' Iberville, to establish a permanent colony. He assembled an eager band of French Canadians, an Italian or two, several Swiss mercenaries, slaves, and assorted Native American guides, as well as his younger brother, Jean-Baptiste Le Moyne, Sieur d' Bienville. The party reached the Gulf early in 1699, where they beached at Ship Island. Exploring the coast, they rediscovered the Mississippi as it entered the Gulf. The official records indicate the date as March 3, 1699. Since the date was Mardi Gras, the Tuesday before Ash Wednesday that kicked off the fasting period of Lent, D'Iberville named his camp in honor of the carnival day.

Next came forts at Biloxi, Mobile, Natchez, and other sites as the French solidified their hold on the region. In the meantime, Louis XIV had died and his great-grandchild took the throne as Louis XV. Since he was just a child, Louis's uncle, Philippe, duc d'Orleans, became regent. Under this administration, Scottish financier and speculator John Law gained the confidence of the duke and was given the go-ahead to exploit the Louisiana Territory. In 1717, Law plunged into the venture with gusto, making the savings and loan scandals of the 1980s look like a Boy Scout picnic. With a twenty-five-year charter under his arm, giving him almost free rein to do what he wanted, Law set about seeking colonists. He fired the first Louisiana governor and installed Bienville. In a scam called the Mississippi Bubble, Law sold worthless stock to European nobility and businesspeople in order to raise money. Law even got the French government to allow him to set up his own bank, one that would grant him unlimited credit.

Promising untold wealth in the New World, Law's agents scoured Europe and recruited hundreds of eager volunteers to populate the new French communities. To flesh out the ranks of the peasantry were prostitutes, the destitute, and debtors literally seized off the streets of France's major cities. For a time, judges were saying "death or Louisiana" to convicted criminals. Of course, all that met the emigrants there was hot air and hard times. There were no riches. They had to work hard to simply survive.

In 1718, Bienville surveyed the land near a large native village called Tchoutchouma, adjacent to the portage (along today's Esplanade Avenue) between the lake and the river. He fell in love with the crescent shape of the Mississippi and figured it would be *the* place for his city, to be called Nouvelle Orleans after the duc d'Orleans. His engineers thought he was crazy for choosing the site, at a bend in the swift-moving, 200-foot-deep river (across from where Algiers is located today). But Bienville persisted and eventually the first stockade and sheds were erected and the plats were laid out for what would become the French Quarter. Thus was a humble New Orleans born.

Bienville was supported by Law, who wanted his major port upriver from the mouth of the Mississippi, which was often closed by sandbars. Law figured that trading vessels from the north could dock at New Orleans, where goods would then be hauled overland and reloaded on other ships berthed on Lake Pontchartrain, connected to the Gulf via Chef Pass.

At first, many of the local Native Americans had to show the clumsy colonists how to make palmetto shelters. They shared their food when starvation loomed. Maize, pumpkins, wild rice, and beans were introduced to the newcomers. African slaves, used to the same semitropical weather, took the lessons to heart. Some escaped captivity and fled into the wilds to live with the tribes. For a time, according to Louisiana Historical Society research, the Native Americans held the balance of power between the two growing groups of whites and blacks. They were the only organized military force in the area, and they knew all the tricks of living in the lush but harsh wetlands. Although they traded with, protected, and cared for those first settlers, the Native Americans were not even considered human beings worthy of being Christianized. Many were enslaved by subsequent waves of better-armed colonizers. Those who escaped the slave-catchers died by the thousands of diseases carried in by the intruders. The survivors fought and died, fled, or were absorbed into the general population.

However, as late as 1795, Native Americans from Alabama were reported selling their baskets and earthenware in New Orleans' markets. Today only two small communities of Native Americans live near New Orleans, descendants of those first people of the Delta. The **Chitimacha Cultural Center** in Charenton (318-923-4830) is located on the Chitimacha Indian Reservation on Louisiana Highway 326, fronting the muddy waters of the Bayou Teche. The tribe and the National Park Service jointly administer the center, where intricately woven baskets and other artifacts made by tribal members can be purchased. The **Tunica-Biloxi Museum** (318-253-8174) is located on that tribe's reservation near Marksville. A building there houses an extensive array of Native American and European colonial-era kitchen utensils, clothing, and weapons.

Eventually, as more and more settlers poured into Louisiana, the city had to grow, following the curve of the river. As Bienville expected, it expanded economically and geographically, eventually absorbing the sugar plantations in the *faubourgs* (suburbs) that had sprung up around the original community. By 1737, New Orleans had become a crown colony, and the future of the city was ensured despite hurricanes, fires, and pestilence.

Through the Treaty of Fountainbleau in 1762 and confirmed by subsequent treaties, the colony was transferred from French to Spanish control. The French Creoles, who had been born in the colony, objected to the changeover and revolted when the new governor showed up. The rebellion was squashed in 1769 when the new administrator, Alexandro O'Reilly, an Irish soldier of fortune, showed up on the city's doorstep with a fleet and more troops.

During the American Revolution, the Spanish controlled New Orleans, sending troops and ships to divert British attention away from the rebellious colonies. They were convinced by New Orleans businessman Oliver Pollack that if the Spanish supported the rebels, they would be backing the winning horse in the race toward freedom. In 1779, England declared war on Spain, but Governor Bernardo de Galvez took his Louisiana-based army and wiped out British outposts from Alabama to Florida. His swift action helped secure the Americans' southern flank.

After the war, the Spanish and Americans signed the Treaty of San Lorenzo, which guaranteed various trade allowances and boosted the port of New Orleans into the big leagues. The harbor swarmed with ships, thousands of eager settlers arrived monthly, and the city was on its way to becoming one of the wealthiest in the New World.

When Napoleon Bonaparte came to power in France, he convinced the weaker Spaniards, under the gun, of course, that it would be in their best interest to hand Louisiana back to France. Under the Treaty of Ildefonso on October 1, 1800, the colony switched hands again. This geopolitical bullying made President Thomas Jefferson nervous, seeing a mighty European power making inroads in the South. He dispatched envoys to France to talk about making a deal hoping to purchase the port of New Orleans and West Florida. Napoleon, faced with the armed might of Europe arrayed against him and strapped for cash, agreed to talk. He subsequently sold not only New Orleans but all of Louisiana, much to the surprise of diplomat Robert Livingston, who headed the American delegation. The Louisiana Purchase was one of the largest land transactions in history. For a mere $15 million, the United States exploded in size, opening a vast new frontier and pointing the country toward new challenges.

Threatened again by the British during the War of 1812, the Battle of New Orleans in 1815 confirmed that the new Republic was slowly on its way to becoming a world power. With the defeat of the British army in front of the ramparts at Chalmette, just outside New Orleans, the United States proved it could stand on its own. Typical of the new America was the hodgepodge of Native Americans, free and enslaved blacks, Caribbean pirates, Kentucky riflemen, French Creoles, and representatives of dozens of other ethnic groups from the city who defeated the British.

Surviving Union occupation during the Civil War, followed by the rigors of Reconstruction, New Orleans continued to assert its economic muscle. Today some 6,000 freighters call on the port each year, making it second in volume only to New York. An estimated 160 million tons of cargo move through the warehouses annually, with Midwestern grain being a major export and Latin American bananas a prime import. Yet earlier in the century, even as New Orleans became financially stronger, the French Quarter slumped just before World War I, with many buildings in the city's heart slipping into decay when their owners moved to the

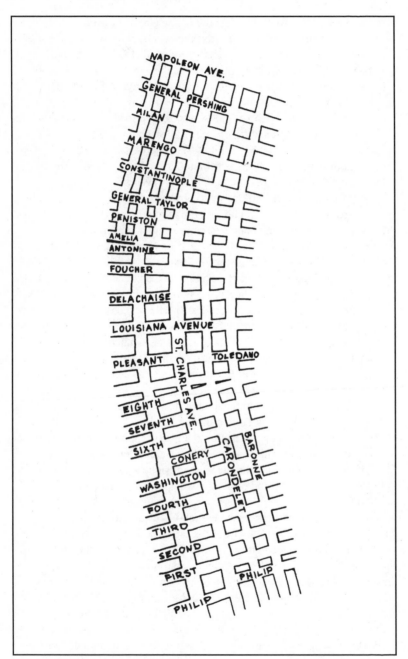

The St. Charles Avenue District

suburbs. However, in the 1920s, newcomers to the city moved in and began rehabbing the old properties. In 1936, the Louisiana legislature created the Vieux Carre Commission with the purpose of preserving the neighborhood's distinctive architecture.

Today, with city ordinances and the effective watchdog eyes of the Friends of the Cabildo, the Vieux Carre Property Owners Association, the Louisiana Landmarks Society, and others, the old quarter has recaptured and retained its charm. However, there is an ongoing battle between developers and preservationists, as more storefronts are gutted of their historic interiors, and souvenir shops and T-shirt outlets pop up.

Exemplifying the "new" New Orleans is the Louisiana Superdome. The 27-story-high structure seats 76,000 patrons, under a dome that covers 9.7 acres and is 273 feet above the surface of the interior football field. The construction of the Superdome cost $163 million; even without a calculator, that comes out to be more than 11 times what the Louisiana Purchase cost in 1803. Daily tours are available from 10 A.M. to 4 P.M., except during some events at the stadium. For tour information, call 504-587-3810.

A Bienville monument, designed by Angelo Gregory, was erected in the explorer's honor in 1955 at Union Station, 1001 Loyola Avenue. The statute depicts the Frenchman looking suitably founderish, along with a priest and a Native American.

The old and the new have a way of meeting in New Orleans.

About the City

New Orleans wants to ensure the best visit possible for its guests. As such, there is help in getting around the Crescent City. If you do get lost, that's part of the fun and excitement of exploring one of the most interesting cities in America. You won't get too far out of the way with all that surrounding water.

The city's tourist and convention commission offers a handy, free visitor's guide that contains listings of attractions and restaurants, plus maps and other pertinent tourist-related information. To obtain details about the city and a copy of the guide, contact the Greater New Orleans Tourist and Convention Commission in the Superdome, 1520 Sugar Bowl Drive, New Orleans, LA 70112 (504-566-5031 or 504-566-5011). Hours are Monday through Friday from 9 A.M. to 5 P.M.

The Louisiana Office of Tourism is located on Jackson Square, 529 St. Ann Street in the French Quarter. The office is open from 9 A.M. to 5 P.M. and is closed on major holidays (504-568-5661). There is also a visitor information center at New Orleans International Airport. You can also snatch up tons of those colorful, glossy guides, maps, fliers, and other printed material beckoning from racks and tables in every hotel lobby, at gift shops, in drugstores, in supermarkets, and at corner jazz clubs. The slick lures feature brassy photos of Hurricane drinks, maw-gaping alligators, splashing paddlewheelers, gleaming trumpets, second-line dancers, heaping plates of red beans and rice, toothy kids, and hat-bedecked mules pulling carriages packed with waving tourists. They tell the delights of old homes, restaurants, tours, gambling, and where to go to have fun. So, armed for late night hotel-room reading, plot a walking-gawking expedition and expect to find adventure at every corner. Well, almost every corner. There is a sign on a battered brick wall at the intersection of Camp and Cravier Streets that reads, "On this site in 1897, nothing happened outside the Commerce Restaurant." But even that is its own fascinating discovery!

New Orleans is a sensory town, where all systems are go when it comes to the eggbeater mix of sights, sounds, and scents. You'll feel your adrenalin pump and nerve endings tingle while strolling past fragrant gumbo shops, their red-pepper pungency exploding through open doors; late-night pinball parlors of flashing lights and whiz-bam-slam clanging jangle; wink-wink-neon strip joints with tuxedoed barkers out front who want to be your best pal; smoky rock clubs where every gyrating kid has a silver nose ring; or expensively cool jazz lounges where the bartenders wear Gibraltar-sized diamonds on each finger.

In New Orleans, the best music in the world is simply a five-minute walk away day and night, ranging from tap-dancing kids on Bourbon to the Neville Brothers in concert. Encircling all this is the powerful, rolling Mississippi River, which has layered its essence on every historical and contemporary aspect of the multiethnic city. Observe, touch, and soak in the elemental humor of the city's in-your-face street life, its business bustle and reflective retreat in backgarden courtyards. Being aware of all this, of soaking up absolutely everything, is the only way to learn what makes the Crescent City keep on rollin' along. Just wear comfortable shoes.

One of the best orientations to the ethnic background of the city, as well as to the entire Delta region, is touring **Jean Lafitte National Park and Preserve** (504-589-3882). The preserve is dedicated to forty different ethnic groups in Louisiana, illustrating the influence that the many cultures have had on the region's history and development. The National Park Service worked with the various nationalities to understand what rich, natural assets were significant to them and how their heritages could be brought to public attention. Subsequently, the preserve was created in

1978 out of small pockets of land scattered around New Orleans and the surrounding vicinity, according to National Park Service anthropologist Allison Pena.

Visitor services are available at the four principal park units that make up Jean Lafitte, each with individual characteristics: Barataria, Chalmette, New Orleans, and Acadian.

The **Barataria Preserve Unit** (504-589-2330) encompasses about 20,000 acres of swamp, hardwood forest, and freshwater marsh, some fifteen miles south of downtown New Orleans on the West Bank of the Mississippi River via the Crescent City Connection Bridge. Take Business Highway 90 (the West Bank Expressway) from downtown to Louisiana Highway 45 (Barataria Boulevard) over Crescent City Connection Bridge. The drive takes about a half hour, so look carefully for signs on the expressway for the Barataria exit; then drive six miles through the suburbs to the preserve. Admission to the area is free.

The visitor center highlights the wildlife in the region and the hunting, trapping, and fishing lifestyles of the Cajuns and Canary Islanders who originally settled here. Barataria was also the home of a pirate fleet that was the scourge of the Gulf Coast in the eighteenth century. The pirates, or corsairs, redeemed themselves during the Battle of New Orleans when their skilled gunners, under the keen eye of Lafitte's lieutenant Dominique, helped crush the mighty British army at the Battle of New Orleans. Eight miles of boardwalk and hard-surfaced trails, as well as twenty miles of canoe tours, allow close-up looks at muskrats, waterfowl, and other wildlife. There are picnic areas, canoe launches, and rest rooms along the way.

The **Chalmette Unit** (504-589-4430) covers the site of the Battle of New Orleans and a national cemetery. The bloody conflict on January 8, 1815 was the final "victory" of the War of 1812, even though it had taken place after the Treaty of Ghent was signed, which supposedly ended the fighting. The preserve's acreage was originally administered by the old War Department, the precursor to today's Department of Defense. It was established as Chalmette National Historical Park in 1939. Tourists can walk along a one-and-a-half-mile marked route that highlights the major aspects of the battle in which Andrew Jackson's ragtag multiracial forces whomped ten thousand spit 'n' polish British led by the Irish-born General Edward Packenham. In the murderous firefight, an estimated two thousand British and only seventy-one Americans were killed.

A visitor center is packed with exhibits from the War of 1812. A must-see is the thirty-minute movie depicting the battle. The on-grounds Beauregard House, built in 1833, is available for touring as well, currently featuring displays on life along the Mississippi River delta.

The Chalmette National Cemetery is adjacent to the battlefield; however, most burials there were Union soldiers from the Civil War era. The Chalmette Unit of the preserve is located on St. Bernard Highway (Louisiana Highway 46) in the town of Chalmette, approximately six miles east of downtown New Orleans.

The **New Orleans Unit** (504-589-2636) is described later in this chapter under the city walking tours. This section of the preserve encompasses the eighty-square-block French Quarter (the *Vieux Carre,* or old square), now a National Historic district.

Since New Orleans is not considered a "cajun" city, a visitor to Louisiana will learn more about Acadian culture by visiting the three units in the preserve that highlight this rich cultural background of the region. The **Prairie Acadian Cultural Center,** 250 W. Park Avenue, Eunice (318-262-6862), shows how the rich grasslands were ideal for crops and cattle raising. A live radio show, featuring cajun and its cousin zydeco music, is featured each Saturday evening in the Liberty Theater, which is adjacent to the visitor center. Call the center to confirm times and entertainers. Turn south off of Interstate 190 on 3rd Street to Park.

The **Wetland Acadian Cultural Center,** 314 St. Mary Street, Thibodaux, is located on the Bayou Lafourche, one of Louisiana's main water arteries. This center showcases the water-based life-style of the Acadians who settled in the area in the 1700s.

The **Lafayette Acadian Cultural Center** (318-232-0789) opened early in 1994 at the corner of Fischer Road and Surrey Street (Louisiana Highway 728-8). It houses general exhibits and displays on the entire Acadian heritage. A film chronicles the Acadian story, with pathos and enthusiasm in the appropriate segments. The Acadians were descendants of some of the first permanent settlers of Canada. Beginning in 1755, they were forcibly evicted from their homes for refusing to swear allegiance to the British crown after the French and Indian War. Thousands eventually made their way to Louisiana, a French colony at the time. The term *cajun* is a derivative of the word *Acadia,* which means *paradise.*

The preserve also has several smaller outlets that house collections of Native American artifacts from the Delta region. Ancestors of the tribes, which once roamed where the city of New Orleans now stands, took care of the early settlers through trading and by showing them how to live more comfortably in the muggy climate. The **Chitimacha Cultural Center** in Charenton (318-923-4830) is located on the Chitimacha Indian Reservation on Louisiana Highway 326, which separates it from the muddy waters of the Bayou Teche. The tribe and the park service jointly administer the center, at which visitors can purchase intricately woven baskets and other artifacts made by tribal members. The **Tunica-Biloxi Museum** (318-253-8174), located on that tribe's reservation near Marksville, houses an extensive array of Native American and European colonial-era items, including cooking gear, clothing, and armaments.

In 1777, Spain authorized the immigration of hundreds of Canary Islanders (the Islenos) to Louisiana, where many continued their professions as fishermen. The park service's **Isleno Center** (504-682-0862) is just south of Chalmette on Bayou Road, one mile east of Judge Perez Drive (Louisiana Highway 39).

Beginning in 1994, in a program running from Memorial Day to Labor Day, Amtrak teams up with the National Park Service and Jean Lafitte National Historic Park to provide on-board educational programs for passengers traveling through Louisiana and the Mississippi Delta region. Talking about natural and cultural sites between New Orleans and Lafayette, volunteer educators, historians, and representatives of various national communities hold free sessions in the lounge car of the Sunset Limited. Announcements about the programs, which cover the ethnic heritage and natural history of the Delta, are made once the train is underway. Sites of interest along the route are pockets of Acadian communities, portions of the German Coast, and the Chitimacha Indian Reservation. For more information on fares and reservations, call Amtrak at 1-800-USA-RAIL.

A tour of the Cabildo offers useful insight into the city's ethnic history. The building is owned by the Louisiana State Museum. The structure, which fronts Jackson Square, was once headquarters of the Spanish rulers. Standing alongside St. Louis Cathedral and the Presbytere, the Cabildo was the manifestation of colonial power. The imposing facade, with its deep foyer and high front arches over the entrance, was a perfect showcase for the might of the colonial administrators.

Today, however, the square in front of the building is now packed with tourists listening to the street musicians and watching the jugglers and portrait painters. The Cabildo is open from 10 A.M to 5 P.M., Tuesday through Sunday but is closed major holidays. Adult admission is $3; seniors and teens pay half price; and children twelve and under get in free.

The state museum took over the building in 1911, refurbishing it in 1993 after a 1988 fire severely damaged the structure. The building was finally reopened in February 1994, with detailed exhibits on the many nationalities and races that give New Orleans its élan. "A Medley of Cultures" ranges from the French to the Germans, the African-Americans to the Jews. Easily read signs lead the visitor on a journey through the city's history, providing vignettes that add life to the past. These observations are nothing new, the museum points out. One display notes that traveler William Darby, who visited New Orleans in the early 1800s, was one among many to comment on the diversity.

"No city perhaps on the globe, with an equal number of human beings, presents a greater contrast of national manners, language, and complexion than does New Orleans," he wrote. Today's New Orleans derives its delightfully "foreign" culture from the mingling of those heritages over the ensuing generations.

Visitors to New Orleans will no longer find specific neighborhoods of individual nationalities as in many other major cities. It is a true melting pot, with ethnic groups melding everywhere. Native New Orleanians, however, grew up fiercely loving their individual *faubourgs*. In the earliest years, these neighborhoods, situated on high points of ground to keep out of the water, were actually separated by canals, swamps, and other physical barriers, rather than by ethnicity. Unlike most other cities that expanded outward, New Orleans matured inward. The geographical impositions of the Mississippi River and Lake Pontchartrain prevented any movement to the far horizon. Politics also played a large role in forming the city's ethos. The Creoles and the Yankees even had separate governments for their respective parts of town, formed after the Louisiana Purchase and divided by the neutral ground of Canal Street. Between 1835 and 1852, the city was even separated into three municipalities. It wasn't until the 1870s that Freeport, Carrollton, Jefferson City, and Lafayette were incorporated into New Orleans proper, according to city historian Mel Leavitt. Even up to 1890, the city actually consisted of at least ten individual townships.

A city study in 1979, "Neighborhood Profiles in Change," delineated seventy-one individual neighborhoods, ranging from only a few square blocks to the larger tracts such as Carrollton. Much of their historical character has been preserved, with ten of the city's neighborhoods now considered National Historic Districts. Leavitt points out that the Uptown Historic District is the second largest in the country, with more than 10,700 buildings included.

Say What?

There's no such place as Noo Orl*ee*ns. Only out-of-towners think that "New Orleans" has an emphasis on the "-eens." Yet to speak like a native is relatively easy, even without a Berlitz phrase book. It's N'*Aw*lins, N'*Or*lyuns, or N'*Yaw*lins. But never, never say Orl*ee*ns; unless, of course, you mean Orleans Parish or even Orleans Street. Both have the "-eens"

emphasis. Confusing. Well, sure. That's why many folks these days simply say, "I'm from NOLA." NOLA? That's the new speak for New
Orleans, LA.

Social Services, Information Agencies

American Express Company (504-586-8201)
American Red Cross (emergencies on nights and weekends,
   (504-586-8191)
Catholic Deaf Center (504-949-4413 for Voice/TDD)
Greater New Orleans Chamber of Commerce (504-527-6900)
Lighthouse for the Blind (504-899-4501)
Travelers Aid Society (504-525-8726)
Tourist Information Service (1-800-639-6753 for toll-free help, twenty-
   four hours a day)

Police

The New Orleans police department encourages visitors to think smart
and use common sense, just as anyone should in a major metropolitan area
elsewhere throughout the nation. Pay attention to surroundings, keep
credit cards and valuable documents in the hotel safe, don't leave personal
belongs unattended or visible in a parked car. If you become a victim of
a crime, immediately call 911 or 821-2222. The police station in the
French Quarter is located at 334 Royal Street and is open twenty-four
hours a day throughout the year. Numerous black bicycles and blue
scooters in the yard around the stately building mark the site. It's often
easier to sweep through the narrow streets and negotiate the crowds by
pedaling or putt-putting a vehicular alternative to the squad car. Horse-
back patrols are also used, placing the officers' head and shoulders above
the throngs of conventioneers, partygoers, dancing girls, college kids on
break, tourists, and international gawkers.

   If tour organizers are interested in taking security precautions one step
beyond the obvious, crime prevention seminars are available for visiting
groups. A session can be set up by contacting the police department's
public affairs division at 504-826-2828; FAX 504-826-2833.

   Most of the city is accessible without a car, and this is especially so in
the downtown area and in the French Quarter. If a car is required, the
police smilingly remind everyone that parking regulations are strictly
enforced, with the emphasis on *strictly*. Since most parking lots and
garage rates are reasonable ($4 to $7) for all-day security, it's often not

worth it to take your chances on the street. So find a nearby lot or ramp, park your vehicle and walk, take the bus, or hop a cab. If found in a No Parking Zone, your car may not be there where you return from a round of New Orleans' festivities or sightseeing. But in this worst-case scenario, the busy tow pound is located at 400 N. Claiborne Avenue (504-565-7450). By the way, the tow fee plus the ticket can be more than $100. So park smart, especially in the Quarter where the meter monitoring and patrol folks are merciless. They've heard every bizarre plea for mercy that anyone could ever dream up. Being from out of town is no excuse.

Transportation

Getting to and from New Orleans is no problem, with major airlines serving the city, plus Amtrak passenger railroad and intercity bus transportation. Interstate highways 10, 59, and 55 run through town. New Orleans is also a port of call for passenger liners that cruise the Gulf of Mexico and the Caribbean.

New Orleans International Airport (NOIA), *Box 20007, New Orleans, LA 70141 (504-464-0831; FAX 504-465-1264).*   Stepping from the plane to the terminal at New Orleans International Airport (NOIA), visitors immediately know where they are. There's no mushy elevator music piped over the sound system; instead you'll hear the city's own strains of sweet, sweet jazz. Concessions offer *beignets* (pronounced běn-yay), those ubiquitous, sugar-coated, holeless doughnuts, along with mouthwatering gumbo and spicy jamabalaya. Video poker machines line the walls of the cocktail lounges. Photos and background notes on the city's famous musicians line the hallways for a refreshing change of pace from the typical blaring advertisements found in other terminals. Colorful posters from the city's multitudinous festivals and concerts carry out the delightful theme that New Orleans is a party town to end all party towns.

The precursor of the current airport was a municipal terminal on Lake Pontchartrain, built in the 1930s. Expansion of that property was too expensive, so a site in suburban Kenner was selected, about ten miles from the city center. World War II interfered with construction and the designated land was taken over by the military for an air base. The property, plus an adjacent 295 acres, was returned to the city in 1947. After civilian amenities were added and runways enlarged in the ensuing few years, the field became one of the nation's busiest almost immediately. The old airfield, formerly Shushan Airport and now called New Orleans Airport, only handles private planes these days.

In the 1990s, the airport came under the direction of Vietnam war hero "Steady Eddie" Levell, one of the city's leading African-American civic figures. The airport accommodates such airlines as Aeromexico, American, Aviateca, Continental, USAir and USAir Express, Lacsa, Northwest, Sahsa, Southwest, Taca, TWA, and United. They provide service to 87 cities throughout the United States and a dozen destinations in Central America and Mexico. Some six million passengers flow through the airport annually, taking advantage of its 277 daily flights. True to New Orleans' tradition as a commercial hub, more than 57,000 tons of freight are also ferried through the system.

For the record, the airport is only four feet above sea level.

—Visitor Information —

Airport and visitor information assistance desks are located in the West Lobby (504-464-2752) and in the East Lobby (504-465-8852). Hours at both are from 8 A.M. to 9 P.M. daily. All service reps are fluent in Spanish, and many can speak three or more languages. After business hours, interpreters are available at the airport through the facility's courtesy phones. The Traveler's Aid booth (504-464-3522) is located in the East Lobby with plenty of tourist leaflets and specific answers for travelers in trouble. Diaper-changing facilities are in the East Lobby women's rest rooms.

—Reception Program, Tax Refunds —

A Gateway Reception Program offers language assistance in 149 different tongues. Foreign visitors also have the incentive of tax-free shopping in many designated terminal stores. There is no duty-free shop, however. A tax refund booth in the West Lobby is available for the convenience of international guests who purchased goods at any of the 1,200 participating outlets throughout Louisiana. Hours are 7 A.M. to 6 P.M., seven days a week.

—Cab, Limo, Public Transportation —

Cab rides from the airport to the Central Business District (CBD) cost about $21, depending on the location of a visitor's hotel. The approximate travel time is twenty-five to thirty minutes. Airport Shuttle limo service (504-469-4555) is just as convenient, costing only $10 for a one-way ride that drops off guests at accommodations throughout the city, including the universities (usually at the respective student union). Ticket booths are located in the baggage pickup area in the basement of the main terminal building. Clerks there are generally very helpful and can even offer tips on what to see and do, so don't be bashful about asking. There's plenty of, "Honey, ya'll want to take in the Audubon Park Zoo cuz it's soooo preeety this time a' year." There's nothing fake about the patter; the folks here want visitors to have a good time and they are proud to suggest off-the-beaten-path sights, as well as the standard French Quarter over-views. Coupons for tour discounts also can be secured at the booths or from the drivers.

The limo drivers are knowledgeable about what's flashing past on the ride into town. Listen up and hear some grand storytelling, with fun tall tales and tourist-tweaking mixed in with the fact. It makes the trip pass quickly—and don't forget to tip.

The Coastline/Mississippi Coast Limousine Service (1-800-647-3957) provides shuttles to the Mississippi Gulf area and to Slidell, Louisiana. The firm's booth is located on the lower level of the terminal next to the U.S. Customs office.

Jefferson Transit offers public bus transportation from the airport every twenty minutes on weekdays and every half hour on weekends during normal business hours. The bus stop is located outside Entrance No. 5 on the terminal's upper level. Transportation from the airport to the central business district is $1.10.

—Parking —

NOIA has on-site parking for 3,000 vehicles. Parking rates are $2.50 for the first hour; $1.50 each additional hour or fraction thereof; and a total of $7.50 for each twenty-four-hour period. There is no weekly rate and parking fees may be paid by VISA, MasterCard, American Express, Discover, and Diners Club, as well as the all-time favorite—cash.

—Car Rental Agencies —

Alamo Rent-A-Car (504-469-0532); Avis Rent-A-Car System (504-464-9511); Budget Rent-A-Car System of New Orleans (504-467-2277); Hertz Car Rental System (504-468-3695); National Car Rental System, Inc. (504-466-4335).

—Banks, Business Service Center —

Whitney National Bank is across from Delta's ticket counter. In addition to normal banking services, Whitney offers cash advances on credit cards, traveler's checks, and money orders; foreign currency exchange; and automatic teller machines. The bank is open Monday through Thursday from 8:30 A.M. to 3:30 P.M. and Friday from 8:30 A.M. to 5:30 P.M. It is closed Saturday and Sunday.

A Mutual of Omaha Business Service Center is easily accessible in the West Lobby. Travelers can buy travel insurance, exchange foreign money, run off photocopies, pick up airline tickets, send faxes, and wire money. Hours are 6 A.M. to 7 P.M. daily.

Amtrak. National rail passenger service is available at Union Station, 1001 Loyola Avenue (1-800-872-5511). Union Station is on the site of what was a turning basin for ships using the New Basin Canal, a waterway linking the Mississippi and Lake Pontchartrain that opened in 1838. Building the canal was a Herculean feat that took the lives of at least 8,000 men, mostly Irish and German immigrants. The riverboat landing, now filled in, was on Rampart Street (called Circus Avenue at the time) between Julia Street and Howard Avenue (then Triton Walk).

Buses. Greyhound and numerous regional bus lines accommodate motor coach passengers at the terminal at Union Station, 1001 Loyola Avenue.

Streetcars. In the old days, several dozen streetcar lines converged on the 171-foot-wide Canal Street, the city's traditional downtown shopping area. The street itself was to be the site of a canal that was never dug, so its width was perfect for the electric cars. And never, no never call them *trolleys.* The term is used solely by Yankees and the unenlightened. Today only the St. Charles line remains, with its 35 olive-green cars running from St. Charles Avenue onto Canal Street from Carondelet and back to St. Charles, just a block away. From there, the line heads Uptown, toward the lush Garden District and points beyond. The other lines have fallen to the bus and automobile. A one-way ride on the streetcar is only $1, with transfers at 10¢. No change is given for the rides into a genteel past. Kids under three ride free with a fare-paying passenger. A good bargain for visitors is an RTA VisiTour Pass, available at $4 for one day and $8 for three days of unlimited riding. Call 504-569-2700 to find out specific locations where the passes can be purchased. Most major hotels have the passes available at their service desks. Many gift shops in the city also have them available. The fifty-two-passenger streetcars run twenty-four hours a day, seven days a week.

Exposed light bulbs illuminate the night, making streetcars visible for blocks away as they rock and roll down the tracks. Brightly varnished wooden seats are polished from years of wear, so don't expect plush modern upholstery. The seats can be reversed, depending on the direction the cars are heading. The cars in use today were designed by North Carolina's Perley A. Thomas Car Company, dating from 1923. A single operator handles the machinery. His single throttle stick controls the speed as he peers down the narrow-gauge line. Riding the streetcar is the perfect metaphor for visiting New Orleans because it allows the traveler to ride looking forward into the future and also looking back into the past.

The streetcars were the successors to the original railroads that replaced the canals as the major modes of transportation. The first line in the city was the Pontchartrain Railroad, which was in operation from 1830 to 1932, running from Elysian Fields out to the lake—a distance of barely more than five miles. Several other train lines were formed in the late 1800s to take passengers to the outer suburbs and amusement parks along Pontchartrain. By 1911, electric streetcars were used throughout the city. But by 1953, only the St. Charles Avenue and Canal Street lines were still in operation. Even the streetcar of playwright Tennessee Williams's *Streetcar Named Desire* fame was shut down. In 1963, buses replaced the streetcars on Canal Street despite widespread opposition. Another tradition went by the boards in 1987 when nuns were first charged fares to ride public transportation. For over a century, the good religious sisters of the city were given free rides because of their centuries of service to the community. The jokes around town at the time pointed out that perhaps the city's politicians were beyond hope after that penurious proclamation, so why pray for 'em anymore.

The St. Charles Streetcar Line currently operates the entire system, which was placed on the National Register of Historic Places in 1973. Other than the cable cars in San Francisco, New Orleans has the only such operational service in the country.

In addition to the St. Charles run, a tourist Riverfront streetcar shuttle service has carried passengers between the convention center and the French Market since August 1988. The seven refurbished cars, dubbed The Ladies in Red, run Monday to Friday, from 6 A.M. to midnight on the nearly two-mile line. Fares are $1.25 each way. A multimillion-dollar expansion of the line has been considered for installation by the year 2000—one that will lay an extra set of tracks, establish a streetcar museum, and offer an extension of the line. A rubber-tired bus that looks like a streetcar makes a route through the French Quarter Monday through Friday only, from 5 A.M. to 7:23 P.M. Fares are $1.00, with transfers at 10¢.

For a free poster of the riverfront streetcar, drop by the RTA offices in the Maison Blanche Building, 101 Dauphine Street.

Beg Your Pardon?

After getting past the countryside with its outlying bayous (a derivative of *bayuk,* from the Choctaw word for *river*), there's no such thing in New

Orleans as north, south, east, or west. The reason for this total disregard for the compass can be laid directly on the meandering path taken by the Mississippi River as it wends its way past the city. So, when in New Orleans, do as the locals do and simply follow the directions the river demands. For instance, Uptown is upriver, Downtown is downriver. Midcity is, well, midcity. The Central Business District (CBD) is easy to find. Look for the office towers, outdoor sculpture, curbside plantings, and crowds carrying briefcases. Lakeside is toward Lake Pontchartrain, and the city's riverside is, of course, toward the Mississippi. It might be necessary to practice these idioms for awhile, but once mastered, a visitor won't get lost. Heading too far in any direction means water. So try it. Uptown—lakeside. Downtown—riverside. And so on. Repeat several hundred times and New Orleans is yours!

The next step is to figure out where you are. Try out the directions on North Peters Street or South Peters Street. Now, having fractured the directional language, experience some of the street names. But start with the French Quarter, more commonly known by hometowners as the *Vieux Carre* (old square) pronounced View Ka-ray. (There are no French Quarter exits on any of the freeways slashing across the New Orleans landscape, so look for Vieux Carre signs.) Burgundy is Bur-guń-dy. There is no disappearing *s* on Chartres, even though French eyebrows would rise at this. It's "Charters." Terpsichore is Terp-si-core and Calliope is Cal-ee-op (that's a loooong *o*). Conti is Con-tie, with Iberville being uttered as Eye-berville.

Street names in New Orleans provide a basic, integral flavoring for the rainbowed personality of this most multinational of American cities. There are more than 500 miles of streets, lanes, avenues, and boulevards in New Orleans proper. In the French Quarter, the city has marked the original Spanish names on tiles set into the walls at various corners. The contemporary names are on the signposts. The French connection is obvious, demonstrating the motherland's delightful vivacity of spirit. In true Gallic tradition, the Creoles dedicated their streets to the feminine gender. Some were wives, others were lovers. Who were the original Elaines, Annettes, and Shirleys? At least old guide books point out that Julia Street was named after a free mulatto woman. On the other hand, the religiosity of the people has always been evident with Religious, Nuns (adjacent to Desire), Ascension, Piety, and others lending a prayerful aspect to the map. Not all streets had Christian roots, however. Especially in the Faubourg Ste. Marie (or St. Mary's, according to the Yanks), there were assorted demigods, muses, fairies, wood nymphs, and sprites who received their due: Dryades, Euphrosine, and so on. Add those to Solomon and Socrates, Poe and Pleasure, and the list goes on and on.

Enthusiasm for Napoleon Bonaparte's military exploits gave New Orleans its Napoleon Avenue, as well as Jena and Austerlitz Streets (named after his famous battles). After Napoleon was finally crushed by the English at Waterloo in 1815, local Francophiles, including the then-mayor Nicholas Girod, wanted to bring him to New Orleans to live in comfort and safety. They even purchased and outfitted a house for him at the corner of St. Louis and Chartres. The general-dictator-emperor, who was called by his contemporaries "an habitual disturber of the peace of Europe," died on May 5, 1821 before a ship could be dispatched to rescue him from his Elba-island exile. The **Napoleon House,** built in 1791, is located at 500 Chartres (504-524-9752) and is now a bar that, according to *Esquire Magazine,* is one of the top 100 taverns in the United States.

Locals also received their street-name due, with long-ago planters such as Montegut and others of his era being honored with appropriate signage. Bernard Marigny, a Creole gentleman gambler who lost his fortune and was forced to sell his plantation, named streets in his new subdivision Craps and Bagatelle to celebrate his favorite games of chance.

However, no one can claim to be a New Orleanian until pronouncing and spelling street names correctly. The true test is leaping through all the phonetic and alphabet hoops of tongue-twisting Tchoupitoulas (Chop-it-ōō-las). When that hurdle is accomplished, you have earned the right to sip *café au lait* daily in Cafe Du Monde, the French Quarter's trendy place to see and be seen in.

Food

Even while wandering New Orleans, seeking out streets and wondering about their spellings, a visitor need never go hungry even if totally puzzled and turned around. Never fear, a five-star eatery is always near. So how about food? It does help to pronounce the words properly with all their ethnic flair. Many nations have contributed to the potpourri of culinary New Orleans. For instance, the basic recipe for gumbo (from the west African word *kingombo,* which means *okra*) was brought to the city by slaves who honored okra's spiritual value as much as its nutrition and taste. Another African-Caribbean derivative is jambalaya, pronounced (jum-bo-lie-ya). This concoction is made with yellow rice, spices, onions, chicken, tomatoes, shrimp, ham, and whatever else you can find in the refrigerator. *Pain perdu* is French toast made with French bread. A "dressed" sandwich has all the works, including what seems to be the kitchen sink along with lettuce and tomatoes. The traditional po-boys and muffulettas weigh in at what is obviously several hundred pounds of meat, cheese, crabs, oysters, and cheese—in addition to whatever else the maker finds close at hand.

A po-boy is a New Orleans' submarine sandwich. (Why go to those chain sub shops when the authentic po-boys are made in every corner grocery store, deli, and sandwich stand at a better price and with more enthusiasm?) The original sandwiches were created by Benny and Clovis Martin, who sold them for 10¢ each during a streetcar strike in 1914. The "poor boys" who were striking could not afford anything else. A muffuletta is a robust hero-sized sandwich with Italian meat and relish, served in a chewy bun as large as a washtub. Then there's *grillades* (gree-yads), which are slices of broiled beef or other meats such as veal. Ask for grillades and grits at any lunch counter and the waitress will think you're honest hometown folk.

Seafood is an integral part of a New Orleanian diet, with each preparation presented in a unique, delicious style. Barbeque shrimp is not slathered in hot tomato sauce as with the standard B-B-Q in Kansas City, San Antonio, Memphis, or Nashville. New Orleans' modus is to prepare a peeled shrimp by cooking it in a heavenly rich butter and garlic sauce. The more garlic, the smoother the taste. Another way of preparing shrimp is adding it to a slurpy, delicious tomato sauce called *étouffée* (ay-two-fay), which means *smothered.)* Sometimes a cousin to the shrimp, the crayfish, is substituted.

These latter crawlers are respectfully called "mudbugs" by the locals because the critters dwell in the bottom mud of slow-moving streams (the popular Mudbugs Restaurant in Kenner gets its name from the little fellas). However, steaming mounds of boiled crayfish, served with plenty of powerful Turbo Dog or Dixie beer, is an unmatched repast. Toss in a round of cajun music and no king ever had a feast so good. But how does a newcomer to crayfish tackle a pile of no-longer-squigglies with their head, legs, and tails still attached. No problem:

Step 1: Tuck a napkin around the neck (yours, that is).

Step 2: Choose a crayfish from the stack. Grab its head between the thumb and forefinger of one hand and the tail between the thumb and forefinger of the other.

Step 3: Twist and firmly pull until the head and tail separate from the body. There will be a slight "ooshing" sound. Discard the head (although some aficionados suck the juice from the appendage) and squeeze the tail between the thumb and forefinger until the shell cracks.

Step 4: Lift and remove the three shell fragments and pull from around the meat. Take the tail and the last shell segment and pull out the meat from inside.

Step 5: Pull the vein free and pop the crayfish in your mouth. Mmmmm!

There's always room for dessert in New Orleans. Try a praline (praw-leen), a wonderful hip-hugging candy made from brown sugar, butter, and pecans. The treat is named after Marcehal du Plessis Praslin, whose cook once needed something to sweeten up the after-dinner tray for a party. The confection was an immediate hit.

To catch up on the latest in the New Orleans cooking scene, tune in to the WWL-TV morning news program, where local chef Frank Davis has long had his "Naturally N'Awlins" show, aired between 7 and 8 P.M. each Tuesday. "I get to cook, go to parties in the middle of the day and they pay me to go fishing," he says. Davis has authored three cookbooks: *The Frank Davis Seafood Notebook, Frank Davis Cooks Naturally N'Awlins,* and *Frank Davis Cooks Cajun, Creole and Crescent City.* Copies are available at most local bookstores. To find them, just follow your nose to the pages that outline old-fashioned New Orleans oyster dressing or his secrets for making apple walnut pie (and don't forget the vanilla ice cream for *à la mode*).

There is a camaraderie among New Orleans' chefs, who often share ideas and sometimes even basic recipes. "We go by what we have," says Gigi Patout, whose family has had a South Louisiana restaurant presence for three generations. They base their award-winning presentations on simple fare. "Heck, jambalaya traditionally is whatever can be cleaned out from the refrigerator. You can end up with twenty gallons of the stuff. In New Orleans, you can make anything you want and call it anything you want so long as it tastes great. I suppose this is a carryover dating from the 1700s. The cooks then simply couldn't wait until the supply ship showed up with the 'proper' ingredients," Patout pointed out.

New Orleans' cooks often learn their craft at home, as with Kevin Belton who absorbed his mom's recipes while doing homework. Belton now teaches creole and cajun culinary styles at the New Orleans School of Cooking in the Jackson Brewery, 620 Decatur Street (classes are held at 11:30 A.M. Tuesdays and Thursdays; cost is $15; for reservations call 504-525-2665). When Belton attended college, his skills provided plenty of lip-smacking alternatives to fast foods for his college buddies. His dorm room, "aka" Belton Bistro, became so popular that the wrestling team made it a home away from home and the coaches complained. But then the athletic management started showing up as well, ostensibly just to check out what was adding poundage to the squad. There wasn't any problem after that, laughs the six-foot-nine, three-hundred-pound Belton.

"My grandmother died at ninety-eight and she had four handwritten cookbooks. There were five recipes for turtle soup," he exclaimed. "She was her own best critic." Like other homegrown New Orleans eatery experts, Belton's own polyglot heritage adds spice. His father was born in

Thibodaux's Cajun country and his mother's multinational ancestral background ranged from Martinique to precolonial America. Belton felt that he also learned his sense of family values around the kitchen table. "When we fixed dinner, we talked. When we ate together, we talked," he explains, adding that he is emphasizing that relationship with his own two young sons Kevin and Jonathan. "And besides, cooking is a fun release for me."

According to Belton, New Orleans food can be considered delightfully decadent or healthy, whichever way anyone wants to look at it. "My uncle ate this all his life and he lived to be 106," asserts Belton. He emphasizes that there are only two questions a New Orleans visitor needs to ask about food: "One. Does it taste good? Two. Is there enough?"

Tours

Leave the drivin' to them. The typical Crescent City tour guide, motor coach operator, cabbie, carriage driver, streetcar conductor, or steamboat deckhand is part encyclopedia, part huckster, part party animal, and part specialist in making the mundane magnificent. It's been the same since the first Bayogoula Indian agreed to show Pierre le Moyne, Sieur de Iberville, the back road to what became Lake Pontchartrain. Each guide has a distinct personality to complement the New Orleans experience. Typifying this breed of wonderful bombast is Annie Bazoon, sometimes known as Annie-Gator or Annie-Thang, a guide for New Orleans Tours. The patter and hometown insight makes any tour a memorable package. She also peddles what she calls swamp jewelry, as well as fish design tote bags, pins, raw shrimp, and luscious crayfish when she's not extolling the wonders of the Ursuline Convent or the Bourbon Street beat on her regular guide route. And Bazoon is only one of hundreds of similar helpfuls who feel their principal duty in life is to show others where and how to have a great down-home time. Call her at 504-866-7929.

New Orleans Tours, *4220 Howard Ave. (504-592-0560).* New Orleans Tours presents six motor coach excursions: a complete city tour, the historic plantation, a riverboat/city combo, New Orleans nightlife, Crown Point swamp tour, and Pete Fountain's Jazz Extravaganza. Spanish-speaking guides are available. The firm has been operating in the city since 1973.

Pick up the tour bus at the Riverwalk, under the overhang at the rear of the old municipal auditorium directly across the street from the World Trade Center (WTC). The building is expected to be converted into a land-based gambling casino by 1995, but until then the motor coaches pull up at Entrance No. 4 (just inside and to the left are restrooms for a last-minute pit stop). By calling ahead for reservations, shuttle buses can also pick up tourists at selected area hotels. The shuttle driver will inform guests as to the proper bus number. Most city, "swamp," and plantation tours depart from the central site across from the WTC. No one wants to end up on the bayous if a downtown tour was expected. Neither should befuddled tourists get on the Department of Immigration and Naturalization Service buses that are usually lined up outside the WTC. Handcuffed deportees from the INS vehicles parked on the street are escorted to immigration offices inside the tower. Deportation proceedings are held there before they are shipped back to their respective homelands. So if fellow passengers are all wearing brown jumpsuits, that's a clue that it's the wrong bus.

While waiting for the correct tour bus in front of the WTC, admire the gold-plated statue of St. Joan of Arc in the median, or as the New Orleanians say, "the neutral ground." The Maid of Orleans, a gift from the people of France to the city, is perched atop her steed and ready for action. It's amazing to remember that she was only 19 when she led French troops into battle and was ultimately burned at the stake for her beliefs before she turned 20. The first "neutral ground," now Canal Street, was just a grassy strip between the Old City and the New, when the Americans flooded New Orleans after the Louisiana Purchase. The site became known as a neutral place where the Creoles and the Yanks could talk business, supposedly without fisticuffs.

New Orleans Tours' complete city tour departs at 9:30 A.M. and 1:30 P.M. daily, running for two to two and a half hours. Adults' tickets are $17, and children's aged 3–12 are $9. The excursion moves up oak-shaded Esplanade Avenue to the marble vaults of St. Louis Cemetery for a stroll through the famous graveyard. There is a stop at the vast grassy expanse of City Park, followed by a run along the choppy waters of Lake Pontchartrain and the yacht harbor there. The motor coach then moves through the streets of old Carrollton, once a suburb and now part of the city proper, and along upscale St. Charles Avenue past the marble and ivy towers of Tulane and Loyola universities and the fresh openness of Audubon Park. The return drive then ventures into the hustle of the Central Business District past the contemporary Superdome and squeezes through the French Quarter. The line's River & City Combo ($28 adults; $14 children 3–12) runs from 9:30 A.M. to 5 P.M., with a motor coach tour of the city followed by a Mississippi River ride on the water-churning *Creole Queen*. The cruise stops at the Chalmette Battlefield, where hero Andrew Jackson whomped the British in 1815—assisted, of course, by Creoles, slaves, freemen of color, Gulf pirates, and a united nations force of Irish, Germans, Italians, Hispanics, and Native Americans of all ages who cast their lot with the new United States. For other tours, call the company for rates and departures.

Gray Line of New Orleans, *1300 World Trade Center (800-535-7786).* Gray Line's tours depart from its ticket office at Toulouse Street and the river, adjacent to the Jackson Brewery. This take-off point is only a block upriver from Jackson Square. Watch the passing crowd while waiting for departure. Locals swear that if one waits there long enough, at least one friend or relative will eventually wander past.

Gray Line has a two-hour Super City tour daily, departing at 9, 10 and 11 A.M., noon, and 2:30 P.M. A paddle and wheel tour, combining a trip on the steamer Natchez and the Super City motor coach tour, leaves at 11:30 A.M. and 2:30 P.M. The line also offers full-day tours of plantations along the River Road; a visit to the historic 1830s home of Oak Alley; a three-and-a-half-hour boat expedition into the bayous; and a tour of the Destrehan Plantation, built in 1787 and one of the oldest plantation homes left intact in the Delta.

Jes Walkin'

Walking tours are available in the French Quarter through several agencies and the National Park Service. Locals chuckle that tourists get hyperbole on the private tours and misinterpretation from the park service folks. Actually they all do an admirable job. The following are among the best.

National Park Service, *423 Canal St. (504-589-3882).* Free tours are offered by park rangers, who lead casual strolls through the French Quarter. Themes vary on cultural aspects of the city during the ninety-minute walking expeditions, starting at National Park's **New Orleans French Quarter Visitors Center,** 916 N. Peters Street (504-589-2636). The programs are held during rain or shine but are not held on federal holidays and Mardi Gras. Programs include a 10:30 A.M. History of New Orleans tour and an 11:30 A.M. Tour de Jour (which varies with the interests of the tour guide and may cover the literature of the city, its architecture, its neighborhood history, or any other topic and sites the guide wishes to highlight). At 2:30 P.M., there is a ninety-minute walk through the lush greenery of the Garden District, called the Faubourg Promenade tour. Take the trolley to the corner of Washington and Prytania and look for the ranger, who should be standing there replete in Smoky the Bear hat and green uniform. Starting June 1 throughout the summer, reservations are required for this tour, with a maximum of thirty guests allowed for the Garden District due to the residential nature of the walk. Call in advance to get the latest information on where the walk starts, in case street work has resulted in changing the location. Just remember that there are no public rest rooms along the way.

At 3 P.M. each afternoon in the visitor center, a program with rangers and volunteers explores Mississippi River Delta cultures in a forty-five-minute show that often involves community residents or slide shows, cooking, jazz, bagpipes, the Japanese culture in New Orleans, and the Cajun background of southern Louisiana.

The French Quarter tour is about a mile, with a maximum of thirty persons (as with the Garden District tour) who have signed up on a first-come-first-served basis. When the tours first started in 1980, sometimes upwards of seventy to eighty people would tag along in Pied Piper fashion, so the numbers eventually were limited. The guide's patter is basically about development since the French founded the city, its architectural styles, and information about restaurants and hotels. How much history is related is up to the ranger.

Tours are essentially bounded by the river and Jackson Square environs. "You can't rearrange the furniture here," one guide chuckles about the lay of the land. But the rangers do not enter historical sites or shops, leaving that up to guests once they have oriented themselves through a walking expedition.

The free tours are comparable to those given by private escorts. For groups, however, the park service serves only nonprofit entities such schools, churches, and organizations for the handicapped because it does not want to compete with other guides for the general public, according to park representatives.

Tours vary depending on the background of the ranger, with each guide bringing his or her own personality and knowledge to the walking expeditions. The majority of those taking walking tours are older adults. It's easy to tell the participants. A tag that says "Jean Lafitte National History Park" is tied with a string around each person's neck to help the guide keep track of his or her charges. The color of the tag changes daily.

Most of the Park Service guides willingly make the effort to learn more about the New Orleans community, if not for their own edification, then to save themselves some embarrassment for not knowing an answer. They regularly get socked with questions that could set back someone with less knowledge at their fingertips. Folks query the guides out of their own experiences. For instance, one escort recalls a plumber asking about plumbing systems in the Pontabla apartments around Jackson Square.

Another person asked when screens were invented, an obvious question after walking past the numerous shuttered first floor windows of French Quarter homes. Many other visitors ask if they can see a jazz funeral on the day of their tour. The guides quickly respond that such processions aren't scheduled in advance, for obvious reasons.

If an answer is not readily available, a guide will recommend a source. Often they will write down the name and address of the questioner and send follow-up information. The staff admits that learning about New Orleans is a constant process that usually entails asking local experts for assistance; studying references; taking tours with other guides; visiting the **Historic New Orleans Collection** (533 Royal Street, 504-523-4662), which contains thousands of written documents about the city; regularly going to the **Amistad Center** in Tulane University's Tilton Hall (504-865-6766) for in-depth reporting on African-American heritage; and visiting other community libraries to pore over histories.

To prepare for their work in New Orleans, the guides receive a generalized, basic background on Louisiana. It is up to them to delve deeper into the background of what makes Louisianians tick and why New Orleans has such a hold on the imagination. In addition to commissioning several histories on the state, surveys of the Acadians, and an ethnographic overview of the Delta, the Park Service has also zeroed in on the city of New Orleans. Wide-ranging topics include the mysterious black Native American social and marching clubs, called the Mardi Gras Indians (researched and photographed by New Orleanian Mike Smith); the development of the second line dance, which follows a funeral service; social and leisure clubs; and jazz. The Park Service Library is open to the public from 8:30 A.M. to 4:30 P.M., Monday through Friday. Call in advance if specific help is required from a librarian. As with the rest of New Orleans' public service agencies, the library is closed during Mardi Gras and on all federal holidays, including Martin Luther King Day.

Since the Park Service route meanders through the urban area, there are some challenges to guests in wheelchairs, with problems occasionally encountered in crossing busy streets in the sometimes hectic, always crowded Quarter. But rangers tend to visualize their route in advance if they know someone might need an easier pathway. Currently, no provisions are made for the hearing-impaired; however, such individuals are encouraged to utilize a printed self-guided walking tour put out by the city's convention and visitors bureau. Groups can secure a signer from the Eastern National Parks Agency and the Monuments and Parks Association, which run the book sale areas in Park Service offices. The latter is a "nonprofit cooperating association" recognized by Congress, which makes interpretative material available to park visitors and the general public.

If you require more ethnic details on New Orleans, contact the National Park Service Center for a copy of the *Ethnographic Overview of the Mississippi Delta Region,* which is packed with details on the ethnic breakdown of the region. To obtain copies, contact the National Park Service, 12795 W. Alameda Parkway, Box 254287, Denver, CO 80225-0287 (303-969-2130). Information is available at 5¢ per page for copies, so be specific with your questons.

Tours by Inez, *Box 56655, New Orleans, LA 70156-6655 (504-486-1123).* Tailor-made tours by Inez Douglas take her guests beyond the pages of guidebooks into the heart of New Orleans life. She knows the personalities behind the walls and doors, where to rent an apartment and how much to pay, inside jokes on local politicians, and which chef has the best Gulf shrimp on any particular day. Her ninety-minute walking tours meet daily at 10:15 A.M. and 2:15 P.M., departing respectively at 10:30 A.M. and 2:30 P.M., in the courtyard of the Hotel DeLePoste, 316 Chartres Street. When necessary, she can call in other guides who speak Spanish, French, Chinese, German, Italian, or Japanese. The cost of a tour is $10 per person. A call in advance is requested. Douglas will wait for an extra few minutes if a client with a tour reservation is late; however, she can't wait too long, so don't abuse the graciousness.

Crescent Tours of New Orleans, *9523 Palm St., New Orleans, LA 70118 (504-486-1631 or 800-643-9198).* Crescent is on call seven days a week, 24 hours a day. The firm offers a kid's-eye view of the city, with tours of museums, the Audubon Zoo, and City Park (children may have the chance to try a spicy-alligator-on-a-stick snack at the central concession booth). Baby-sitting service is also available while moms and dads take off for a day of street roaming or a night of whooping it up.

Magic Tour, *Box 70766, New Orleans, LA 70172 (504-593-9693).* This strolling tour is a relaxing way to meander from the French Quarter to St. Louis Cemetery No. 1 on Rampart Street. The ninety-minute walks leave daily at 10:30 A.M. and 1:30 P.M. from the Coffee and Concierge shop, 334B Royal Street. Adults' tickets are $7 and kids' are free. Translators are available upon advance notice.

Derwent Company, *421 Frenchman St. (504-943-6182 or 800-521-3481).* This firm specializes in tours for overseas visitors, with guides who can speak French, Spanish, Chinese, Japanese, Italian, Hebrew, Swedish, and Dutch, among a smattering of others.

Friends of the Cabildo, *632 Dumaine St. (504-523-3939).* Tours of the historic Cabildo and surrounding French Quarter are offered at 9:30 A.M. and 1:30 P.M. daily except Monday mornings. The Friends is a volunteer association of New Orleanians that supports the Louisiana State Museum located in the old Spanish administration offices. The group operates a gift shop in the Cabildo.

Algiers Point Association, *Box 740045, New Orleans, LA 70174 (504-366-9127).* A view of the New Orleans skyline is best from the Algiers dockside or from the deck of the chugging ferryboat that links both cities. This walking tour of the National Register Historic District in Algiers is a photographer's dream. Brochures describing the tour highlights can be picked up at the Dry Dock Cafe near the ferry terminal at Algiers Point.

Other Tours

Airboat

Rajun Cajun Airboat Tours, *one-half mile east of Louisiana State Highway 433 on Highway 90, Slidell (504-847-9875).* Okay, so this isn't the best way to see the French Quarter, but a bayou adventure near the city is fun on these open airboats. There's the chance to see wild boars, 'gators, and waterbirds up close—real close. The boats can accommodate the physically impaired. This is a weather-permitting operation, so be sure to call ahead. When everything is a go, the boats depart daily from 10 A.M. to dark. The cost is $15 for adults and $12 for kids. Hang on tight.

Bicycle

Olympic Bike Rentals & Tours, *1506 Prytania St. (504-523-1314).* Mountain bikes with five, ten, or fifteen speeds can be rented with delivery and pickup at a hotel for no extra charge. You can also drive to the rental outlet and park there if you prefer. Helmets, children's seats, water bottles, and maps are provided. Olympic even sends out the cavalry in case of a breakdown. A repair truck is a phone call away. As a help for the international traveler, several folks at the rental shop speak Spanish.

Carriage

Gay 90's Carriages, *1824 N. Rampart St. (504-943-8820).*   Although established in 1941, the carriage rides seem to have been a part of the New Orleans scene forever. The mule-drawn buggies are a common sight clip-clopping through the French Quarter and nearby streets. Drivers try to outdo each other in shouting stories at their passengers. The louder it gets, the more outrageous is the tale being related. Boarding is at Jackson Square for the half-hour ride. No reservations are required, but a driver likes to fill her or his carriage before shaking the reins so there may be a wait until other folks clamber aboard. Pay the $8 in advance for the thirty-minute ride. Tips are greatly, repeat greatly, appreciated. Gay 90's even has a special training school for its drivers, where they pick up historical tidbits and learn that mules have minds of their own.

Riverboat

John James Audubon **Riverboat,** *1300 World Trade Center (504-586-8777 or 800-233-BOAT).*   This boat cruises between the Aquarium of the Americas to the zoo in Audubon Park, departing at 10 A.M. and noon, and at 1, 3, and 5 P.M.

Cajun Queen **Riverboat,** *Poydras Street Wharf (504-529-4567 or 800-445-4109).*   Tours cruise past the French Quarter in all the style of the good old steamboat days when the docks were jammed with gaily painted paddlewheelers. Cruises depart at 11 A.M., 1:15 P.M., and 3:30 P.M. Adults pay $10, and children ages six through twelve pay $5.

Cotton Blossom, *2 Canal St. (behind the World Trade Center) (504-586-8777 or 800-233-BOAT).*   The Cotton Blossom departs at 11 A.M. daily from the dock behind the Jackson Brewery for a forty-five-mile cruise.

Creole Queen **Paddlewheeler,** *Poydras Street Wharf (504-529-4567 or 800-445-4109).*   Cruises leave the dock at 10:30 A.M. and 2 P.M. Adults pay $13, kids three to twelve pay $6. The *Creole Queen* has a Dinner on the River & All that Jazz buffet cruise, with boarding at 7 P.M. and departure at 8 P.M. New Orleans bandleader Otis Bazoon usually wields the baton as the bright lights of the city slide past. Adults pay $39, and children ages three through twelve pay $18.

Louisiana Cruises, *No. 2 Canal St. (504-523-5555).* Cruises are offered at 10 A.M. and 3:30 P.M. daily except for Christmas and Mardi Gras Day. Spanish, German, Italian, and French translators are available for groups of overseas visitors.

Natchez **Steamboat,** *No. 2 Canal St. (504-586-8777 or 800-233-BOAT).* The city's only sternwheeler, the *Natchez* departs at 11:30 A.M. and 2:30 P.M. daily, with a 7 P.M. dinner and jazz cruise. The dock is located behind the Jackson Brewery. At 10 P.M. Saturdays, a romantic moonlight dance cruise gives a special glow to the Crescent City horizon. A buffet with creole and cajun foods rounds out the experience. Bring the back cover of the Greater New Orleans Convention and Visitors Guide to the landing and present it to the deckhand for a free cocktail on board. The coupon has to be presented when getting on the vessel.

Seaplane

Southern Seaplane, *1 Coquille Dr., Belle Chasse (504-394-5633 or 504-394-6959).* Tours take guests over the city, scooting low over the Superdome and the French Quarter, over the Mississippi River, and then on to the bayou country.

Take a Cab

Several cab companies operate in New Orleans, with competency, cleanliness, and comfort mostly an individual driver's prerogative. All cabbies have to turn on their meters when driving around the city. During special events such as Mardi Gras, the fare is $3 per person or the meter rate, or whichever is greater. Taxis must always be marked with the company's name and a CPNC number. If you wind up in Dallas instead of dining at the **Old Dog New Trick Cafe** (307 Exchange Place, 504-522-4569, the city's only vegetarian restaurant), not only can you yell at the driver, you can also file a complaint. Note the company name, CPNC number, date, and time of the problem. The problem should then be related to the Taxicab Bureau in City Hall, 504-565-6273).

Publications

Daily newspaper

The **Times-Picayune** costs 35¢ from Monday to Saturday and $1 on Sunday. Newsstands are on many street corners, with hotels carrying the paper in their notions shops. The word *picayune* means *small*. Originally the term applied to the newspaper's cost, which was one picayune, the smallest colonial Spanish coin, valued at 6.25¢. Two picayunes amounted to one "bit." Two bits made a quarter, according to New Orleans historian and television commentator Mel Leavitt. The newspaper offices are located at 3800 Howard Avenue, 504-826-3279. Its Friday entertainment guide, *lagniappe* (lan-yap, meaning *a little bit more*), outlines the entire range of who's doin' what in Crescent City. The term came from long-ago presupermarket days when it was Acadian custom to give a customer a bit of extra grain weighed out from a woolen cloth sack called *la nappe*. To make up for any grain stuck in the sack or spilled, asserts historian Leavitt, the seller would say, "This is for that caught in the sack" (*C'est pour la nappe*).

Entertainment newspapers

Offbeat Publications, *921 Canal St., No. 908 (504-469-3575).* This free monthly guide lists the hot, hotter, and hottest spots in town, with complete listings of clubs and concerts, plus galleries, theater, special events, and festivals. There are articles ranging from the zen of gumbo to Zin, a self-described Haitian *nouvel jenerasyon* (huh?) group that performs zouk music from Guadelupe and Martinique. And let's not miss the features on female rappers Da'Sha'Ra, the ever-popular Fats Domino, or the Dirty Dozen Brass Band. *Offbeat* is everywhere, but first look in hotel newsstands.

This Week in New Orleans, *3200 Ridgelake Dr., No. 403, Metairie (504-832-3954).* This publication features weekly entertainment updates. Copies are available in gift shops, hotels, and other news outlets.

City Magazines

Where Magazine, *921 Canal St., No. 703 (504-522-6468).* *Where* is a monthly visitor publication that is distributed through some 150 hotels and shops in the Greater New Orleans area. It tells where to find the latest in Newcomb pottery and where to see rare white alligators (secret: at the Audubon Park Zoo, on Magazine Street across from Audubon Park, the 340-acre site where the World's Industrial and Cotton Centennial Exposition was held in 1885).

Arrive Magazine, 111 Veterans Blvd., No. 1810 (504-831-3731). Featuring a twelve-page map section, *Arrive* points out the locales of trendy restaurants, theaters, galleries, and clubs.

Guest Informant, 635 Gravier St. (504-524-5213 or 800-275-5885). This hard-cover guide to shopping, dining, and recreation has been distributed to hotels throughout the city for more than fifty years.

Mardi Gras

This is the festival to end all festivals when it comes to crowds, parades, bizarre behavior, and let-it-all-hang-out fervor. And it is a legal holiday for New Orleans. Mardi Gras is an important part of the rhythm of the city, to say nothing of it bringing in millions of dollars, with some 1,800 parades staged in the city since 1857. It is a brilliantine mixture of streamers, music, balloons, almost-anything-goes, hype, and hoopla. The pageant's official colors are green for faith, gold for power, and purple for justice. Planting the seeds a thousand years ago, the ancient Romans celebrated their Lupercalia, a wild rite of spring that culminated in three days of unbridled enthusiasm for wine, sex, and song. More often than not, the partying degenerated into drunken orgies. Then Christianity came along, throwing a cloak of respectability over the pagan holiday by making it a time of feasting before Lent's forty pious days of fasting. The religious gloss of the old bacchanalia spread throughout the Christian world, evolving into what is now called Carnival, a "farewell to the flesh." The term *Mardi Gras,* which means *Fat Tuesday,* was coined by the French to denote the day before Ash Wednesday. They carried the tradition with them to their new colony, with the first recorded Mardi Gras noted in 1699 when Pierre Le Moyne, Sieur d'Iberville, marked a map with the site of a Mass said on that feast day. He named the site, sixty miles south of New Orleans, Point du Mardi Gras.

The feast is movable because it is based on the timing of Easter, which itself is determined by the appearance of the full moon after the spring equinox (usually around March 21). According to the Church calendar, the first Sunday after the full moon that follows March 21 is Easter

Sunday. Forty weekdays and six Sundays before that is Ash Wednesday. The day before that is Mardi Gras. When in doubt over the exact day, and to save counting on your fingers, simply call the Greater New Orleans Visitors and Convention Bureau (504-566-5031 or 504-566-5011) for the correct date. At midnight, everything is supposed to shut down and the penitential season (supposedly) begins. As such, the festival could be staged any time between early February and March.

The Mardi Gras theme tune is "If I Ever Ceased to Love," taken from a musical comedy dating from 1872. Whenever Rex, king of one of the most famous carnival courts, is toasted along his parade route and at official functions, the song is played. After the hundredth hearing, it is enough to drive one mad, especially with the refrain, "If I ever cease to love, may cows lay eggs and fish grow legs." The courts of Rex and Comus, another of the famous carnival kings, both hold balls in the Municipal Auditorium, each paying respects during the night. At 11:20 P.M. the two royal couples sit together until midnight, when Carnival ends and everyone departs.

As the city grew, so did the concept of Mardi Gras, evolving from a bawdy street bash into today's internationally known parades, concerts, and festivities. Balls were held from the birth of New Orleans, lending a fantastic gentility to the rough-and-tumble town. One of the first disputes between the Creoles and the new Yankee administrators when the United states took control in 1804 was the result of an argument over what sort of music would be played at that year's Mardi Gras dance. The first street parade was recorded in 1837, with a group of torch-carrying masked revelers (the *flambeaux*) tramping through the French Quarter and throwing out fruit and cakes. Soon mounted horsemen were parading as well, dumping bags of flour on bystanders' heads. This practice was not always appreciated by the people standing in the streets, and the annual trooping of the horses often ended up in a brawl. Local newspapers called for an end to what they called the vulgar aspects of the festival.

In 1857, several displaced lads from Mobile met in an upstairs French Quarter bar and formed what they called the Krewe of Comus. Since there had already been Carnival parades in that Alabama city for several years, the Founding Fathers felt that New Orleans needed their "stability" to bring order back to the parade. And thus was the official Mardi Gras parade born. In 1870, Comus was joined by a new krewe, the Twelfth Night Revelers. When Russian Grand Duke Alexis visited New Orleans in 1872 to woo the buxom burlesque singer Lydia Thompson, several businessmen organized a day parade in his honor. They chose a "king," now called Rex, to be King of Carnival, which is the highest award given to a local New Orleanian for civic leadership.

Other krewes were organized over the ensuing years, with Les Mysterieuses, the first women's organization, holding its initial ball in 1896. The
all-black Zulus were formed in 1909 to mock the white krewes. A big
boom followed World War II, with additional eager groups joining the
thundering ranks of paraders.

There had long been an unhealthy racist and sexist undercurrent in the
Mardi Gras formations that persisted until 1991, when the New Orleans
City Council passed an ordinance that ordered krewes to open their ranks
to persons of any religion, race, or gender. The antidiscrimination clause
resulted in fluttering and posturing by some of the older organizations,
with Comus and Momus boycotting the 1992 parade. But by 1993, everyone was back on board again. No one could stay away from Mardi Gras
for long, especially for such reasons. For the record, the only times Mardi
Gras parades were not held were during the Civil War, both World Wars,
and a police strike in 1979.

Currently there are some fifty parades and more than seventy balls to
help the city let off psychological steam. Lists of the major parades (from
the Slidelians to the Elks) are available from the city's tourism office. The
parade season now starts twelve days before Christmas and leads up to
Mardi Gras. Several parades precede the Rex procession, which starts at
10 A.M. and attracts hundreds of thousands of people, packing every
available inch along Canal Street. The best place to watch, at least for
families, is on St. Charles Avenue. But get there in the predawn hours to
ensure a watching post. Some folks even camp out all night along the
curbs and ferociously defend their turf. And anyone with a house along
St. Charles always seems to have dozens of friends on Carnival day.
Parking is horrendous, so don't even try to approach Midcity or Uptown
in a car of your own, especially if you are unfamiliar with the street layout.
For parades in Metairie, the lake side of Veterans Boulevard between
Clearview Avenue and Martin Behrman is considered the best by Linda
Bays Powers, a writer for *Where Magazine.*

Here are some tips for enduring a fun day, gleaned from long-time,
devoted parade-goers:

- Leave your vehicle at your hotel parking lot and take a cab or bus—or
  simply walk.

- Be sure to establish a reunion place in advance in case you are separated
  from friends or family, which is easy to do in the rush. And stick to that
  timetable for reassembly so no one worries.

- Dress for the weather and wear walking shoes. Travel light, even if you
  are only going a few blocks. Don't carry a dangling purse or loose

wallet. A backpack works well. Valuables have a way of disappearing via unwanted lightfingered visitation, even though police have a highly visible presence. Cop outposts are located on the 700, 900, and 1100 blocks of Canal Street and on the busy corner of St. Charles Avenue and Poydras Street in the Central Business District. First-aid stations are scattered along the routes.

- Be aware that the French Quarter festivities may not be suitable for young children. For instance, the Drag Queen Costume Contest is usually an eye-opener for folks not accustomed to outlandish costuming and behavior. However, Bourbon Street is always a great place for people watching.

- Bring some juice or water if the day is hot. You never know if you can get close to a concessionaire because of the mobs. Fruit, candy bars, granola sticks, and other pick-me-ups come in handy as well.

- Before the parade, purchase an inexpensive periscope from any of the gift shops in the city or street vendors. These enable you to look over the heads of the crowds. Or bring a stepladder for looking over everyone (skip the stilts). Never stand behind a tall person.

- Shout, "Hey, Mister," as loud as you can. That's the time-honored refrain seeking "throws" to come your way. Certainly it's not politically or gender correct these days, but the more flirting that goes on the better between watcher and krewe member. A throw is a necklace, doubloon, or other gift tossed into the crowd from the floats (the Zulus hand down their prized coconuts to a few select folks along the route).

- Keep your good humor, stay calm, be polite, and smile even if someone steps on your toes.

Entering into the full Carnival flavor is the best way to enjoy yourself. Gift shops throughout the city offer masks that range from the simple to the fantastic. Look for the deals that offer three masks for $9 or other bargains. There are several costume shops in New Orleans. For more elaborate outfits, you can try **A Little Shop of Fantasy,** 304 Decatur Street (504-529-4243), **Serendipitous Masks,** 831 Decatur Street (504-522-9158), and **Mostly Mardi Gras** in the Jackson Brewery (504-524-4089 or 504-581-3199). The sky is the limit for pricing. Or make your own, save bucks, and have just as good a time.

The Greater New Orleans Archivists, with the help of the Friends of the Cabildo, the Historic New Orleans Collection, and the Amistad Research Center, have assembled a helpful free guide locating historical information about Mardi Gras. The easily accessible sites include several at Tulane University, reachable from the St. Charles Streetcar line. They include:

The Amistad Research Center, *6823 St. Charles Ave. (504-865-5535).* The center, founded in 1966 to chronicle the civil rights movement, is one of the country's premier archives on minority affairs. Located at Tulane University (on the St. Charles Streetcar line), the Amistad holds more than ten million documents, a library of 20,000 volumes, and an extensive art collection. The Mardi Gras portion includes films of Zulu coronation balls and sheet, manuscript, and taped music, including compositions by pianist Basil J. Bares, a former slave who wrote *"Le Folies du Carnival"* in 1866 and other tunes that were the hit of the Reconstruction era. There are also files on the Mardi Gras Indians, black marching societies that incorporate elements of Native American costuming and traditions into their parading. These were "outlaw" groups during the segregation years.

African-American influences are at the root of many Mardi Gras traditions, ranging from the flambeau carriers with their intricate Africanlike dance steps to the "second line," a parade after a parade. The famed Zulus, who were organized in 1909, were a parody of white marching societies.

Howard-Tilton Memorial Library, *7001 Freret St. (504-865-5685).* The university library's special conectons include the Comus Carnival collection, the Rex School of Design deposit, the Coralie Davis Costume Designs collection, and numerous others. Doubloons, float plates, press releases, scripts, police parade assignments, films, diaries, videotapes, and dissertations abound. The William Ransom Hogan Jazz Archive on the library's fourth floor contains 2,000 taped reels of oral history on the life and culture of New Orleans, including Mardi Gras.

Newcomb College Center for Research on Women, *Newcomb Campus, Tulane University (504-865-5238).* The research center is located in the Caroline Richardson Building on Newcomb Place near the university. The extensive oral history archive includes information on Olga Peters, a Newcomb graduate in 1920 who designed hundreds of Mardi Gras tableaux, floats, and ball scenery. The Newcomb Photograph Collection also has hundreds of prints of Mardi Gras balls held at the college from 1918 to 1948.

Other large collections of Mardi Gras materials can be found throughout the city. Among the best are:

The Historic New Orleans Collection, *533 Royal St. (504-523-4662).*   The HNOC is a museum/research center with extensive collections relating to Louisiana's heritage. Mardi Gras photographs, sheet music, dance cards, contracts, fliers, and manuscripts are included in the collection. Among the most interesting are the interior drawings, etchings, and photos of halls where the elaborate balls were held, such as the French Opera House, built by James Gallier in 1859 at the corner of Bourbon and Toulouse. The building was destroyed by fire in 1919, but it survives in the HNOC files. The collection is in the heart of the French Quarter, with midday gallery tours of the exhibits at 12:30 P.M. every Wednesday.

Louisiana State Museum, *751 Chartres St. (504-568-6968).*   The museum actually consists of eight landmark buildings in the French Quarter. Seven of them are in the Jackson Square area, with the Mardi Gras collection in the old United States Mint at 400 Esplanade Avenue. The well-documented displays take guests from the earliest Mardi Gras through contemporary parades, in explosions of colorful costumes, prints, and posters. There are enough feathers, spangles, and lace to outfit several kingly courts. Wandering through the collection is good for at least two hours of enjoyment, perfect for a rainy New Orleans afternoon. This exhibition features the metro area carnival krewes. The state museum was created by a legislative act in 1906 and opened in 1911. The Mint is open from 10 A.M. to 5 P.M., Tuesday through Sunday.

Loyola University, *6363 St. Charles Ave. (504-865-3186).*   The university's Special Collections and Archives Department was founded in 1970 as part of the library. Carnival items, reports, and correspondence are among the papers donated by Moon Landrieu, a New Orleans mayor from 1970 to 1978. While not as broad a collection as some of the others, the Loyola archives provide interesting looks into the behind-the-scenes political and governmental aspects of Mardi Gras management.

New Orleans Notarial Archives, *421 Loyola Ave. (504-592-9100).*   Located in the Civil District Court building near the Superdome, the legal archives contain a still-growing thirty-five million pages of documents. Mardi Gras-related materials include charters, leases, and mortgages for krewe-owned property such as the "dens" where they store floats during the off-season. The files contain such rare notary records as the articles of incorporation for the original Krewe of Rex (April 28, 1874) and the building contract for the first Rex den on Calliope Street, dating from 1883.

New Orleans Public Library, *219 Loyola Ave. (504-529-7323).* The Louisiana division of the library has its origins in the Cabildo archives established by Governor (good old "Bloody") O'Reilly in 1770. An extensive carnival collection contains memorabilia from the 1860s to the 1990s. There are even records from the New Orleans police department cataloging arrests made during Mardi Gras from 1826 to 1966. Books, films, and numerous official city records are included in the collection.

Southern University at New Orleans, *6400 Press Dr. (504-286-5296).* SUNO's Center for African and African-American Studies, founded in 1989, holds numerous photos and documents pertaining to the black influences on Carnival that have been donated by organizations such as the Young Men [*sic*] Illinois Club, Capetowners, and Mardi Gras Indians.

Touro Infirmary Archives, *1401 Foucher St. (504-897-8090).* The infirmary, founded in 1859, is the oldest private hospital in New Orleans. Located near the more popular parade routes, the hospital has always had a close affiliation with Carnival. Many of its administrators and staff have been kings and queens of Mardi Gras balls. As such, the hospital's archives are packed with newsletters, staff correspondence, "throws," and photos featuring the hospital's involvement. The Touro Archives were moved to renovated quarters in the Selma Feitel Gumbel Building, 3450 Chestnut Street, in 1992.

University of New Orleans (UNO), *Earl K. Long Library (504-286-6543).* The archives and manuscripts department at UNO is the official repository of the Louisiana State Supreme Court, the Orleans Parish School Board, and the local chamber of commerce. Interesting Carnival-related materials are documents and souvenirs from the truck parades that followed the krewe processions on Mardi Gras day. These pageants featured gaily decorated trucks of all kinds carrying ordinary citizens, family groups, and schools immediately after the larger parades. The library also has material on the Zulu balls and photos of the Krewe of NOR parades.

Xavier University Archives, *7325 Palmetto St. (504-483-7655).* Xavier University has been assembling material on African-American culture since 1915, including the black influence on Carnival. The Allen Family Papers contain a great deal of detail on the Young Men [*sic*] Illinois Club, a noted African-American krewe.

Archdiocese of New Orleans Archives, *1100 Chartres St. (504-861-9521).* Housed in the old Ursuline Convent in the French Quarter, the archdiocesan archives in the Archbishop Antoine Blanc Memorial contain nineteenth-century pastoral letters from city bishops outlining Lenten obligations. There are also church historian Roger Baudier's weekly newspaper columns from 1932 to 1960, which often told about creole Mardi Gras and Lenten customs. Built in the 1750s, the building is one of the oldest in the United States. The Ursuline order donated the structure to the bishop of New Orleans in 1824 and it has been owned and occupied by the archdiocese ever since. The archivists also collect and preserve records on the eight civil parishes in Louisiana included in the New Orleans archdiocese. Some records date back to 1718.

Music

The heartbeat of the city is its musical scene. One can never go wrong in New Orleans when it comes to the glorious strains of jazz, blues, rock, opera, and the other sweet, sweet sounds. New Orleans journalist Honey Naylor rattles off dozens of notable New Orleanians among the country's top entertainers. She includes jazzmen Louis Armstrong and Louis Prima; Al Bernard, the rockin' writer of "Shake, Rattle and Roll"; the Boswell Sisters, a noted singing trio whose professionalism set the tone for women performers in the 1930s; clarinetist Jimmy Noone; bandleader Joseph (King) Oliver; Grammy-winning singer Harry Connick, Jr.; trumpeter Al Hirt; R&B great Fats Domino; gospel singer Mahalia Jackson; the Marsalis family, including Branford of "Tonight Show" fame and trumpeter Wynton; the popular Neville Brothers; and opera star Norman Treigle. And the list goes on and on—from Preservation Hall to the street musicians trying to make it into the big time.

Bright young talents in contemporary bands are becoming popular on the national circuit, carrying the Crescent City banner with them on tour. Among them are the Iguanas, whose "Nuevo Boogaloo" album is a well-received mix of New Orleans R & B, Tex-Mex, rock, and Caribbean sounds. The group was formed in 1989 and was given the Big Easy Award for the best emerging talent in 1990 and the Big Easy Award for the best new rock band in 1991.

Musical roots are deeply sunk in the city, with various strains providing an intricate, rich tapestry—from slaves playing their homemade instruments in Congo Square to today's Bourbon Street strip clubs and Blood and Grits, whose brand of "swamp jazz" on the Bymymamas Music label has everyone rocking at Kadli's Coffeehouse or Lucky's Bar.

Culturally, the city has always been known as America's Paris. The city was the first in North America to have a permanent opera company, with lavish Italian and French productions being staged well before the Civil War. In fact, the first recorded opera was in 1796, with a performance of Gretry's *Silvain*. The Spectacule de la Rue St. Pierre, the Salle Chinoise (renamed the Theatre de la Rue St. Philippe around 1810), and other halls echoed with the most modern extavaganzas of their era. Many were American premieres. The nationally acclaimed Theatre d'Orleans, which was open from 1806 to 1866, presented at least 140 operas between 1827 and 1833. After a decline in the 1920s and 1930s, the opera scene rebounded in the late 1940s. Currently, the city's company hosts at least ten operas during its season from November to May, with performances being given at the plush **Theater of the Performing Arts,** 801 N. Rampart Street (504-565-7470).

The Philharmonic Society, founded in 1824, laid the base for New Orleans' strong tradition of classical music. In the late 1830s, a Negro Philharmonic Society, with more than 100 white and black musicians, presented concerts for city residents who objected to sitting in segregated theaters. Noted nineteenth-century performers such as violinist Ole Bull and singer Jenny Lind always included New Orleans in their tour schedules. The Louisiana Philharmonic Orchestra (the New Orleans Philharmonic Symphony Orchestra when it was founded in 1936) offers a season running from October to May, with a subscription series featuring leading international artists as soloists or guest conductors. The orchestra is headquartered at 821 Gravois Street (504-523-6530) and usually performs at the **Pontchartrain Center,** 4545 Williams Boulevard, Kenner (504-465-9985) or at the **Orpheum Theater,** 129 University Place (524-3285). The New Orleans Friends of Music sponsors chamber music concerts at Dixon Hall on the Tulane University Campus. For details, contact the university's box office at 504-865-5269. The city's other universities also host numerous classical concerts.

Since parades are a focus of New Orleans life, the brass band has become a symbol of the city's vibrancy. Newspapers reported that brass bands were "a real mania" as early as 1838, with thumping drums, thundering horns, and crashing cymbals often filling the air from dawn to the wee hours, especially on Sundays. Funeral processions, complete with bands, were nothing new in the early 1800s, with notices posted in the local papers and everyone invited to join in. Everybody from firefighters to Freemasons strutted to bury their dead. They all had their brass bands, the core of many of them consisted of contracted Sicilian musicians, who had brought their marching traditions with them from their island homeland. A traditional ponderous dirge generally led the mourners to the gravesite, with a light, happy flair in the "second line" parade on the return from the cemetery where they "turned the body loose." Jelly Roll Morton's "Dead Man Blues" captures those brass band airs.

The African-American marching band tradition originated well before the Civil War and flourished during Reconstruction, laying the roots of jazz. The *New Grove Dictionary of American Music* relates how the black influence in these bands welled up from spirituals, ballads, reels, rags, blues, gospel, and military music. The Tuxedo Brass Brand, still performing today, burst on the scene in 1900 as a typical street band. The Dirty Dozen Brass Band and the Treme Brass Band carry the New Orleans style of music to all parts of the world. Other famous black brass bands have been the Excelsior, Alliance, Eureka, and Onward. At the same time, Papa Jack Laine was a leading white musician whose tootin', rootin' bands were popular at turn-of-the-century processions.

All this sound boiled into what became known as jazz, with its traces of upcountry blues music. Dozens of famous black musicians received their early training in highly structured street bands, in the rough-and-tumble world of bordellos and dance halls, and on the street corner. The cornet seemed to be the instrument of choice prior to the 1920s, with the likes of Chris Kelly, Freddie Keppard, King Oliver, Buddy Bolden, and others putting their brassy stamp on the always-evolving style. Clarinetists Jimmie Noone, Sidney Bechet, Johnny Dodds, and Edmond Hall, plus trombonists Kid Ory and Honore Dutrey, were also extremely popular. White musicians edged into what could be called Dixieland or riverboat jazz, epitomized by bandleader Nick LaRocca, a protégé of Papa Jack, whose Original Dixieland "Jass" Band was the talk of Chicago when he exploded on the scene as World War I ended.

For all you ever wanted to know about jazz, visit the William Ransom Hogan Jazz Archives (504-865-5688) at Tulane University during regular business hours on weekdays. The archives were founded in 1958. Librarians there can answer questions on just about anything musical. Just ask.

Since 1969, the New Orleans Jazz & Heritage Festival each spring celebrates the old-time styles, as well as the most modern versions of the sound that made New Orleans famous. The foundation that directs the festival is located at 1205 N. Rampart Street (504-522-4786).

Some of the best music can be found in neighborhood bars and other out-of-the-way sites. Strike up a conversation with any New Orleanian, who can usually relate any number of secret places yet undiscovered by motor coach operators. For instance, the **Elks Lodge,** 2215 Cleary Avenue, Metairie (504-888-8152), hosts the Metropolitan Jazz Club jam sessions from 1 to 5 P.M. on many Sundays. Call to confirm, however. Mark these others on your must-hit list: **Crescent City Brewhouse,** 527 Decatur

Street (504-522-0571); **Columns Hotel,** 3811 St. Charles Avenue (504-899-9308); **Maison Bourbon,** 634 Bourbon Street (504-522-8818); **True Brew Cafe,** 200 Julia Street (504-524-8441); and the **Palm Court Jazz Cafe,** 1204 Decatur Street (504-525-0200).

The following are some of the popular jazz outlets in the city. Some require cover charges or a drink minimum, depending on which performer is scheduled.

Preservation Hall, *726 St. Peters St. (504-522-2841). Music starts around 8:30 P.M.* This is the mecca of traditional jazz in New Orleans. Long lines of folks who didn't make the open seating always crowd around the door hoping to hear a few strains from whoever is on tap that particular evening. They may be lucky to spot Kid Sheik, the Olympia Brass Band, Wendell Brunius, or the Humphrey Brothers. Call for information on cover charges and whether reservations are required.

***Creole Queen* Paddlewheeler,** *Poydras Street Wharf (504-524-0814 or 800-445-4109).* The ship offers nightly All That Jazz cruises nightly, from 8 to 10 P.M. Bandleader Otis Bazoon has long been a fixture on board. Music begins at 7 P.M., with departure at 8 P.M. from the Canal Street dock at Riverwalk. Reservations are necessary. A buffet is served.

Hotel Inter-Continental, *444 St. Charles Ave. at Poydras (504-525-5566 or 800-332-4246). Nightly in the lobby.* Jazz pianist Carl Franklin along with bassist Richard Moten perform in the upper level lobby lounge. The staff at the hotel speaks Lebanese, Vietnamese, French, German, Spanish, Hebrew, and Japanese, subsequently covering most of the bases when it comes to ordering drinks.

Le Meridien Hotel, *609 Common St. (504-525-6500 or 800-543-4300).* The Louis Armstrong Jazz Club is the place to be from 9:30 P.M. to 12:30 A.M., Tuesday through Saturday. On the lower level of the hotel, the club is easy to find. Various artists perform, so call ahead or check the papers.

Maxwell's Toulouse Cabaret, *615 Toulouse St. (504-523-4207). Open daily 3 P.M. to whenever.* The Dukes of Dixieland, Harry Connick, Sr., the Jimmy Maxwell Orchestra, and Rene Netto and the Sounds of New Orleans are regulars.

New Orleans Hilton Riverside, *No. 2 Poydras St. (504-584-3988). Open 9 P.M.–2 A.M., Monday through Saturday.*   The Horizons Club in the hotel is a hot spot for local wheelers-and-dealers wishing to show-case their city to guests. Pete Fountain's Nightclub is on the third floor (reservations required; call 504-523-4374).

Tricou House, *711 Bourbon St. (504-525-8379). Open daily from 11 A.M.–11 P.M.*   Pianist Al Broussard is a regular entertainer at the casual Tricou. Bands also often play there from 1:30 P.M. to an open-ended closing time.

Snug Harbor, *626 Frenchman St. (504-949-0696). Two shows nightly at 9 P.M. and 11 P.M.*   The city's main jazz showcase has upper- and lower-level seating, with attending cover charge. But an attentive guest can sit in the adjacent bar and hear plenty of that good music if the barkeep doesn't have a New Orleans Saints football game tuned in on the television.

Tipitina's, *501 Napoleon Ave. (504-895-8477). Open 3 P.M. until sunrise, Monday through Friday, Saturdays at 6 P.M.*   New Orleans' own Neville Brothers often drop by for a riff or two or three or four. One never really knows who might show up to jam with the band on stage. While mostly offering jazz, an occasional cajun, zydeco, or R & B group might slip in. Check the local entertainment listings for that night's performers.

Other Good Stuff to Know about New Orleans

Banking

Most banks are open from 9 A.M. to 3 P.M., Monday through Friday, except holidays. Only a few (ask the concierge) are open from 9 A.M. to 2 P.M. on Saturday.

Post Office

The central Post Office, 701 Loyola Avenue (504-589-1135), is open from 8:30 A.M. to 4:30 P.M. on weekdays, except for holidays, and from 8:30 A.M. to noon on Saturday. Branch offices are located throughout the city, so check the Blue Pages in the South Central Bell phone book for addresses and phone numbers.

Mosquitoes

Don't worry about them, unless you are taking a bayou tour. Then load up on repellent, especially during the summer.

Telephones

Local calls are 25¢. Long-distance rates apply as they do elsewhere in the country.

Tax-free shopping

International guests may wish to take advantage of Louisiana's tax-free shopping possibilities. After roaming trendy shops in the Riverwalk or Jackson Brewery, who needs to pay more? Information about the program is available from some 1,200 businesses, as well as from hotels and the Louisiana Office of Tourism on Jackson Square. For more information, call 504-568-5661.

Weather

Summer is simple to describe: hot, hotter, hottest (like the city's nightclubs)—and muggy. Some wag once said summer in New Orleans was like wearing a rubber suit all day. The thermometer often gets to be more than 95 degrees Fahrenheit (35 degrees Celsius) for weeks and weeks, tempered only by crushed ice and sweet lemonade. But days and nights from October through May are simply wonderful. New Orleans is gardenia fresh in the evening and almost-cool in the day. With that in mind, just remember the slogan: New Orleans is always "cool" at night, even when it's "hot." And dress accordingly.

Drinking

City Ordinance 828MCS42-96 prohibits carrying open glass or metal containers on any New Orleans public street or sidewalk. The law applies both to soft drinks, as well as alcohol. However, cups are allowed on the streets. The legal drinking age is 21 years. New Orleans and Las Vegas are the only two American cities with no closing law; as such, the bars can remain open twenty-four hours a day. For the record, New Orleans ranks third in per capita consumption of alcohol, after Nome, Alaska, and Washington, D.C.

Scams

Watch out for quick-talking hustlers who seem to know every sideline in the book. One of the longest running is the "I know where you got your shoes at" routine. This is a variation on a routine that is at least a century old, whereby a local comes up to a tourist, shakes his hand and bets that he knows where the visitor "got his shoes at." The rube thinks he is betting on where his shoes were purchased. Wrong! The right guess is that the shoes are right there on a New Orleans sidewalk, on the bottom of your feet. If the fleece is lucky, he'll get a shoe shine out of the lesson. As Dan "the Shine Man" explains, "My grandfather told me never to shake to another man's game." Shine Man, who speaks enough Japanese and French to try the trick with international guests, even has a sliding scale for polishing: $5 for sandals, $10 for tennis shoes (for whitener), $20 for dress shoes, and $40 for boots. "Hey, man, I'm a professional at what I do. I don't hit people, I don't rob them. You bet fair and square and take your chances. And I give entertainment, teach a lesson and give a pretty good shoe shine on top of it all," he laughs. Shine Man and his fellow artistes can make upwards of $250 or more a night on a busy street such as Decatur or Bourbon where conventioneers think they know it all. Most take it as a joke when they lose the bet. "I had one Australian fella who said he came 3,000 miles to get that shine, after I won," says Shine Man, who also works as a waiter at a French Quarter restaurant.

The Shine Man's secrets of success: Look for couples with nice shoes. "The man always wants to prove to his woman that he's a good gambler and ain't afraid to take chances. But I get 'em every time." Never bet with a guy who is over sixty-five. "If they've been in military service or around the block a bit, they know the routine. Besides, they'll never bet more 'n a dollar, anyway."

On a more nefarious side, watch wallets and purses on Bourbon, which is called Grand Central Station by the pickpockets who lurk around the fringes of crowds. They often strike at folks craning to get a look at the fire-eaters, jugglers, acrobats, dancers, and other street performers who fill the nighttime street. They notice when a watcher pulls out a billfold to drop in a tip. One bump and the stash disappears.

But that doesn't mean that all New Orleans is out to "git ya." Far from it. Most city residents will not just bend over backwards to help a guest but will perform all sorts of contortions. The visitor needs only to think smart and not walk around slack-jawed and over-awed. Keep showy, one-of-a-kind valuables in a hotel safe, and always have an extra quarter secreted on your person somewhere for any emergency phone call. Whether in New Orleans or back home in suburbia, these words to the wise are no different. Remember, don't go for something that seems too good to be true, even if brash Bourbon's bright beat blasts your soul and the red carpet seems to unroll forever. New Orleans can be a tantalizing one-night stand, a hustler's heaven, a Big Daddy/Maggie the Cat kind of town where you wake up with a heartache the next morning.

Or it can be the most invigorating, albeit unabashed, urban playground you've ever visited. Most of what happens is your choice.

Creole/Cajun New Orleans

History and Settlement

Before you go another step, you need to know the proper pronunciation: Cajun (cay-jun) and Creole (cree-ole).

Who are these Cajuns and Creoles whose motif with the small *c* is on almost every other restaurant and gift shop in New Orleans? New Orleans' Chef John Folse, who opened a culinary school in 1988 in what was then the Soviet Union, was quoted by historian Mel Leavitt as saying the major difference between the two was that the Creoles ate in the dining room and the Cajuns ate in the kitchen.

In reality, the difference between Creoles and Cajuns is not quite so simple. In the strict definition, a Creole would have been white or black, either a full-blooded descendant of an early Spanish or French settler or of an African slave. The word *Creole* comes from the Spanish word *crillo,* which means literally *child born in the colonies,* as opposed to a baby born in Europe or Africa. New Orleanians "of color" were mulattoes, quadroons, and octoroons—children of relationships between full-bloods. To compound the ethnic stew, as late as 1873, public directories in New Orleans were calling anyone born in the city a "Creole." This meant there were German Creoles, Chinese Creoles, Jewish Creoles, and Bohemian Creoles, as well as those of French, Spanish, and African descent.

Cajuns, on the other hand, were descendants of French Canadians who had lived in Nova Scotia since 1604. The land was so fertile there that the settlers called it *l'Acadie,* or *heaven on earth.* In 1713, the English seized control of the area after a war with France. The fiercely independent Acadians promised to remain neutral if the British crown would leave them alone after the takeover. However, in 1755, the English governor demanded that the Acadians swear allegiance to the crown. They refused, feeling that the authorities went back on their word, which, of course, they had. Faced with rebellion, troops were sent in to confiscate the Acadian property and the entire population was ordered into exile. Some returned to Europe, some moved west into French-speaking Canada, and others went to other French colonies.

In 1765, Acadian political leader Joseph Brossouard arrived in New Orleans with 200 of his family and friends. Life in the big city did not agree with them, so they moved to Breaux Bridge, Louisiana, and began farming. Over the next decade, these original settlers were followed by almost 10,000 others, among whom were several thousand refugees who had first gone to France and then returned to America in 1785. The Acadians' forced migration was immortalized in poet Henry W. Longfellow's *Evangeline,* first published in 1847. The epic poem told of two Acadian lovers separated by the exile. The term *Cajun* is a bastardized version of *Acadian.* Both whites and blacks in Louisiana can legitimately claim that heritage.

So just what is the difference between Creoles and Cajuns?

For more than a century, the Creoles were the economic, social, and cultural leaders in New Orleans. Upper-class and urbane city dwellers, they spoke French, educated their children in France, clung to French traditions, and considered themselves far superior to any other residents of New Orleans. Those Creoles who remained in Louisiana were generally uneducated but felt cultured because they spent time at the French Opera House and hung out at cafes and the theater. They were especially contemptuous of crude, pushy *Americaines* who arrived in New Orleans after the Louisiana Purchase in 1803.

Creole residents were glad that the Yankees and other "outsiders" lived primarily on the far side of Canal Street, in the Uptown area of New Orleans rather than in the French Quarter. But nothing the Creoles could do would stop the influx of newcomers. Within the next decade, at least 250 businesspeople were recorded as setting up commercial establishments in the city. The majority were Americans who moved into Faubourg S. Marie, immediately dubbing the suburb a Yankeefied "St. Mary's." Their homes and businesses pushed out from New Orleans into what had once been Creole sugar plantations. The area today is the glass and steel muscle of the city's Central Business District (CBD), a true monument to early Northern expatriate entrepreneurs, such as builder and developer Samuel J.

Peters. He was among many outsiders who burst on the New Orleans scene at that time to set the city's then languid business community on its ears.

The Creoles were hard pressed to keep up their traditional control over all aspects of New Orleans commerce. They bitterly complained as English slowly became the language of enterprise in what had been their bailiwick for generations. On the other hand, the Americans muttered that street lighting and the few other civic improvements being made at the time seemed to be going into the Vieux Carre instead of the suburbs where they lived. Of course, travelers to New Orleans complained about the muddy streets in both parts of town, not caring whether Creoles or Yanks were in charge of the purse strings.

In fact, there were two distinct New Orleans communities. The Creoles had their Place d' Armes (Jackson Square), while the Americans had Lafayette Square. The Creole social and business community focused around the St. Louis Hotel on St. Louis Street, while the Yankees congregated at the lavish St. Charles (which was surrounded by pigpens, according to New York journalist Abraham Oakley Hall, who wrote numerous columns about the Crescent City). The Creole Mansion Row was along Esplanade near the United States Mint, while the Americans built their palatial homes along St. Charles. The Americans had the venerable St. Patrick's Church, and the Creoles worshipped in St. Louis Cathedral.

The expansive, tree-shaded, and flower-laden boulevards between the districts were called *neutral grounds,* a term still used today for the grassy dividers separating the traffic flow. There Creoles and Americans could warily—and relatively safely—conduct their business transactions, supposedly without getting into fights. The original neutral ground was what is now Canal Street.

The personification of the Creole was Bernard de Marigny, son of businessman Pierre Philippe de Marigny, who had made a commercial fortune under the Spaniards and was considered one of the richest people in America at the time. Young de Marigny's grandfather was Antoine Philippe de Marigny de Mandeville, stepson of the French royal engineer. Grandpa Marigny spent millions of francs building a villa north of Lake Pontchartrain where he could keep an eye on his vast land holdings. The mansion site is now the town of Mandeville (named after that distinguished, and rich, early colonist).

Little de Marigny might have gotten his easygoing contempt for money by watching his father in action. According to legend, the middle Marigny once hosted guests from France at an exceptionally fancy dinner, serving supper on special golden tableware that was then tossed into the Mississippi after the meal. The gesture meant that no one else was worthy of eating from the service.

De Marigny inherited seven million dollars when he turned fifteen in 1803. He spent much of it almost immediately on gambling and wild times and was subsequently forced to sell his beautiful estate, the Faubourg Marigny, to pay his debts. But de Marigny got in one last word, even as the papers were signed taking away his plantation. One of de Marigny's favorite games was Hazards, a dice game nicknamed *le crapaud* (*the toad*) by its players who squatted on their haunches like toads while playing. Because of his love for the game, he chose the name *Craps* for a lane in the new subdivision that had once been his property. Years later, the name was changed to Burgundy, following complaints by four churches on the street. They felt that such a gambling designation was inappropriate for their respective mailing addresses. When he was eighty-three, de Marigny died alone and almost destitute in a two-room apartment in his beloved French Quarter.

Another Creole noted for his opulent life-style was Charles Durand, whose beautiful Pine Alley plantation was on Bayou Teche near New Orleans. Preparing for the weddings of two of his daughters who were being married on the same day, Durand imported spiders from China to spin webs on three miles of trees leading to his mansion. Gold and silver dust was then sprinkled on the dewy webs early on the wedding morning much to the delight of the arriving guests. But such romantic opulence was not to last forever. The plantation was devastated during the Civil War and the buildings were destroyed. Today all that remains of the site just off Louisiana Highway 86 are the pine trees shading a long, narrow road leading to an empty field.

The Cajuns were more low key and fiscally conservative than the Creoles, finding sanctuary in parishes outside the city. Consequently, a contemporary visitor will have a hard time finding an "original" Cajun in New Orleans, much less an entire cajun neighborhood. However, an estimated one million people in Louisiana can trace their ancestry to the Acadian refugee families. People of the land, they still primarily make their living in the bayous as hunters, trappers, boatmen, fishermen, or off-shore oil rig workers. A hard-working people who love life, their philosophy remains *laissez le bon temps rouler* (*let the good times roll*). Yet for years being Cajun was considered lower class. Children were forced to speak English in schools and many of the family traditions began dying out as the bayous were developed, television intruded, and families dispersed in search of jobs.

Although few persons in New Orleans speak only French today, the Cajuns retain their unique speaking style and idiom. Their patois is similar to that spoken by residents of Quebec. Both dialects are akin to the language used by their ancestors, the first French Canadian settlers of 300 years ago. And in the past twenty years has there been a slow resurgence in appreciation for what is typically cajun.

New Orleans, however, has long been proud of both the creole and cajun influences that provided much of the underpinning of its cuisine, its emphasis on tradition, and its wonderful music.*

A walk through the French Quarter will bring the creole life-style to reality. Although most buildings are privately owned, several typical properties of the creole heyday can be explored. The **Hermann-Grima House,** 820 St. Louis St. (504-525-5661), is open from 10 A.M. to 4 P.M. (last tour leaves at 3:30 P.M.), Monday through Saturday. The house is closed on major holidays. Interpreters show guests around this multistory home that looks plain and withdrawn from the shuttered street side but is open and cheery within. The architectural style is typical of an era when family life went on behind the scenes, well separated from the muddy bustle outdoors.

As a bonus for visitors, on Thursdays from October through May, cooks prepare nose-tingling demonstration meals in the building's restored kitchen. The meats, breads, and desserts spotlight authentic creole cooking styles from the 1830s to the 1860s. It is necessary to call ahead for times of the programs, as well as for reservations. The builder of the house was Samuel Hermann, an early Jewish businessperson in New Orleans.

Food

New Orleanians, whether Creole, Cajun, or Castillian, love their food, making any major meal a center point of their day. Conversation, deal making, and flirting are integral parts of any social occasion involving the culinary aspects of life. Of course, the wide range of multiethnic restaurants available in the city always means a delightful dilemma for the hungry diner, whatever the motive beyond simple pumping of protein. It seems that almost every New Orleans eatery, however, has creole or cajun in its name or on its menu—whether serving pizza, kosher potato dumplings, or fried rice. Yet there is a difference between cajun and creole menu presentations.

Cajun cooking is more down-home, with the best chef probably being a bayou *grand-mere* who learned her culinary secrets from her *grand-*

---

* *A reminder:* Remember that capitalized *Creole* and *Cajun* mean the people from those ethnic backgrounds, while the lowercase *creole* and *cajun* are used as adjectives.

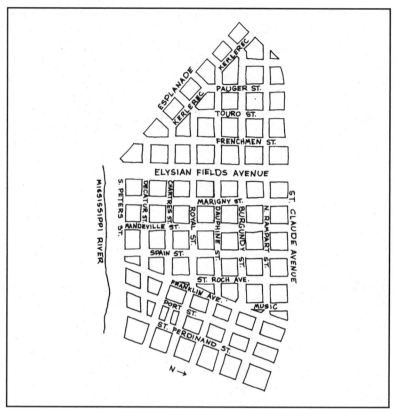

The Faubourg Marigny District

mare. While cajun cooking might seem spicy to the uninitiated, it needn't be explosive to the palate. Unlike the gallons of Louisiana Hot Sauce or pounds of peppers applied to anything that doesn't move, as in the trendy, pseudo-cajun watering holes of Hollywood and Manhattan, true cajun cooking has a more subtle fire. The base of cajun food preparation is the roux, a delicate mixture of fat and flour used for thickening strength and seasoning. The first question a cajun mama would traditionally ask her son when he said he was going to be married was usually, "Is she a Catholic?" The second question, often even more important, was, "Can she make a roux?" If the answers to both were "yes," the young woman was well on her way to matronly approval.

Sausages, pork, chicken, duck, and seafood are the primary ingredients simmered in cajun crackpots, flavored with the roux. Whether slow-moving or fast, turtle, rabbit, venison, and alligator can also find themselves simmering as well. Foods in the cajun mode are prepared as bisque, gumbo, *étouffée,* and *piquante.* The bayou recipe book can be expanded even more. Another cajun delight is *boudin,* an industrial-strength pork sausage stuffed with rice and herbs. The competition is intense to see who has the most succulent sausage. There must be several hundred butchers in southwest Louisiana who have proudly proclaimed themselves Boudin King for their hometowns. A Louisiana guest simply has to sample them all to be sure who's the best.

Creole cooking, on the other hand, is an urban phenomenon. Emphasizing sauces, it tends to be traditionally hotter than cajun cooking because a wider selection of spices was available in the old colonial city when the recipes were taste-tested. While the list is almost endless, *oysters bienville* is a well-known creole dish. A juicy sausage called *andouille* is often used in creole meals, especially served with heaping mounds of flavorful red beans and rice. The latter is a heavy, tummy-warming mixture of kidney beans, with rice, seasonings, spices and, of course, chunks of the chubby sausage. Monday is traditional red beans and rice day in creole homes, when all the weekend's leftovers were cooked together. For variety, "dirty rice" also utilizes all the leavings from Sunday's big meal. The rice is sautéed with green peppers, onions, celery, giblets, and other remainders.

Whether Cajun or Creole, both ethnic groups enjoy their *café au lait,* which is coffee mixed with milk, or *café brulot* made from coffee, spices, orange peels, and liqueurs. The *café brulot,* when presented in a restaurant, is often served flaming in a chafing dish for dramatic effect. Coffee flavored with chicory is a signature item at the Cafe du Monde in the French Market. The herb is dried, ground, and roasted before adding to the drink, providing extra power to the caffeine kick.

Don't be fooled by lexicon "barbecued" shrimp in New Orleans's creole restaurants. In the Crescent City, such delectable shrimp is actually simmered in a peppery, garlic-butter sauce to make a great appetizer.

Joe Cahn, director of the New Orleans School of Cooking, points out that once the basics of cajun or creole food preparation are learned, the rest is easy. "We do pot cooking. Why cook for two persons when you can cook for one thousand?" he asks. "So what if nine hundred don't show up. You then have plenty for tomorrow." Cahn speaks from the viewpoint of one who knows how to rise to such challenges.

Cahn opened his school in 1973 and moved it to the Jackson Brewery building in 1984. He holds a daily three-hour cooking class for eager pupils, both out-of-towners seeking the ultimate munching thrill or locals wanting to bone up on the latest kitchen techniques. "The idea is to put your heart and soul into your preparation because you are cooking for family, whether 'family' is the Queen of England, the Rolling Stones, the folks next door, or kinfolk," he emphasizes.

In New Orleans, eating is how people get to know each other, according to Cahn: "We want to show people we care, so we prepare good food, break bread together, and talk."

The cooking school kitchen is in the back room of a storefront in the upscale mall that once was the city's largest brewery. Six tables, with five to six chairs each, sit in front of a food preparation area, with an overhead mirror to show all the stirring and swirling processes. A glass door separates the school from the sales area out front where there are sacks of rice, boxes of beignet mix, and shelves of regional cookbooks with such delightful titles as *Who's Your Mama?, Are You Catholic and Can You Make a Roux?* by Marcelle Bienvenu. A rack with a sign saying "Joe's Stuff to Spice Up Your Life" groans with everything from paprika to onion salt. Green, red, orange, and mustard-colored hot sauces hunker in all their explosive energy, packing one section of the store: Louisiana Red Sauce, Panola Cajun Jalapeno Sauce, Campfire Hot Sauce, Cajun Chef, Panolo Gourmet Hot Sauce, Trappey's Louisiana Hot Sauce, Cajun Power Garlic Sauce, and West Indian Style Pepper Sauce are only a. few of the brands of bottled dynamite on display, all of which can readily double as rocket fuel.

Gigi Patout, who came to New Orleans from hometown New Iberia in 1979, often holds classes at the cooking school. She and her brother Alex have been fixtures on the city's culinary scene ever since. Ms. Patout, a petite five-foot-one, even took her cajun charm to Los Angeles in 1989. She stayed for five years, building up a rollicking sort of place that became a hangout for the towering, ball-bouncing L.A. Lakers, glowering actor Jack Nicholson, and assorted others in the Hollywood pack. But when it was time to return to the stability of her Louisiana home, there were no regrets.

All five kids in her Patout family were in the restaurant business at one time or another, learning the secrets of crawfish preparation from their parents and a grandma who owned a hotel. Subsequently when she and her brother Alex opened the first of several restaurants in New Orleans, the door was always open for any relative who wanted work. "We cooked instead of playing golf," says Patout, who started out as an office manager for an off-shore oil rig company before her brother convinced her to join him as the hands-on chef.

Cookin' Cajun Cooking School, 1 Poydras St. (504-586-8832 or 504-523-6425), also presents eager, and hungry, visitors an opportunity to learn about oysters Rockefeller, andouille sausage, creole bread pudding with amaretto sauce, bananas foster, fried eggplant fingers, and the tried-and-true shrimp creole. Classes are held from 11 A.M. to 1 P.M. Monday through Saturday, with breakfast, lunch, cocktail hour, and dinner available for groups. Seating at long tables, covered by bright red-and-white checkered tablecloths make for a comfortable introduction to the city's cuisine. The school is located in the Creole Delicacies Gourmet Shop in the Riverwalk Festival Market overlooking the rolling Mississippi River. Cost for a class is $15 per person, with seating available for up to eighty folks. Participants get 10 percent off on purchases in the gourmet shop.

There is a camaraderie obvious among the long-time New Orleans chefs, including the sharing of recipes. These recipes naturally metamorphize into distinct personalities as each kitchen artisan takes the basics and adds his or her own touches.

Cajun Restaurants

Patout's Cajun Cabin, *501 Bourbon St. (504-524-4054), daily 11 A.M.–11 P.M.*   One of several noted Patout family restaurants where Gigi Patout holds sway in the back kitchen and has the freedom to do what she wants when it comes to stoves, ovens, and pans. "You can make anything you want and call it anything you want," she laughs. Fried turkey, crawfish, and seafood are often on the menu. Their on-site banquet room accommodates upwards of 300 persons. A tiny bundle of energy, Patout is diva of the Bourbon Street restaurateurs. Live music is a regular addition at her place, with Mamou, Appaloosa, the Cajun Playboys, and other regulars playing bayou washboard-accordion-guitar favorites.

Other family operations included the now-shuttered original **Patout's Restaurant,** which was an old home at 1391 St. Charles Ave., dating from 1842. Then there was **Patout's Cajun Festival,** 620 Decatur St. (504-581-3437), started by the family but now owned by New York native Greg Leighton, who jokes about his Bayou Yankee management style.

Michaul's, *701 Magazine St. (504-522-5517), Monday–Thursday, 6–11 P.M., Friday–Saturday, 6 P.M.–midnight; closed Sunday and most Catholic holidays. Live cajun music Monday–Thursday, 7–11 P.M.; Friday and Saturday, 7:30 P.M.–midnight.*   For fun, a visitor can't beat the good time *fais-do-do* feel of Michaul's, a high-ceilinged old warehouse with plenty of dance floor room in the city's artsy district. A *fais-do-do* literally means *falling asleep.* The term was adapted from country cajun where family dancing went long into the night and the kids in attendance soon fell a-snoozing while listening to the music. Long tables covered with red-checkered tablecloths encircle the knotty pine foot-stompin' area, fronted by a low stage. Michelle Babineux opened her original Michaul's in Algiers as a local eatery for homesick Cajuns seeking a dose of good alligator sauce piquante.

She soon outgrew the first place and moved across the river where she and musician husband Al (a regular on the "Grand Ol' Opry" radio program) opened up the existing 500-seat restaurant-dance hall. The food remained superb. Ask for the catfish pecan ($15.95), with the fish dipped in egg batter with lemon and butter sauce, then rolled in pecans.

Her staff makes sure everyone gets up and dances; there is usually a half-hour of instruction before the band blasts away. With their love of the razzmatazz Louisiana style of music, Michaul's owners have made their place an unofficial headquarters of the Cajun French Music Association, so only the best in backwater bands play there: Allen Fontentot & the Country Cajuns, Don Duet & the Cajun Pals, LaTouche, the Cajun Troubadors, and Don Montecet often appear. Michaul's also often holds special house concerts with the likes of Zachary Richard, the Bruce Springsteen of Cajun bandleaders. Paul Simon, Huey Lewis, Guns & Roses, and other name-brand entertainers often drop by Michaul's when they are in town, so the place is great for celebrity spotting.

Steve LaFleur's Mamou is considered Michaul's house band, if "regular" is the word for what some trendy music critics gleefully have called leather and motorcycle music rip-roarin' straight from the deepest bayous. Wearing his trademark battered black fedora, earringed LaFleur pushes the traditional cajun syncopation to the nth degree, tossing in some monster R & B backlicks and zip-zap zydeco for flavoring. "Cajun music is fun, it's the rock 'n' roll of folk music," says LaFleur, who has recorded with Rounder and MCA labels. But don't panic thinking that Mamou only plays for the under-thirty set. Michaul's is a hot spot for senior motor coach tours and LaFleur knows how to wink for the blue-haired ladies, as well as the blue-jeaned groupies. It's amazing watching lines of active oldsters whamming away to the tune of Mamou's wild "Ugly Day Stomp."

Mulate's, *201 Julia St. (504-522-1492), Monday–Saturday, 11 A.M.–11 P.M.; Sunday 12:30–3:30 P.M. Live music nightly.*   Mulate's is one of the state's best-known cajun restaurants, with restaurateur Kerry Boutte opening up his first property in 1980 in the town of Breaux Bridge. Ten years later, his New Orleans site was launched across the street from the convention center. The large warehouse space is decorated with paintings by Louisiana artists in a regularly rotating exhibition.

A cajun buffet lunch is served from 11 A.M. to 2 P.M., Monday through Friday. The house speciality is Catfish Mulate's, a catfish filet topped with crawfish *étouffée* sauce, a dish now also served at Euro Disney's American Cuisine Restaurant. The most fun is in the evening, when cajun bands are on tap; a daytime eating experience is fairly tame, especially when there's a room full of conventioneers and motor coach tourists nervously sampling their first fried crawfish. It's best to return for leg kickin' music after 9 P.M., when the place rocks.

In addition to the Breaux Bridge and New Orleans restaurants, another Mulate's is located in Baton Rouge.

Olde N'Awlins Cookery, *729 Conti St. (504-529-3663), daily, 11 A.M.–7 P.M.*   Blackened redfish with sautéed crab fingers, alligator sausage, and soft shell crab enliven the menu here. Dress is definitely casual. On comfortably warm days, guests can sit in a courtyard. Lunches range from $5 to $10, with dinners from $10 to $15.

Creole Restaurants

Pelican Club Restaurant & Bar, *312 Exchange Alley at Bienville St. (504-523-1504). Lunch, Monday–Friday 11:30 A.M.–2:30 P.M.; dinner, Sunday–Thursday 5:30–10 P.M., Friday and Saturday 5:30–11 P.M.*   Reservations are suggested for the Pelican, which has its own haunted elevator leading to upstairs offices. But don't worry about any spectral appearances between the soup and salad courses. Dining is on the first floor and only owner Richard Hughes and his crew need to contend with Things That Go Bump in the Night. Today elegant is the word for the Pelican Club, a far cry from the turn of the century when the building supposedly was a house of ill repute. Hughes's partner and chef Chin Ling adds an interesting dash to the creole menu with his native Singapore flair, presenting such dishes as tea-smoked duck and spicy curry. Hughes and a third partner, Ricky Lemon, are native New Orleanians. The three met while working the restaurant scene in New York and figured that the old hometown needed them. Their cosmopolitan touch extends to the languages spoken by the staff: French, Spanish, and Chinese, in addition to N'Awlinian.

The Pelican Club has some 135 wines from California, Australia, France, and Italy in its bins, earning rave notices from *Wine Spectator* magazine. Thirteen vintages are served by the glass. Holiday *reveillon* is always one of the best times to dine in New Orleans, with the Pelican holding up well against the competition. A holiday dinner might consist of turtle and alligator soup or smoked duck and shrimp gumbo, followed by turkey and vegetable spring rolls with cranberry sauce. The main courses consist of a choice of roasted boudin and andouille sausages with green peppercorn and roasted pepper sauce; pecan-encrusted fish of the day with tangerine salsa and roasted potatoes, duck breast with kumquat coulis, smoked jalapeño and honey-lime jam; or filet mignon with mushroom cabernet sauce. It's all topped off with coconut cream pie, Mississippi mud cake, or apple cranberry bread pudding. And don't forget the egg nog. The total bill is about $30 per person, not counting the wine.

In the old days, Exchange Alley was not considered appropriate for ladies because of the nearby dueling schools. But now the restaurant has become a local landmark and the sign of the Pelican is often used as a reference point for strollers.

Alex Patout's Louisiana Restaurant, *221 Royal St. (504-525-7788), open for dinner 5:30–10 P.M. nightly.* Gigi Patout's brother owns the Louisiana, a restaurant always seeming to pull down a fantastic review from *Gourmet, Food & Wine* and other glossy magazines. They'll even validate nearby garage parking. Reservations are recommended. *Reveillon* at Patout's is another superb tummy tickler, starting with Louisiana won tons stuffed with shrimp and crabmeat on a bed of mango chutney and sweet soy. Diners then move on to smoked salmon, sweet potato praline casserole and vegetables, and lemon cheesecake.

Antoine's Restaurant, *713 St. Louis St. (504-581-4422). Lunch, 11:30 A.M.–2 P.M.; dinner, 5:30–9:30 P.M.* The Grande Palace of New Orleans dining, Antoine's has been operating under the aegis of the same family since the doors swung open in the 1840s. Fifth-generation Bernard R. Guste currently holds the reins. Oysters rockefeller tops the lists of foods here, which explains why there are usually lines waiting to get in for a taste treat. Reservations are strongly recommended, unless you know the maitre d' personally. Even if you do, don't bet on getting to skip to the head of the line. French and Spanish, of course, are both spoken here. Presidents and dictators, divas and comedians, tourists and tycoons can all be seen in Antoine's.

Arnaud's Restaurant, *813 Bienville St. (504-523-5433). Lunch, Monday–Friday 11:30 A.M.–2:30 P.M.; dinner, Monday–Sunday 6–10 P.M.; Jazz Sunday brunch, 10 A.M.–2:30 P.M.* Arnaud's specializes in French and creole cooking in an elegant setting. Gentlemen, wear jackets. Delicate mosaic tiles on the floor, soft thwup-thwup-thwup rotating of ceiling fans, and leaded glass windows overlooking the French Quarter provide an ambience well suited to the cuisine. Dinners here are $20 and up, so prepare the pocketbook.

The Court of the Two Sisters, *613 Royal St. (504-522-7273), daily jazz brunch, 9 A.M.–2:30 P.M.; dinner, 5:30–11 P.M.; closed Christmas.* There's hardly a better way to spend a blissful morning than with a breakfast brunch at The Court of the Two Sisters. Romantic gaslights illuminate the patio at night. Making a selection, however, is downright difficult, with more than sixty items from which to choose. Spanish and French are spoken here, catering to the continental crowd who make the restaurant a must-stop on their stateside excursions.

Decatur House Restaurant, *1119 Decatur St. (504-523-7702). Open for lunch and dinner only Friday, Saturday, and Sunday, 11:30 A.M.–9:30 P.M. The bar opens at 11 A.M. and sometimes closes when the sun peaks over the horizon.* Trout pecan, veal Pontchartrain, and soft-shell crab *meunier* are among the house specialties. The Decatur House is intimate, seating only sixty either in the dining room or an interesting little courtyard. Lately a younger crowd has been settling in at the bar.

Delmonico Restaurant, *1300 St. Charles Ave. (504-525-4937). Open Monday–Saturday, 11:30 A.M.–9:30 P.M.; Sunday, 11:30 A.M.– 9 P.M.* Delmonico's has been a New Orleans tradition since 1895, with turtle soup, stuffed shrimp, red snapper, and broiled catfish favorites for a century. Expect moderate dinner prices, from $15 to $20.

Festivals

Creole Christmas, *c/o French Quarter Festivals, 1008 N. Peters St. (504-522-5730).* For tradition, it's hard to beat anything New Orleans has to offer. Harking back to Yule days of 200 years ago, the historic French Quarter opens its doors to holiday revelers. Tours of antebellum homes, caroling in Jackson Square, a Jewish-Catholic Chanukah service at St. Louis Cathedral, and creole cooking demonstrations at the New Orleans School of Cooking bring civility back to the holidays. Nightly motor coach tours are offered via Gray Line and New Orleans Tours to the Celebration in the Oaks lighting display at City Park ($16 for adults and $11 for children) and for caroling cruises aboard the *Natchez* steamboat. Papa Noël, the creole Santa Claus, visits stores, schools, and museums.

Rejoice on the River, caroling by ethnic groups in Spanish Plaza at Riverwalk, precedes a tree lighting the first Sunday of December. African-American, Vietnamese, and Hispanic young people perform traditional music, along with adult gospel choirs and jazz musicians. A "second line" procession then sweeps up all the participants, audience, and passersby as it jives along Decatur Street to the tree lighting site at Decatur and North Peters, just outside the Cafe Du Monde (504-581-2914). The lighting ceremony features nationally known musicians and loads of kids, elves, carolers, politicians, and community leaders. This may be the South, but be prepared for cool evening weather by bringing a sweater or jacket. Naturally there's more music at the lighting ceremony, with "*Le Anges dans no Campagnes*," "*Belle Nuit*," and other French carols interspersed with "*Venid Fieles Todos, La Primera Navidad*" and others in Spanish to capitalize on the mixed heritage of the district. Hymns in Yoruba, Wolof, and other African dialects, such as the beautiful "*Ise Oluwa*" (Whatever Is God's Will Is God's Will) and "*Eh Jalli Ah Assh*" (It Is Through the Creator), bring home the African traditions of the French Quarter as well.

In the 1800s, creole families celebrated the *reveillon* on Christmas Eve and on New Year's Eve. The first was primarily a religious service, with midnight Mass followed by breakfast at home. A traditional dessert at the time was a jelly-filled cake dripping with rum and covered with whipped cream. New Year's was more partylike, with families moving from home to home to eat, drink, and catch up on the news. A huge dinner always followed back home, with dancing and singing. Several of the French Quarter's best creole-style restaurants participate in an updated version of the *reveillon* by offering holiday-special meals throughout December. Prices are set from $15 to $45 and include at least four courses, plus *café brulot* and eggnog to top off the meal. Participating restaurants have included the Pelican Club, Arnaud's, Bacco, Begue's, Gumbo Shop, Ralph & Kacoo's, Tujague's, the Rib Room, Steaks Unlimited, Mr. B's, Louis XVI, Galatoire's, and Brennan's.

Commercial tours upriver can be made via motor coach to watch the Christmas Eve bonfires along the Mississippi. Tinder in the shape of tepees, boats, and houses are lighted to help Papa Noël find his way to New Orleans along the River Road levee in Gramercy and Lutcher. Call Gray Line Tours (504-587-0861) for details. Tours depart at 3 P.M. from the firm's ticket office at Toulouse Street and the Mississippi River, one block from Jackson Square adjacent to Jax Brewery. Tickets are $45 per person ($25 for children) and include a tour of Tezcuco Plantation and dinner at a restaurant along the way.

French Quarter Festival, *c/o French Quarter Festivals, 1008 N. Peters St. (504-522-5730).* Throughout the second weekend in April since 1984, the Crescent City has celebrated what it calls the world's largest jazz brunch and fireworks display. The fest started as a local street fair to celebrate the much-heralded conclusion of street repairs in the Quarter (remember, New Orleanians don't need much of an excuse to have a party). While the creole connections are tenuous, the free street extravaganza is held throughout the Vieux Carre and in Woldenberg Park near the Aquarium of the Americas. The French Quarter Is for Everyone is the theme for the three days of outdoor concerts, courtyard tours, talent and bartender competitions, a family Mass (11:15 A.M., Sunday, St. Louis Cathedral), and enough parades to satisfy any die-hard marcher. The Guess the Weight of the World's Largest Praline competition is also a popular feature. Since this is truly family oriented, organizers emphasize that the Quarter is for kids with pony rides, face painting, music, storytelling, historical dress-up, and plenty of hands-on activities at the Louisiana State Museum in the Cabildo.

Lillian Boutte, Banu Gibson, Wanda Rouzan, Michael White, the Dukes of Dixieland, Ronnie Kole, Storyville Stompers, Camellia Jazz Band, Zion Harmonizers, John Du Bois, Charmaine Neville, and dozens of others bring more than 100 hours of jazz, gospel, cajun, and classical music to the numerous stages set up around the French Quarter. Not only is there such food for the musical soul, but there's food for the body as well, with an emphasis on updated creole-style cooking: alligator sausage, cheesecake with praline sauce, eggplant dressing, and crayfish chili served by area restaurants and caterers.

Packages, which include hotel rooms, can be secured through Travel New Orleans (1-800-535-8747), Tours by Andrea (1-800-535-2732), and Destination Management (1-800-366-8882).

chapter three

Irish New Orleans

History and Settlement

New Orleans' Irish, who pretend their veins course with green blood, are always proud to proclaim that the sons and daughters of the Gael have been on hand since the city's founding. When Jean Baptiste Le Moyne, Sieur de Bienville, returned to the wild Louisiana frontier in 1730, there were Irish soldiers of fortune in his camp. Many belonged to the storied "Wild Geese," who were Catholic landed gentry, and their retinues and descendants—expatriates fleeing their home after bitter revolutions against the English through the 1600s and 1700s. In fact, according to historians, an estimated 450,000 Irish died in the French armies between 1691 and 1792. Hundreds of Irish were in the French military expeditions into the New World, with New Orleans only one of many outposts that had a Gaelic flavoring from the beginning.

Two brothers, named Jean Jacques and Barthelmy MacCarthey-Mac-Taigs, were perhaps the best known (their name was later abbreviated to Macarty). Their rebellious father had been a captain in an Irish regiment but was forced to escape with his family to France in the early 1700s. There he became a major general in the French army, and his sons learned the military trade. Seeing economic opportunity in the New World, the two young men came to Louisiana to stay, where they married local women.

Other early Irish arrived in more peculiar circumstances. When the Spanish took over the governing of Louisiana in 1762, they had a difficult time dealing with the recalcitrant French locals. It took another member of the Wild Geese faction to bring them to their politically correct senses.

Spanish Governor Alejandro (Alexander) O'Reilly was an Irish native, an exile like many others who joined the armies of Catholic countries that were England's enemies. While living in Havana, Cuba, he became friends with the Protestant expatriate and fellow entrepreneur Oliver Pollock, who had earlier made his way to New Orleans and become a successful businessman. When named governor of Louisiana by the Spanish king, O'Reilly awarded his pal a monopoly on the trading rights along the Mississippi. He did this because Pollock had brought a shipload of supplies to New Orleans during one of its early—and many—food crises.

Pollock and Governor O'Reilly were great friends, due in large part to their common heritage and revolutionary inclinations. Pollock's offices in the French Quarter were on Chartres Street, in back of what is now the Royal Orleans Hotel. Near the rear door of WSDU-TV on Chartres Street, a wall plaque identifies Pollock's former place of business.

Pollock gave his fortune to support the Spanish army that defeated the British in the Battle of Pensacola in 1781, which helped drive the redcoats from the Gulf Coast during the American Revolution. If the English had remained secure in Florida, the American colonies would have had a harder time securing their independence.

Veterans of the Walsh and Dillon regiments, Irish units that fought with French General Lafayette in the American Revolution, came to the area following the war and were absorbed into the hustle and bustle of the adolescent city. To accommodate this polyglot mix of citizenry, the Spanish administrators also encouraged English- and Irish-speaking priests from the Spanish seminary at Salamanca to volunteer for the Louisiana missions. One of these hardy clerics was Father Patricio Walsh, vicar general and administrator of St. Louis Cathedral when Louisiana became the second diocese on the American continent in 1793.

The Irish brought their love of life with them when they moved to New Orleans. In 1809, New Orleans' first recorded St. Patrick's Day parade was held.

Irish immigrants fought on both the British and American sides during the War of 1812, a nasty conflict that culminated in the historic Battle of New Orleans. There was a wry historical footnote about Irish-born General Edward Pakenham, killed while commanding the British forces on January 8, 1815. As was the custom of the era, his body was sealed in a keg of rum to preserve it on the long voyage back home to Ireland for burial. Somehow the keg was misplaced and the corpse was not found until some months later when the barrel was tapped for use in a pub in Ireland. The Irish-born mayor of New Orleans at the time of the battle, Augustin Macarty, must have smiled about the panic he imagined at the bar when the general was discovered. Some wags have claimed that it was the prime example of someone getting really "stiffed."

Out of the early Irish came some of New Orleans' most famous sons and daughters. Many of the city's most magnificent buildings and private residences were designed by James Gallier, Jr., who emigrated from Dundalk with his family. It was believed that their original name was Gallagher, gaelicizing it to better mix in with the French Creole social and business world. The Galliers designed New Orleans' old city hall across St. Charles Street from Lafayette Square. Gallier is the traditional site where Rex, king of Mardi Gras, greets city officials during the parade. The Galliers also completed the interior of St. Patrick's Church and devised a means to shore up the massive structure when it began to sink into the underground muck as construction proceeded.

The **Gallier House Museum,** 1118-1132 Royal St. (504-523-6722), has been refurbished in an 1860-style of decor. An adjoining building houses exhibits on the architect's life and times. Free parking is available and guides speak German and Italian to accommodate international visitors. An imaginative visitor can almost see Gallier himself coming downstairs to say hello.

It is difficult to determine the exact numbers of Irish who settled in New Orleans in those days. Before 1820, census rolls tossed the Scots, English, and Irish into the same "British" stewpot. By the 1860s, census record keeping was more exact. About 25,000 Irish were recorded as living in the city just before the Civil War. This contingent did not arrive dockside with silver spoons in their mouths. From the earliest days of heavy emigration in the middle of the 19th century, the majority of Irish came to New Orleans as low-paid laborers.

New Orleans was the second largest port in the United States in those days, following hard on the heels of New York. Of course, the streets were thought to be paved with gold in all American cities. If it was a tossup between the blustery climes of the Northeast or balmy days in the South, it was often an easier choice to come to Louisiana. Another major factor in attracting the Irish was the fact that New Orleans was an intensely Catholic community, unlike New York with its smorgasbord of religions. A keen contemporary ear can pick up a twang in New Orleans speech similar to that in New York or Boston, however. Coming to mind are "dese" and "dose" for "these" and "those." They go to "woik" and the ladies carry a "poise." These linguistic quirks can be traced to Irish who emigrated to different stateside cities during the same era.

Many Irish were recruited to work on the six-mile-long New Basin Canal, linking Lake Pontchartrain to the Mississippi River. In charge of the project were Yankee entrepreneurs Maunsell White and Beverly Chew, hardfisted, tight-pocketed types who had organized the New Orleans Canal and Banking Company. Their mission was to build a sixty-foot-wide, six-foot-deep trench that would make it easier for hauling freight and, incidentally, break the Creole monopoly on existing port facilities. A turning basin in the city was to allow shops to return to the lake.

Seeking economic security and fleeing hard times at home, the Irish abandoned their Auld Sod cottages and slums, lured in part by the promise of fortune in this canal project. From 1832 to 1838, between 20,000 to 30,000 Irish were estimated to have joined hundreds of Germans who also expected that a fantastic new life would be open for them on the Louisiana frontier.

In reality, if Paddy and Hans survived the ocean voyage, they found disease-carrying mosquitoes, 100-degree-plus temperatures, and back-breaking labor. While there was indeed mistreatment of slaves, the ordinary laborer of the period didn't have it much better. Although the white workers were nominally free and could appreciate the potential of upward mobility, they often took the worst jobs because slaves were usually, but not always, protected from the most dangerous work. Slaves were capital investments, simple property to be bought and sold. As such, no savvy overseer wanted to have "damaged goods" on his hands. If a slave was injured, a master could lose thousands of dollars on the investment. And if a slave died, it was up to the master to bury the slave. But if an ordinary citizen sickened or died, friends or relatives were responsible for his/her care.

Besides, if a "free" Irishman would work for fifty cents a day, plus room, board, and $6.25 a month for whiskey, management figured it was coming out ahead, especially since purchases were usually made at the company store. Nobody really cared if the strong-backed Irish died or not; there were always plenty more arriving dockside almost daily.

Laborers lived in fetid tent camps along the canal. Those who died were buried almost where they collapsed, in and along the banks of the deep ditch. If there was a mudslide, trapped workers were usually abandoned and then entombed by the slimy earth. It is estimated that 8,000 men died building the New Basin Canal.

When roadworkers were ripping up Canal Boulevard at Seapark to improve the traffic flow near St. Patrick's Cemetery in the late 1980s, they unearthed a mass grave of several hundred of these dead unfortunates. Most were unidentified victims who died of cholera, typhoid, yellow fever, and other diseases. Others died from injuries incurred while digging their way by pick and shovel through the swamps. In the predynamite days, black powder was available for blasting, but it wouldn't work in the wet Louisiana muck and huge cypress and oak stumps had to be dug out by hand. It was a common occurrence that men were seriously injured doing such hazardous work.

But those who survived made up some of the city's best success stories. They were in the front lines of workers available as longshoremen, teamsters on the dray wagons, warehousemen, and in other muscle jobs that opened up after the completion of the canal. Eventually they moved into service jobs in police and fire departments and into politics and other professions. More than one Irish New Orleanian today can be proud of his or her family's rise in status: from newly arrived great-grandparents who couldn't read or write, to grandparents who made it through grade school, to parents graduating from high school, to their own college educations, and on to their children's masters and doctorates. A typical example of the Irish-born immigrant is the great-grandfather of Monsignor John Reynolds, pastor of St. Patrick's Cathedral in the mid-1990s. He worked in the Pennsylvania coal mines, moved to New Orleans, fought with the Confederates, and was captured by the Union. Wounded four times, he lived through the war to eventually become New Orleans's police chief.

Economists look at maps of New Orleans and point out how the Great Basin Canal changed the financial life and overall look of the city. The channel doubled the previous dock space along the Mississippi fronting the French Quarter. With the canal and the turnaround basin built for barges, the city grew even faster.

Through the years, the Irish continued to leave their mark on New Orleans. During the Civil War, feisty Father James Mullon, the Irish-born pastor of St. Patrick's, openly opposed the city's occupation by the federal army. He supposedly told one commander that he'd be happy to bury all Union occupiers from his church. And he wasn't just saying that out of a spiritual gesture. But in a cavalier gesture, Yankee officers allowed St. Patrick's to keep its bell, making it the only church in the city spared in the metal-meltdown effort of the war. According to local legend, Mullon had gallantly served in the U.S. Navy during the War of 1812 and, thus, his church escaped the looting.

By the 1890s, the Irish had risen to many positions of authority in the city, just as they did in Boston, New York, Chicago, and other immigrant cities.

However, as a flood of arrivals came from other nations, there was a growing animosity between them and those who came earlier. Fearing for their jobs, the old-timers objected to the newcomers, although they had been in the same situation themselves. In one celebrated incident, popular New Orleans Police Chief David Hennessy was shot to death by unknown assailants as he left his French Quarter home in 1891. Although there was never any proof, it was rumored that some Italians had committed the murder. Eleven Sicilians were subsequently plucked off the street and arrested. Despite being held in jail, they were lynched by a vengeful mob that attacked the prison and overpowered the guards.

It took a generation before both communities were reconciled over that ethnic trauma. Today, though, the Irish and Italians work closely together in all aspects of city life, from politics to law enforcement to cultural activities. There is even an Italian-Irish St. Patrick's Parade Committee that stages its own March 17 High Holy Hoopla in Metairie. There is a street fair, corned beef and spaghetti stalls, and a procession of gaily decorated floats and rousing bands.

The Irish have always been proud to show off their beloved adopted city. After Mayor John Fitzpatrick was elected in 1892, New Orleans hosted the raucous national convention of the Ancient Order of Hibernians. An Irish Heritage Festival, an hours-long parade, and fancy-dress dinners were the order of the day. In 1992, another national convention of the Hibernians set the city's ear on end again with all the Gaelic goings-on. Also in 1892, Gentleman Jim Corbett, the noted hard-knuckle boxer, trained at Uptown's Berhman Gym at the corner of Washington and Prytania streets. He and John L. Sullivan, another famed bruiser, then battled it out on the riverfront. Corbett was the exhausted victor in the twenty-first nose-crunching round.

Most of the Irish worked the docks, living in the Uptown neighborhood known as the Irish Channel, located in the lower Garden District. Boundaries of the Channel were (and still are) more a state of mind than of actual geography. But the main concentration of the Gael could be found in the blocks bounded by the Mississippi River, Magazine Street, Jackson Avenue, and Felicity Street. Historians have said that the original Irish Channel was the two-block-long Adele Street, between St. Thomas and Tchoupitoulas. But the Irish were never ones to be bounded with anything like maps, so their population spread along Constance, Division, Annunciation, Laurel, Magazine, and Camp streets.

There are several accounts of the origin of "Irish Channel." One tale says that the narrow lanes in the Irish section flooded so often that they were like river channels. Another story claimed that sailors coming toward the tricky bend in the river near where the Irish lived could spot the lights of the Ocean Home Saloon, the Bull's Head Tavern, the Isle of Man, and other waterfront dives well known to the dockers. The man on ship-

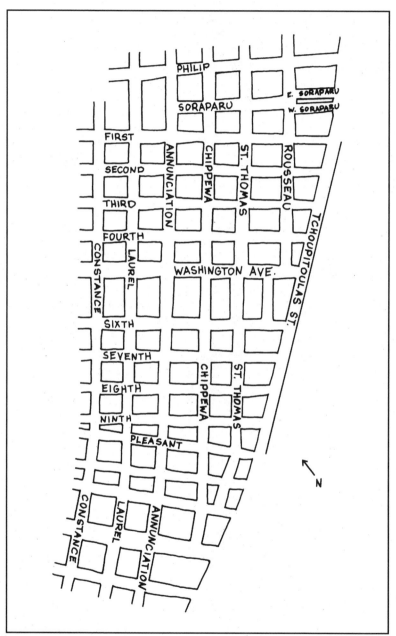

The Irish Channel District

board watch would yell out, "There's the Irish Channel!" to the helmsman so he could make the proper maneuvers to avoid running aground. Yet the simple reason that the Channel got its name was the fact that it was where the Irish settled. It was close to work, close to church, and close to friends. So who needed more?

Today's Irish Channel is a typical changing urban neighborhood, one with a tough edge to it these days. Most of its original families have long gone to the suburbs, especially to Metairie. Bargain-minded shoppers can still find great deals, some treasures, and lots of bizarre odds and ends in the numerous antique shops and secondhand stores that now line Magazine Street, once the heart of the Channel's long-ago thriving commercial district. Because of its low rents, many artists have moved back into the area, with vegetarian restaurants and coffee shops opening and closing like sprouting mushrooms after a Kilkenny rain.

Parasol's Bar (504-899-2054), a rambling and somewhat battered white frame building with green doors and window frames, is tucked into a corner on Third and Constance streets, just off Magazine. The pub no longer has a regular Irish clientele yet remains the staging area for a "practice" parade several days prior to St. Patrick's Day. Streets around the bar are packed with parade-goers flocking to hear the latest rock 'n' roll bands, drink green beer, and get caught up on gossip. It's all under the guise of learning their marching position in the Irish Channel procession for St. Paddy's Day. This event used to be a spur-of-the-moment street party, but now the police erect barricades to help control the traffic flow. Die-hard old-timers lament that even this tiny bit of officialdom gives a bit too much formality to the day. The run-through is usually held the Saturday prior to St. Patrick's.

The Irish Channel was on the upriver side of the French Quarter, just beyond the large homes where the first Yankee businesspeople lived after the Louisiana Purchase. The Irish in the neighborhood were served by priests at St. Patrick's, 724 Camp Street (504-525-4413), and St. John the Baptist, 1139 Dryades Street. The story of St. Patrick's parallels the rise of the Irish in New Orleans. The church's cornerstone was blessed on July 1, 1838 by Bishop Antoine Blanc, with the aforementioned Londonderry-born Father James Mullon saying the first service. Designed by Dakin and Dakin Architects, the structure was completed by Irish architect James Gallier. St. Patrick's is now on the National Register of Historic Places, standing proudly at the edge of the city's bustling financial and business district.

From the time of the founding of the city in 1718 until after the Louisiana Purchase by the United States in 1813, French-speaking priests cared for all the city's Catholics. Yet after the fire of 1788, the city expanded upriver and many immigrants and Yankees moved into the district between Canal and Howard, known as Delord Street at the time. They wanted their own place of worship.

A wealthy French creole businessman, Pierre Foucher, built a small church in that district, which again was staffed by French priests. As the Irish flooded into the neighborhood and adjacent blocks in the 1820s and 1830s, they demanded their own church and priests. In 1832, a group of Irish leaders called for an architect to build St. Patrick's. All those Irish mothers wanted Irish clergy to hear their confessions in Gaelic, a language they could understand, not that "French stuff." But it was almost a decade before the effort finally got off the ground and construction started.

A sheriff's sale in the mid-1840s, in which debts owed by the church were repaid by the rental of pews; attacks by the anti-immigrant know-nothings in the 1850s; and a fire in 1861 weren't enough to halt the parish's expansion. Eventually most of the city's influential businesspeople and politicians of Irish extraction were parishioners. Today the church is noted for its Christmas concerts, usually held on the first two Sundays in December. A monthly Latin mass is said at 9:30 A.M. on the second Sunday of the month.

St. John the Baptist Church, established in 1848, has not fared so well Its home neighborhood looks as if it has struggled through too many losing prize fights. Tumbled-down homes and garbage-littered gutters ring the old church, padlocked except for Sunday services. Crack dealers lurk in nearby doorways. Even police are more wary when answering emergency calls there.

But there are islands of quiet amid the surrounding urban decay. During the last century, Irish-born Margaret Gaffney Haughery supported many orphanages in New Orleans and was known for distributing food to poor young people. Today her plump visage, shoulders covered by a sweater shawl, now stands permanently in marble with her left arm protectively comforting a child. She died in 1882 and her statue was erected in 1884, making it one of the first in North America to honor a woman—"other than the Blessed Mother," joked one Irish wag. The statue can be seen in the tiny, parklike Margaret Place at the intersections of Clio, Camp, Gaeinnie, and Coliseum near the old telephone company headquarters.

Appropriately, across the street is the Louise Day Care Nursery at St. Theresa of Avila Church, 1135 Coliseum Street, with a mural of playing children painted by the New Orleans Youth Corner Studies program.

The third wave of Irish, after the wealthy gentry in the first contingent and the ditch diggers in the second, were the wretched survivors of the Potato Famine that ravaged Ireland in the 1840s. The latest arrivals had to begin their climb up the social ladder from the minute they arrived ashore, just as the previous émigrés had done. Since the Channel was already packed with residents, the new Irish moved "Downtown," to the far side of what is now Esplanade.

Their cozy "shotgun" and "camelback" houses are still clustered throughout that neighborhood. A typical shotgun house is very narrow, with all the rooms opening end-on-end for ventilation purposes. The design got its nickname since it was assumed that a gun could be fired through the house with the shot traveling through the center of the home, traversing each room without hitting anything—presuming the doors were open and grandma ducked, of course. The rear end of what was called a camelback house has two stories, while the front of the building is only one story. This design avoided a tax on the number of windows fronting the street. The tax collectors probably weren't fooled, but the style provides another delightful addition to the rich variety of New Orleans' architecture.

The Downtown Irish were envious of the Uptowners. For one thing, the Uptowners had two Catholic churches, while the Downtowners still had only French-speaking parishes to attend. It was considered an intolerable situation for the faithful, so they saved their pennies and quarters and eventually had enough to build their own St. Alphonsus Church in 1857, served by Irish priests. The front door of the imposing structure sits almost on Constance Street, except for a narrow sidewalk.

Many of this wave of Irish became "screwmen," according to historians, whose job was "screwing," or packing, cotton into the holds of freighters and steamships. For generations, the Uptown and Downtown Irish wouldn't mingle. Now, of course, they do. One cooperative effort was the erection of a Celtic cross in 1990 atop the now filled-in New Basin Canal. Paid for by the Irish Cultural Society of New Orleans, the Connemara marble cross remains a strong reminder of the human cost of the project. Capsules buried in the monument contain several thousand names of contemporary Irish-American New Orleanians who contributed funds to the project. Many could count their ancestors among those memorialized. A public rededication ceremony is generally held the first Sunday in November.

The cross was originally rimmed with flowers; however, the mud hauled in to build the mound on which the monument was placed was full of seeds of the British Horsetail, a hardy weed that can quickly reach up to three feet high if not regularly trimmed. So now instead of the floral arrangements, the Irish Cultural Society members attack the bushy intruders with clippers and cutters. That "the Brits got their revenge" is the running joke among the volunteer gardeners. The memorial site is just behind a rundown relic of another fearsome age: a nuclear bomb shelter that was built to protect New Orleans city officials if ever the now-dissolved Soviet Union attacked.

· The advent of the railroad put an end to the waterborne freight hauling. By bits and pieces, the original canal became filled in, so only a small section remains adjacent to the Southern Yacht Club on Lake Pontchartrain. Yet the face of the Irish remains strongly evident in New Orleans. Throughout the twentieth century, the Irish in New Orleans continued to prosper. In 1920, Andrew McShane became mayor and served for five years. His successor died in office, and Arthur O'Keefe became mayor, serving until 1929. One of O'Keefe's great-grandsons, Sean, even served as a secretary of the Navy.

Social Organizations

There's nobody like the Irish to turn out for a parade. Marching clubs celebrate St. Patrick's Day with a vengeance bordering on madness in a city known for strutting its stuff for the slightest reason, or virtually no reason at all. The Algiers, Downtown, Irish Channel, and Italian-Irish marching clubs are only a few of the major paraders who favor the color emerald. They are primarily informal social organizations, bringing together folks who simply like to party. This, of course, is one of life's basic tenets according to New Orleanians.

In addition to the marching clubs, the Ancient Order of Hibernians and the Ladies Hibernians have chapters in the city.

Irish Cultural Society, *6126 Clara St. (504-861-3746).* These friendly sons and daughters of Erin are more into preserving authentic culture than quaffing green beer, at least in public. But they certainly aren't shillelaghs-in-the-mud. They meet monthly at their clubhouse on Clara Street, the basement of an old home in the Tulane University neighborhood. "People look at the word *culture* and think of it being solemn and not fun. It certainly isn't that way; it's just that we don't push Tin-Pan-Alley Irishness," explains one officer.

Regular business meetings are held the second Friday of the second month (February, April, June, August, October, December). Social gatherings, where everyone brings munchies to serve, are held on the alternate Fridays. There is a Dutch treat bar and anyone is welcome to drop by for a bit o' chat and plenty of *craic,* the Irish term for *a good time.* Either a guest speaker is invited or there might be a spirited discussion on some aspect of Irishness. Meetings begin around 7:30 P.M. Out-of-towners are welcome.

Each year, the association presents awards to someone working hard to preserve Irish heritage in New Orleans. A certificate is given to the *caomnh noir* (preserver), honoring him or her for protecting the "treasure" of Irish culture. On a certificate is the society's coat of arms, depicting a *fleuer-de-lis* (a harp and a key). The *fleuer-de-lis* represents the French heritage of New Orleans.

The family of Society President Henry Scanlon is typical of New Orleans's Irish. He can trace his roots back to the famine émigrés who arrived in the 1840s. Since they were at the bottom of the social ladder, they settled on the fringes of the Irish neighborhoods, living alongside Germans and Italians. There is German blood in Scanlon's veins. On his English-Irish mother's side, he can follow his roots back to 1746, with the Teutonic influence derived from tough stock originating in Germantown, Pennsylvania. That part of the family came to New Orleans as part of a wave of Northerners after the Civil War.

"We didn't talk much about that Yankee line," laughs Scanlon, a foreman for the New Orleans electric company. His lilting brogue, tinged with a touch of Southern drawl, is a fooler. Like many in New Orleans, his accent could almost pass for that of a Brooklynite. His Irish ancestors came to the Crescent City at the same time as many other émigrés were being shunted into New York, and their speech patterns remain similar.

In addition to monthly get-togethers, the society marks special occasions as well. For example, there is Founder's Day in the spring, honoring club president emeritus Dr. Rodney Jung, city health director from 1962 to 1970 and from 1981 to 1983. Now in private practice, Jung is also professor emeritus in tropical medicine at Tulane University.

Again demonstrating the New Orleans heritage gumbo, Jung doesn't have any Irish in him at all, but he formed the society in 1977 because of his interest in and love of the Gaelic culture. Jung even speaks Irish, to the point of singing the national anthem in the Old Tongue. He is also writing a book on Irish folk songs. Growing up in the Irish Channel, Jung is Spanish on his mother's side and German on his father's.

"The Irish of my day there worked on the docks. They were proud but had pretty well forgotten what it was like to be really Irish," Jung explains. "All we had were stereotypical pictures of a guy in a green suit and peculiar hat celebrating St. Pat's by throwing cabbages and drinking beer," he says. Despite this, because of social contacts he had with the Irish, Jung became very enamored of the nation's traditional culture and was a member of the New Orleans Friends of Ireland, the precursor of the Irish Cultural Society. The Friends disbanded in the late 1970s and the cultural group was then formed.

One of the organization's major activities is sponsoring Irish language classes at O'Flaherty's Irish Channel Pub, at about 4 P.M. on Wednesdays, taught by Sister Bernadette McNamara.

The New Orleans School of Irish Dance, *717 Adams St. (504-283-1391). Mailing address: 635 St. Charles Ave., New Orleans, LA 70130. FAX 504-524-0607.* Classes are held Saturday, beginning at noon for children under six. Classes run until 7 P.M. Every Saturday from 9 P.M. until everyone drops, *ceili* (traditional folk dancing) and set dance lessons are held at O'Flaherty's. *Seisuns* (Irish jam sessions) are held in The Informer, the pub on the noisy side of the building, where everyone can whoop and kick out a leg at no charge except for the price of a pint. Adult sessions for formalized *ceili* and set dancing are held at 6:30 P.M. on Tuesdays. School Director Mary Ann McGrath Swaim was certified by the Irish Dance Commission in Dublin in 1984 and was the first Louisianian to receive the coveted certification. Swaim is also an attorney who practices with her husband and brother in an 1836 building designed by the famed New Orleans Irish architect James Gallier. She was named Irish Person of the Year in 1991 by the local chapter of the Ancient Order of Hibernians.

McTeggart School of Irish Dancing, *4921 Jefferson Highway, New Orleans, LA 70121 (504-831-9676).* Maureen McTeggart Hall is a Denver-based instructor who has been teaching classes in New Orleans since 1984. A teacher for 40 years, she has dance schools in Dallas, Houston, and Denver, in addition to New Orleans. The McTeggart School was established in 1939 in Cork by Peg McTeggart, Maureen's older sister. The family immigrated to the United States in 1958, bringing their love of dancing with them. Maureen McTeggart began teaching in Denver in 1976 and helped organize the Irish Step Dancers of Colorado. She is a vice president of the Irish Dancing Commission and adjudicates every year at the North American and World championships. Classes are held from 5 to 8:30 P.M. on Friday and from 8:30 to 10 A.M. on Saturday at the St. Francis School Auditorium, 444 Metairie Road, Metairie.

Shops

Irish Shop of New Orleans, *723 Toulouse St. (504-523-6197 or 1-800-927-0321).* Tapes, flags, books, jewelry, hats, tea towels, trinkets, sweatshirts, and custom-made, coat-of-arms golf shirts fill the shelves in the Irish Shop. Owners Don Rusina and wife Barbara Fahy offer an extensive collection of Irish souvenir items. The store opened in 1988 "with special things for special people," assert Rusina and Fahy.

Pubs

The warmth and charm of Ireland is best exemplified by the Irish public house, or the pub. New Orleans has several great hangouts for the Gaelic set. Some are more Irish than others, and a shamrock on the door doesn't necessarily mean that you'll be meeting Mick from Monahan inside. But the fun of New Orleans is exploring the Irish-named pubs to find the right match. Here are a few that would please even Brendan Behan, whose love of the pub scene rivaled his literary skills. Hours are early to late. In New Orleans, bars only need to be closed two hours a day for cleaning. If there are any questions about hours of operation, just call.

Fahy's Irish Pub, *540 Toulouse St. (504-586-9806).*   This is a cozy French Quarter bar, owned by Don Rusina and his wife Barbara Fahy. The couple also operates the Irish Shop of New Orleans a few blocks away. Fahy's has a decent happy hour from 3 to 7 P.M., Mondays through Fridays and from midnight to 3 A.M. Darts and pool round out the setting for conversation with locals.

O'Flaherty's Irish Channel Pub, *514 Toulouse St. (504-529-1317).*   There's nightly entertainment in this wonderfully dim, wood-paneled building, the High Court of Tara for the real Irish of New Orleans. Actually, an alley and rear courtyard separate the two large rooms that make up O'Flaherty's. On the left is The Informer pub for serious or light conversation and a drink or two or three. On the right is The Ballad Room in which owner Danny O'Flaherty runs a tight ship whenever there are performances. Silence is requested to show "respect for the entertainers," says O'Flaherty, who arrived stateside from Connemara in 1975.

"It's bad manners to be talking when someone is singing," he emphasizes (O'Flaherty has been known to request that talkative guests leave and go next door). A Gaelic speaker, O'Flaherty writes many of his own arrangements, some of which have to do with the Irish in New Orleans history. He and Welsh harpist Robin James-Jones team up to comprise Celtic Folk, a duet that has appeared at concerts and festivals around the nation. Don't ask for him to sing rebel songs or "Danny Boy." What you'll hear are authentic tunes, with plenty of the bittersweet story lines that make real Celtic music so distinctive. At Christmas, the pub holds a Celtic

Christmas celebration. Special concerts also are held throughout the year. Call for the latest on the Gaelic grapevine.

The pub offers a "Celtic Circle" for $100 a year, entitling music fans to the best seats in the house, an opportunity to meet touring performers and, best of all, the chance to cut to the head of the line waiting for bar service on St. Patrick's Day. O'Flaherty's has become the center for Irish entertainment in New Orleans, with out-of-town entertainers on the bill, as well as locals. *Ceilis* are offered at varying times.

There's also a well-stocked gift shop in the courtyard area, offering books, knitwear, flags, and other quality items—with no leprechaun statues in sight.

The Kerry Pub, *331 Decatur St. (504-527-5954).*   Co-owner Noel Walsh performs from 9 P.M. to 1 A.M. Sunday and Monday, with other groups, such as Highland Paddy or Dave Sharp and the Hard Travelers, performing throughout the remainder of the week. Guests never know who might drop by or tip a pint, whether a touring performer, such as Danny Doyle, or a local politician. A Songwriter's Night is held each Monday showcasing local folk and acoustic talent. There is no cover charge. Nash, who also owns Harty's Tavern in hometown Ballybunion, has a passel of folks from the Old County working the place. Belfast, Wexford, and Craigavon accents are commonplace.

Ryan's Pub, *241 Decatur St. (504-523-3500).*   This is a fairly recent addition to the French Quarter scene, but owner Martin Doherty, of County Tyrone, has made it one of the top local pubs in the neighborhood. The corner site has been a bar for generations, most recently the popular Lord VJs, before Doherty took it over early in 1993 and cleaned it up. There's a good mix of local folks, especially with the young waiters and waitresses who come over after their restaurants shut down for the evening. So there's always plenty of action around the pool table, dart boards, and jukebox. Earringed manager Craig Brown is a Scot, with years of experience running such popular Glasgow hangouts as Napoleon's, the Tunnel Club, Panama Jack's, and Jackie O's. Many of the barkeepers are young folks from the Old Country.

Pictures of famed Irish authors such as James Joyce and Brendan Behan adorn the walls. The old wooden backbar must be one of the most impressive in the city.

Molly's Irish Pub and Restaurant, *732 Toulouse St. (504-568-1915 or 568-1916).*   Said to serve the best Irish coffee in the French

Quarter, Molly's is mostly a hangout for young rocker types after 9 P.M. Piped R & R is loud and brassy, but this is the place for the under-thirty set to mix and mingle in a definitely casual atmosphere. You won't get much more Irish here than the coffee, however. But if black leather and a predisposition for The Pogues or The Ghost of an American Airman is your game, then give Molly's a roll. Small, with seating for only 45, Molly's is open twenty-four hours a day.

Molly's at the Market, *1107 Decatur St. (504-525-5169).* Jim Monaghan, the King of the French Quarter Irish, holds sway at Molly's. Monaghan is a former mining engineer who opened the first of several pubs in the Crescent City some twenty-five years ago. He usually holds sway looking out on the throngs along Decatur Street from an open window facing the street near the end of his bar. Molly's at the Market is a great place to meet authentic fiery-haired lads and lasses. Monaghan makes his place hop. There's an eclectic mix of bikers, business types, off-duty waiters, struggling poets, passing jazz artists, and recently arrived Old Sod types. Molly's offers great pub grub, ranging from burgers to soup.

Monaghan, whose dad was from Sligo, throws a heck of a St. Patrick's Day parade. Every Tuesday from 10:30 P.M. to midnight, he hosts a Media Night with a celebrity bartender. Louisiana's governor, among others, has poured taps at Molly's. Manager Regina McGoldrin, from County Meath, keeps everyone in line, including Monaghan—who is certainly a handful.

Pat O'Brien's, *718 St. Peter St. (504-525-4823); Sunday through Thursday, 10 A.M.–4 A.M.; Friday through Sunday, 10 A.M.–5 A.M.* Supposedly Pat O'Brien's serves more liquor than any other bar in the world. While that might just be part of the O'Brien's legend, it is true that the place invented the fabled Hurricane drink, a sweet but powerful concoction made of dark rum, with cherries and other garnishes and served in a commemorative lantern-shaped glass. There's nothing like sitting in the bar's inner courtyard with a table of friends, while the French Quarter crowd surges past in the fresh New Orleans evening.

Yet is it Irish? Not quite, despite the gift shop packed with O'Brien memorabilia and shamroguery green stuff. More touristy than anything else, O'Brien's now has an outlet in Cancun, Mexico, of all places and is considering another property on Memphis' Beale Street. George (Sonny) Oechsner II, the current owner, acquired the famous French Quarter watering hole in 1978. His father, George Sr., had managed the bar since the 1940s. And yes, there really was a B. H. (Pat) O'Brien, a well-known

Irish New Orleanian who died in 1983 at the age of eighty-three. O'Brien opened his bar in 1933 and went into partnership with Charlie Cantrell in 1937, moving around to several sites in the French Quarter. The current O'Brien's was originally the Tarbary Theater, the first Spanish theater in colonial America.

Here are a couple of other late-night Irish hangouts, more local than anything else, but snug and comfortable:

Mick's Irish Pub, *4801 Bienville Ave. (504-482-9113).*

Timothy Shanahan's, *7600 Maple St. (504-866-3712).*

Festivals

The Highest Holy Day parade to end all parades in New Orleans is held on St. Patrick's Day (March 17), with a fervor matching, if not surpassing, all that preLenten frenzy of Mardi Gras. Primarily a walking event, participants move from pub to pub in the French Quarter. Riders on the few floats that make their way through the crowd of revelers often toss cabbages and carrots in a parody of Mardi Gras trinket-tossing. This is mostly a green-beer crowd that is into wearing silly plastic hats and waving mock shillelaghs.

The Irish Channel parade begins with a 1 P.M. Mass at St. Mary's Assumption, 2030 Constance, with marching starting at Race and Annunciation streets. The 400-plus strollers—including the usual motley collection of green-derbied politicians, tongue-lolling Irish sellers, and creamy-cheeked lads and lasses—meander to Magazine Street and on to Louisiana Avenue. After making a serious attempt at a stylish *U*-turn on Prytania Street, the Green Gang returns to Louisiana Avenue and heads to Washington Avenue, to disperse at Tchoupitoulas.

Two marching clubs parade through the Vieux Carre on the weekend prior to St. Pat's Day. The Decatur Street Irish Club starts and ends at Molly's at the Market, 1107 Decatur Street, in a procession that also tosses out enough veggies to make an Irish stew. To capture a cabbage, a girl has to kiss the guy doing the tossing. This raucous ensemble weaves down Bourbon and various side streets before being routed back to Decatur.

The Downtown Irish Club, numbering some 200 members and innumerable hangers-on, marches on St. Patrick's Day itself, usually starting around 6:30 P.M. But remember, this is Irish time. Be prepared to quaff another Guinness in case the carousing Celts get a late start, rolling from the corner of Alvar Street and St. Claude Avenue.

The drums go bang and the cymbals clang loudly for Metairie's Italian-Irish Parade committee during St. Patrick's week, kicking off with a street party at the Clearview Shopping Center two days before St. Patrick's Day. For multicultural imbibers, there's free wine and beer, beginning at 4 P.M., with Irish-Italian sandwiches and a presentation of the organization's parade grand marshals. Both the Irish and the Italians choose their own marshals, who don't actually have to be of either ethnic background. True to the wonderful rainbow makeup of the city, even Chinese and other ethnic business and political leaders have received the nod to lead the procession.

On the closest Friday to St. Pat's, the committee holds a dinner dance at the Pontchartrain Center, 4545 Williams Boulevard, Kenner. There's a grand mix of corned beef and cabbage and Italian sausage and peppers. The parade is usually the Sunday after St. Pat's, if the date does not fall on a weekend. Beginning at the Clearview Shopping Center, the route meanders through Metairie, concluding at the corner of Martin Behrman Avenue and Veterans Boulevard.

For information, write the parade committee at Box 1562, Metairie, LA 70004.

Nationally known talent usually performs at O'Flaherty's Irish Channel Pub on St. Patrick's, for a serious celebration of culture. Music, theater, and dancing round out the bill. O'Flaherty's is located at 514 Toulouse Street (504-529-1317).

Distinctly more serious and educational, but loaded with just as much fun and great music, is the annual Celtic Nations Festival of Louisiana held early in October. Booths and stages line the banks of the Tchefuncte (Cha-funk-ta) River in Madisonville, the oldest permanent settlement in St. Tammany Parish. The town was officially incorporated in 1811, only seven years after Louisiana's establishment of statehood. Performers from the Celtic nations of Ireland, Scotland, Wales, and Brittany are represented.

Newspapers

The Irish American Post, *301 N. Water St., Milwaukee, WI 53202 (414-273-8132). The Irish American Post,* the only Midwestern Irish monthly newspaper, regularly features New Orleans and other Louisiana Gaelic goings-on with both news and features from stringers based in the Crescent City. An extensive calendar is usually the best place to find out the latest in entertainment and programming around the area.

Copies can be found at most of the Irish bars in New Orleans and from the Irish Cultural Society. Newsstand issues are $1; yearly subscriptions are $12.

Irish Echo, *309 Fifth Ave., New York, NY 10016 (212-686-1266);* **Irish Voice,** *432 Park Ave., South, Suite 1000, New York, NY 10016 (212-684-1198).* These two major East Coast weeklies can be found in selected New Orleans outlets, such as O'Flaherty's. Both papers offer excellent coverage of Irish and northeastern United States Irish news but not much about local Louisiana or New Orleans happenings. $1/issue for the *Echo* and 75¢/issue for the *Voice.*

Irish Eyes, *c/o Masterpiece Publishing, 1314 N. 3rd St., Suite 120, Phoenix, AZ 85004 (602-252-3161).* Occasionally copies of *Irish Eyes* pop up around the city, with news from Arizona and other southwestern states. The free paper can often be found at O'Flaherty's.

Southwest Celtic Music Association, *8204 Elmbrook Dr., Suite No. 135, Dallas, TX 75247 (214-630-9068).* The association's newsletter offers good bimonthly coverage of happenings in Texas, Mississippi, and Louisiana. A calendar is helpful. Nonmember subscriptions are $8/year, $1.50/copy.

Celtic-American Heritage Society, *Box 5166, Jackson, MS 39296-5166 (601-992-2054 or 601-984-5806).* The association's monthly newsletter tells of the latest Irish news in the South, with an emphasis on Mississippi and Louisiana. Complimentary subscriptions are possible by writing to the society. Membership is $15 a year and allows free admission to the early September CelticFest held annually in Jackson, which draws a good contingent of New Orleans' Irish music fans. It also provides discounts for other society concerts and events.

chapter four

German New Orleans

History and Settlement

The first Germans arrived in Louisiana in the early 1700s, lured to the colony by the empty promises of land developer John Law who had spread word throughout Europe about fabled riches and an easy life-style in the New World. His promotional broadsheets and fliers were printed in several languages, including German. One pamphlet promised a land overflowing with gold, silver, copper, lead, and medicinal herbs.

It is estimated that more than 10,000 Germans and several thousand Swiss set out for Louisiana between 1718 and 1724, attracted by Law's glowing words. Most were from the Rhine River valley, leveled during the Thirty Years War that raged from 1616 to 1648. The region was barely recovering from the onslaught of fire and sword when Law's agents rode through the countryside tossing out dreams like gold coins. The peasants were happy to head anywhere they were promised freedom from disease, war, and starvation.

Of the those who signed on to seek their fortunes, barely two thousand actually reached their goal, landing at first in Biloxi or on Dauphin Island off the Bay of Mobile. Hundreds of eager émigrés had perished just waiting for passage from Europe or on the long voyage from German ports to the colony. Yet, in 1721, a large contingent of exhausted, hungry survivors under the leadership of Karl Freidrich D'Arensbourg eventually made its way up the Mississippi, some twenty-five miles north of what was then just the hamlet of New Orleans.

No one was impressed with the village; a description of the place at the time was not as rosy as the scoundrel Law had painted, at least seen through the eyes of a newly arrived German settler. Writing home to his family, he told of houses made of reeds and bark and how most people slept outside on the ground.

But the Germans kept coming. A number of them were called "redemptorists" because they could redeem the debt incurred for their passage money by working as blacksmiths, laborers, teamsters, brewery workers, and in other jobs.

Many rushed on upriver to the Arkansas frontier, hoping to make it big. Villages were enthusiastically plotted out along the Mississippi River and tiny farms hacked out of the forests with hand tools. Despite their dreams of success, these communities struggled to survive. Confronted with harsh weather, unfriendly Native Americans, and long distances back to the city's primitive support system, many eventually gave up the struggle on that far frontier. By 1722, they returned to the relative comfort and safety of adolescent New Orleans. Law's tenuous land venture had collapsed by that time and the bankrupt wheeler-dealer was forced to flee France to the safety of neighboring Belgium, barely a carriage length ahead of his outraged creditors. The Louisiana settlers wanted to return home to Europe, but no one would pay their passage since Law's venture was already kaput. Governor Bienville, sensing an opportunity to solidify his colony's food production capabilities, eloquently pleaded for the Germans to stay. He promised to reward the disgruntled émigrés with rich farmland near where D'Arensbourg's earlier community was slowly gaining self-sufficiency. Although leery of more promises, the stranded Germans decided to take another chance and so they remained. Subsequently, the area in which the Arkansas Germans and the D'Arensbourg Germans settled became known as *La Côte des Allemands* (the German Coast) or, more simply, *Des Allemands* (the Germans).

Many German names vanished from the record books at this time because French priests recorded the baptisms, marriages, and deaths. For instance, Weber often was twisted into Webre or Fabre, the Traegers became Tregre, Zweig was literally turned into Labranche, and Dups became Toups. The well-known creole name Schexnaydre was originally Schneider. First names also underwent changes as the Germans married into French families. In the first generation of settlement, Hans and Otto were still popular as given names. By the second generation, there were more Maurices, Marcels, and Anatoles. Today's New Orleans phone book is replete with such examples.

The German Coast started some twenty-five miles north of the city and continued on for about another forty miles. With only axes, spades, and hoes, the settlers cleared the virgin timber and established their log homes. Floods, wild animals, and tribes unhappy with their new neighbors were only a few of the problems that were compounded by the distance from the city and the difficulty in receiving supplies. Yet the situation wasn't considered as bad as their previous endeavors much farther north in the Arkansas territory. The tenacious Germans made the best of the situation and eventually gardens, comfortable houses, and profitable farms evolved from the wilderness. On Sundays, families rowed downstream to New Orleans to sell their produce in front of the cathedral and in the French Market. On several occasions, their agricultural products arrived in time to save the struggling city from famine during its early years. The Germans worked so hard that the New Orleans Creoles often referred to any difficult task as one that "takes the Germans to do it." The phrase is still sometimes heard in Louisiana.

Between 1848 and 1900, the Germans were the largest group of foreign speakers in the city, according to Joan B. Garvey and Mary Lou Widmer who wrote a popular history of New Orleans called *Beautiful Crescent* (Garmer Press, New Orleans, sixth edition, 1992). According to their research, a large number of the German newcomers settled in what was the City of Carrollton and others moved to Lafayette City (then on the fringes of New Orleans) or lived in homes throughout the old Ninth Ward. Between 1850 and 1855, another 126,000 Germans poured through New Orleans, eager to find riches in America. Since owners often leased out their slaves, competition with slave labor forced many of the newcomers to settle elsewhere in the country or continue their journey on to Mexico or Central America. The threat of disease during that era also kept many of the Germans on the move. The dreaded, mosquito-borne yellow fever that arrived regularly each summer was enough to convince some arrivals that even the windswept Texas plains sounded better than strangling to death in some pest house.

But those who stayed made an impact. The Germans were the strong middle class—as butcher, baker, and candlestick maker for New Orleans. Jorge Stillet was a well-known upholsterer whose name demonstrated the blend of ethnic cultures. There was Aston Frey, whose meat shop in the French Quarter always served only the best cuts (he said). And the long-gone Ninth Street market was also crowded with other German butchers whose open-air stalls were groaning under the weight of smoked hams and freshly cut beef sides.

Old-time New Orleanians still remember a now-closed German bakery on Pleasant Street that was famous for rye bread. Today the **George H.**

Leidenheimer Baking Co. Ltd., 1501 Simon Bolivar Avenue, 504-525-1575, still gets a rise out of its *brot* business. Managed by four generations of the same family, the bakery was established in 1896. The firm carries on the tradition of producing fresh French bread daily, but, alas, it doesn't do pumpernickel. Leidenheimer is the largest French bread wholesaler in New Orleans, with seventy-five employees supplying restaurants, hotels, and grocery stores in Alabama, Arizona, Florida, Hawaii, and Texas.

Engineer Fritz Jahncke paved the first city streets during a four-year project that cleaned up Canal and other major thoroughfares between 1876 and 1880. Jahncke also formed the Sewerage and Water Board and was instrumental in coordinating the digging of the infamous New Basin Canal forty years earlier. Hundreds of his countrymen labored on that project alongside strong-backed Irish navvies. Regardless of their nationality, thousands of the workers died of injuries and fever as they toiled under the broiling sun. The unfortunate deaths kept folks like mortician Jacob Schoen busy carrying the deceased who weren't simply buried where they fell.

Other noted Germans in New Orleans included Philip Werlein, who, in 1853, published what became the Confederacy's battle song, "Dixie." The tune, which was often sung by the troops as they moved into battle lines during the Civil War, was written by Dan Emmett. The term *Dixie* was often a nickname for New Orleans before it gained broader acceptance as a tag for the entire South. In the early 1800s, a ten-dollar bill was printed for use in the city. One side of the bill had the English word *ten,* and the other side had the French *dix. Dix* became the trademark of the city, since, according to historians Garvey and Widmer, New Orleans was the only place where it was used.

While most small-time grocers in New Orleans originally were Sicilians, the grandfather of Louisiana Public Service Commissioner John Schwegmann started his own food market. The family-owned Schwegmann supermarket chain now has stores as far north as Baton Rouge. Schwegmann carries on the tradition of his father, who was also on the Public Service Commission, which regulates the offshore oil industry. Schwegmann's wife Melinda was Louisiana's lieutenant governor in the early 1990s. The family home is near Lake Pontchartrain behind the University of New Orleans. The first small Schwegmann store was near the French Quarter at the corner of Elysian Fields and St. Claude Avenue, not far from Rampart Street. The old building is still maintained as a supermarket but under different ownership. Another early Schwegmann's store is located at 1325 Annunciation and more stores are scattered throughout the city. In addition to the supermarkets and a chain of pharmacies and discount stores, the family owns the Schwegmann Bank & Trust Company, with four locations in the greater New Orleans area.

Naturally the German influence meant that brewing became a big business. Peter Laurence Fabacher was one of the more famous biermeisters, serving on the board of the Jackson Brewery. The brewery itself, located along the docks across the street from Jackson Square, was a mainstay of New Orleans from 1891 to the mid-1970s. The old brewery building was saved from demolition by far-sighted developers who renovated the structure and turned it into a warren of upscale shops and eateries. A multilevel lounge on the upper floors affords a romantic view of the Mississippi River, especially at night with the lights glistening from passing freighters and from the streets of Algiers across the flowage. With all that slosh available, numerous *biergartens* sprang up all over the city before the turn of the century. For five cents a dance at the long-ago Tivoli, a dashing bon vivant could ask any sweet young woman who worked there to twirl around the floor with him as the orchestra played soul-stirring waltzes.

During the Civil War, many of the city's Germans marched off to fight in gray uniforms for the glory of the South. Thousands never returned, their bones littering battlefields from Virginia to Texas. Yet the German community remained strong and closely knit. By the turn of the century, there were at least eight daily German-language newspapers (today there are none). As with many major urban areas at the time, the city was ripe for control by political machines as more wide-eyed, innocent immigrants poured in, ripe for the plucking. Corruption was rampant.

Despite several reform movements in the 1880s and 1890s, New Orleans' legendary political world remained bold and brassy. Graft, gambling, prostitution, and a host of other more decadent arts were regular parts of life. The police were under the direct hands-on control of the individual mayors, all of whom used the force as a private army of shakedown artists in a citywide protection racket. In the 1880s, John Fitzpatrick was the boss of the Regular Democratic Organization (RDO) and kept many politicians in his vest pocket. One of his protégés was Martin Behrman, a young German shopkeeper who became an assistant assessor's clerk because he was a hardworking vote-getter for the machine. When the RDO was tossed out of office by reformist Joseph A. Shakspeare, all the in-crowd lost their jobs, including Behrman. But Fitzpatrick returned with a vengeance, armed with thousands of ballots under his arm. He was elected mayor in 1892 and again helped out crony Behrman, who was appointed clerk to several city council committees and progressed to a number of state posts as his career advanced. In 1904, he became the first German mayor of New Orleans and assumed the mantle as boss and titular head of the so-called Choctaw Club of Louisiana. The "club," a closeknit cadre of backroom politicos, was organized in 1864 and had evolved into the regular Democratic Party by the 1890s. Behrman's coterie of political hacks, stump-pounding orators, wardheelers, gamblers, police on the take, cigarillo-puffing hookers, and related guiding lights of society was also called the "Behrman Ring." Law-abiding folks had less complimentary names, most unprintable, for the gang. Up against Behrman on the state level was another eager group of reformers hoping that any new governor would change the New Orleans government corruption and break Behrman's political stranglehold on the Crescent City. His opponents were derisively called the "Goo-Goos," a name taken from their organization, the Good Government League.

None of their tactics worked; even appeals to decency fell on deaf ears. Behrman was re-elected in 1908 and held office for three more terms until 1920 when he finally lost to another alleged reformist: Andy McShane, a fast-talking Irishman who himself was no stranger to smoky pool halls and backroom deal-making. But this was New Orleans, where almost anything went in the civic area and political maneuvering was considered brilliant form—if your candidate won. Despite McShane's victory, no one could keep a good Behrman down. He was re-elected in 1925 as his supporters gleefully shouted, "Papa's Back!" However, even power politics had to end sometime: Behrman died the next year with his boots on while still mayor, the only New Orleans political leader to hold office for five terms.

By 1930, the city's population was 27 percent Italian, 21 percent German, and 13 percent French. This was the last time the census was broken down on such ethnic lines, according to Charlie Hadley, a professor of political science at the University of New Orleans. Hadley is also president of the Deutsches-Haus, an umbrella association of several German organizations. A Massachusetts native, he leads classes in American politics at the university, having come to New Orleans in the 1970s after a stint of teaching in Austria. "Before I knew it, I got on the Deutsches-Haus board and then was elected president," he laughs, referring to his English and Scottish heritage. "Not a drop of German in there," he says.

According to Hadley's research, the oldest German neighborhoods were along Louisiana Avenue, called "Grand Route Wiltz" before the Civil War. The thoroughfare was named after a German lumber mill baron who owned most of the land there and sold it all off in the housing boom that came after the war. The name was changed during the Reconstruction era when many of the prewar, not-politically-correct tags went by the wayside. This "Germantown" spread along Magazine Street and continued past Jackson to Race. German merchants had their offices in the venerable commercial district on Magazine Street, anchored by the Germania Bank that disappeared in the crash of 1929. Often the Germans

lived next to the Irish, but each fiercely kept its independence for generations. The Germans built their St. Mary's Assumption Church (504-522-
6748) directly opposite the Irish St. Alphonsus Church (504-522-6748)
on the corners of Constance and Josephine streets. The Irish Channel
parish is still functioning quite well, but the nationality lines have blurred
after a century of love and intermarriage. Today only St. Mary's Assumption Church is still in use.

As with many central city areas, the neighborhood has dramatically
changed over the years, white flight taking many of the younger residents
out to the suburbs. Facilities such as the St. Thomas Housing Project were
carved out in the heart of the district in the 1960s. While Magazine Street
has remained mostly white, more African-Americans now live closer to
the river where most of the German families used to live. Several former
German churches in the vicinity are now owned by black congregations
of various denominations.

Yet the evangelical background of the German community remains
strong. At 2 P.M. on the first Sunday of each month, German-language
services are conducted in the St. Matthew United Church of Christ at 1333
S. Carrollton Avenue (504-861-8196). A social hour follows, giving
parishioners the opportunity to chat and catch up on the latest news.
German-born minister Heinz Neuman is chaplain at German Seaman's
mission. St. Matthew's congregation dates back to 1836. Its first building
received the nickname "Rooster Church" because of the bird-shaped
weather vane atop the steeple. When a new St. Matthew's was built in the
1920s, the plucky chanticleer was moved to a place of honor in a showcase near the vestibule. Happily ensconced, it now doesn't make any
difference any more if the weather is foul or fair.

Many Germans were buried in Lafayette Cemetery No. 1 (in old City
of Lafayette) across the street from the popular **Commander's Palace**
restaurant, 1433 Washington Avenue (504-899-8221). Not to worry, there
is no direct link between the two.

Somewhat typical of today's younger German New Orleanians is car-
penter Hubert Vahrenhorst, Jr., born in 1970. His dad was also a carpen-
ter, who came to New Orleans in 1923 to seek work after several years as
a seaman on a banana boat managed by the Lykes Steamship Line. Hubert
Sr. secured a job renovating French Quarter houses and eventually became superintendent of the local carpenters' union. A strong athlete, the
elder Vahrenhorst returned to Germany to compete in the 1936 Berlin
Olympics as a member of his homeland's powerful soccer team. When he
tried to return to New Orleans, he was harassed for participating in the
games and was called a spy by unfriendly neighbors. However, his U.S.
citizenship convinced authorities he wasn't a Nazi agent. During World
War II, Hubert Sr. built decks in the Delta Shipyards. Even in generally

open-minded New Orleans, the war years (as they were also during World War I) were tough on such residents of German descent, but they kept their clubs open and associations functioning. Now, with the official designation of October 6 as national German-American Day, they proudly stand alongside all the other ethnics who make up the strong backbone of the city.

In fact, the National Park Service is developing a German Heritage Museum in Gretna, refurbishing a former school to hold papers and artifacts pertaining to the Teutonic influence in the region. Another site is also to be constructed near Lafayette. Both facilities are expected to be completed by the end of 1995 or early 1996. Many key records from the German community can be currently found at the **Historical New Orleans Collection,** 533 Royal Street (504-523-4662). The staff conducts tours at 12:30 P.M. on Wednesdays. Scholars can always call for appointments.

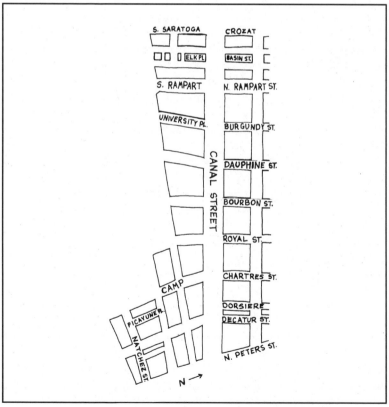

The Canal Street District

Organizations

German Heritage, Cultural and Genealogy Society, *Box 2802, Gretna, LA 70058-2802.* The society can help track family backgrounds and will refer questioners to the appropriate books, records, and research papers.

Deutsches-Haus, *200 S. Galvez St. (504-522-8014).* The brick two-story building, which used to be the Southern Telephone Exchange Company office, was purchased by the German community in 1928 as a gathering place for readings, lectures, discussions, and general sociability. Currently some 300 members belong, several of whom fought each other during World War II. One veteran even belonged to both the German and American armies. The Deutches-Haus is conscious of getting younger members to keep itself alive, viable, and meaningful. Subsequently, it launched a student membership program in 1993. Maintenance of the house is funded through revenue generated by festivals and parties held there and by the selling of $10 shares to members. In the old days, a member could buy as many shares as he or she wanted when joining. Since there are only a limited number of shares available, a new member now can become a shareholder during the second year of membership by purchasing a single share.

The facility is two blocks from Canal toward the Uptown area (just turn left from Canal on Galvez, between the Shell Station and Cox Cable offices). The club's former bowling alley is now a meeting hall, but there remain a well-used, open-air *Biergarten* and a cozy *Bierstube,* both of which are open to the public for happy hour. In true New Orleans fashion, the "hour" runs from 4 P.M. to midnight, Wednesdays through Fridays. Naturally thick and frothy German-made beer is sold in bottles, and there is a wide variety of fermented hops on tap. A thirsty guest should try Dixie Brewery's powerfully dark, brooding Voodoo beer or the smoothly flavorful Turbo Dog, both made locally.

Deutsches-Haus is homebase for several German-themed organizations, keeping steward Len Montecino busy. Montecino, who is studying mathematics at the University of New Orleans, is a third generation New Orleanian with a Spanish-German-Cajun background, so he fits in well just about anywhere in the city. The *Männerchor,* or men's choir, meets on the third Friday of each month, while the *Damenchor,* or women's singing group, meets on the second Friday. Bayou Steinverein, a beer stein collecting fan club, and the Crescent City Homebrewers, a beer-making and drinking club, also meet there regularly. *Schlaraffia,* a High German language association that originated in Prague in 1869, holds regular intellectual gab-fests from 8 to 10 P.M. on Thursdays, from autumn until the end of May. For the beginner, however, German lessons are given at 7 P.M. each Wednesday by volunteer teachers, including retired seaman Karlheinzen Von Bargen and Katchia Dell, a young German national who is married to a local businessman. Also headquartered at the Haus is Volksport, a walking club that conducts excursions and tours throughout Louisiana and Mississippi, often to visit historic German sites. A Deutches-Haus women's auxiliary meets in the building the third Friday of every month as well. A Thursday night movie series features documentaries on German history, cultural issues, and related topics.

Throughout the year, the Deutches-Haus remains the center for social life for the New Orleans German community. Most events are open to the public. An annual Crawfish Fest is held in April, with the exact dates determined by the timing of the harvest and availability of the "mudbugs," as the delicious little water creatures are affectionately called. But for other parties, the fabled Usinger's sausage and bratwurst from that other Germanic city, Milwaukee, Wisconsin, are the featured delicacies. Oodles of the best wurst are dished out when the Haus sponsors its *Tirolnacht* (Tyrolean night), a Friday night festival held during the school year in honor of Austrian exchange students. For the past several years, a large contingent of young European collegians have attended the University of New Orleans, which provides an excellent excuse for another get-together in the *Bierstube.* Traditionally on the Saturday before Mardi Gras, a lively *Fasching* (carnival) gets the members and their guests in a pre-Lenten holiday mood. Everyone attending is encouraged to wear colorful costumes and masks. In recent years, whenever a German freighter would be in port, the sailors and officers would be invited to the *Fasching,* where beer and schnapps freely flowed. Annually at the end of May or the first of June, the Haus also stages a *Volksfest* (people's party) in the *Biergarten.* Members are admitted free with one guest; other visitors are asked to pay a small ticket charge.

The Deutsches-Haus features an annual Oktoberfest, held on the Friday and Saturday of the last week in September and during the first four weekends in October. The German Heritage Festival Association conducts a lively parade the first Saturday in October, which romps past the convention center near the river and ends at the Deutsches-Haus, covering a distance of about two miles. Confirm the date, time, and route by calling Deutches-Haus or the local newspaper. Plenty of oompah-oompah band music and high-jinks let the city know the Germans are coming.

German Protestant Orphan Asylum, *5342 St. Charles Ave. (504-895-2361).* Offices for this social service agency are located in the Jewish Community Center. The association was formed more than one hundred years ago to care for orphaned children. Of course, today there is no longer an actual asylum building, and the GPOA acts primarily as a family counseling service.

German Seaman's Mission, *6612 Canal Boulevard (504-482-0465).* A recorded message in both German and English alerts callers to leave their name and phone number, as well as any questions about services. Chaplain Reverend Heinz Neuman responds to questions.

Restaurants

The Versailles Restaurant, *2100 St. Charles Ave. (504-524-2535).* Chef and owner Gunter Preuss came to New Orleans from Germany in 1967 brimming with experience working in the hotel industry. He first worked at the Fairmont Hotel before starting his own business. Preuss has been running the Versailles Restaurant since 1974. While billing itself as a French creole restaurant, the Versailles does offer several hearty German dishes, including leek soup, Wiener schnitzel, potato pancakes, wild game with red cabbage and dumplings, smoked pork loin, lentil soup, stuffed beef filet, and *Kaiserschmarren,* which is a sugared, cut-up pancake with raisins. The restaurant has dozens of glass beer steins displayed in cases throughout the building. The restaurant seats 160.

Fairmont Hotel, *123 Baronne (504-529-7111).* The Fairmont has been open for 100 years, originally as the Grunwald Hotel. The name was changed to the Roosevelt in the 1920s because of anti-German sentiment. In 1965, the elegant hotel was bought by the Fairmont hotel chain based in San Francisco, and the name changed again. The award-winning property has 732 rooms, and its lobby has been renovated in a traditional Old World style with plenty of comfortable chairs and couches for lounging and people watching. The hotel's Sazerac Restaurant now features Creole-American food, where years ago there used to be heartier Germanic fare. In the 1980s, the hotel general manager was a Berliner who used to import German bands and chefs. While no longer touted as a German property, many German visitors still register, especially in the summer holiday months. A majority of the staff speaks German.

Kolb's Restaurant, *125 St. Charles St. (504-522-8278), 11 A.M.–10 P.M. daily; the menu changes for dinner at 4 P.M. On many October evenings, a German band performs.* Kolb's has been a fixture on St. Charles Street since its heavy leaded glass doors swung open in 1899. Across the trolley tracks that run down the center of the narrow street is

Meyer the Hatter, 120 St. Charles St. (504-525-1048), whose hats probably graced the heads of the solid burghers in turn-of-the-century New Orleans. Sam Meyer's family establishment, packed with Borsalino, Kangol, Stetson, and Biltmore headgear, predates Kolb's by five years. In the old days, there were cobblers, clothiers, and accounting clerks on this street, and German was often spoken more regularly than French or English, at least in the back rooms and warehouses. Kolb's attracted them all with its scents of savory sausage and schnitzel.

Antique ceiling fans, run by a belt-and-pulley system, are still used to keep the air circulating on hot Louisiana afternoons. The dim interior remains comfortably cool, shaded as it is with stained oak sideboards and wainscoting. It's the perfect late-day place for a foaming stein of St. Pauli Girl or Beck's beer and a knockwurst sandwich. On the National Register of Historic Places since 1985, Kolb's has gone through a succession of owners since the properly goateed Conrad Kolb (shown in the ornate painting in the back dining room) started the restaurant and ran it until he died in 1932. The family managed the facility for forty years until selling out in the early 1980s. In those dietary days, hip-hugging German food wasn't on the menu for svelte Fräulein who preferred carrot sticks to strudel. Kolb's business slumped, hit with the recession's double kidney punch and the take-it-easy-on-the-gravy craze. Subsequently, a group of area business executives had to purchase the declining restaurant as an investment, slowly rebuilding the clientele. Homesick German tourists and locals who still appreciate pork shank have made their way back to the Central Business District, drawn by Kolb's local chefs. They now temper their cajun and African-American culinary heritages with red cabbage and sauerkraut again, favoring the Rhine River over the Mississippi.

Managing the bar since the early 1960s is native New Orleanian Joe Balthazar, whose lanky, tuxedoed frame presents a proper Teutonic elegance. So what if he can trace his heritage through an assorted mixture of Spanish, French, Native American, and African-American grandparents, great-grandparents, and great-great-grandparents. Always cool, his neatly trimmed mustache doesn't quiver when three perspiring patrons from Texas flop through the front door, hunker down on his bar stools, and demand some of "that German stuff," pointing to the taps of Warsteiner.

In the back dining room, white-coated waiters starchily set tables for the nighttime meal and arrange bottles of Mosel and Rheingau wine in the display racks. Their Delta drawl is lost behind the low rattle of cutlery, but Kolb's Germanic ambience still boldly speaks out as it always has.

chapter five

Italian New Orleans

History and Settlement

There's nothing new about spaghetti on the bayou. An Italian mercenary, Henri "Enrico" De Tonti, was second in command to Robert Cavalier, Sieur de La Salle, when the flamboyant French explorer made his tortuous way down the Mississippi River searching for gold and silver. Tonti's signature, in fact, was directly under La Salle's on the papers that declared Arkansas and Louisiana French territories. Tonti then sailed down to the Gulf of Mexico and mapped the area in 1699, a full nineteen years before Jean Baptiste Le Houpe, Sieur de Bienville, actually drove the first rampart stake into the ground, establishing New Orleans. Italians have made their mark on the Crescent City ever since.

After his Louisiana sojourn, Tonti went on to be governor of the Delta region, with headquarters both at Missouri's Fort St. Louis and Fort Chartres in Illinois. The globe-trotting Tonti family had more colonial connections in the New World. Henri's younger brother Alphonso was a cofounder of Detroit whose daughter Teresa was the first white child born there.

By the time the Louisiana Territory came under American control, several Italians had already gained prominence in New Orleans. Among them was the DeReggio family of shipowners and land developers, some of whom are among the early "residents" of St. Louis Cemetery No. 1.

The *de* was eventually dropped from the name. Today there are eighteen Reggios prominently listed in the New Orleans phone book.

Recruiters for the British Army during the War of 1812 sent circulars around the city in 1812, urging "Spaniards, Frenchmen, Italians, and Britons" to join the crown forces. Few, if any, of the Italians in New Orleans took up the offer and enlisted, preferring the camaraderie and comfort of their adopted homeland. Of course, the British eventually went down in flaming defeat at the Battle of New Orleans, with the Italians on the opposite side of the cotton bale fortifications.

Some Italians who came to New Orleans, or who were born here, eventually returned to their homeland. Yet the siren lure of New Orleans always remained strong. Dr. Felix Formento, who was born in the city in 1837, went back to Turin to study medicine. But the pull of America was too strong, especially at the outbreak of the Civil War when his home state requested that he put his medical expertise to use. Formento gave up his lucrative Italian practice to help organize the Louisiana Confederate Hospital. Other Louisiana Italians also were notable for their efforts on behalf of the Southern cause in that terrible conflict. For instance, famous Confederate General P. G. T. Beauregard was always proud of his Italian family tree. Prior to the Civil War, he had been superintendent of the U.S. Military Academy at West Point and already had a long and distinguished military career.

The initial important step announcing that the Italians were a major force in New Orleans came on July 4, 1843, when the Societa Italiana di Mutua Benefiza in Nouvo Orleans was incorporated as the city's first Italian community and social organization. Subsequently, many additional benevolent associations sprang up, such as the St. Bartlemo Apostolo (Bartholomew) Society, which was founded on March 13, 1879, to serve emigrants from Ustica. In the 1880s and 1890s, another 25 Italian-American organizations were started up in the city. Included among them was the Lega dei Presidente, established in 1898 to provide free health care for Italian immigrants. The Sala della Unione Italiana at 1020 Esplanade was purchased for use as a social center around the same time, serving in that capacity through the 1950s. The structure is now an apartment building. Most of the organizations were formed by immigrants from particular cities or regions wishing to retain their individual traditions. From humble beginnings, they have become well known in the community for years of service. Eight Sicilians from the town of Contessa Entellina gathered on September 8, 1886, in New Orleans and formed La Societa Italiana di Beneficenza Contessa Entellina. This society is a bit different from some of the others in the Crescent City because its members were descendants of the "Arbreshe," or Albanian settlers who founded their village more than seven hundred years ago. The association celebrated its one hundredth anniversary in 1986 with a Mass at St. Joseph's Church on Tulane Avenue and a well-deserved party at the New Orleans Hilton.

By 1850, New Orleans had the largest Italian community in the United States, with 924 families registered by the census, according to local historian Giovanni Schiavo. Only 900 Italian families were recorded in New York City during the same head count. That slim lead held up for another twenty years as craftworkers, engineers, and other middle-class professionals and their families left the turbulence of a fragmented Italy to seek their fortunes. One arrival, Angelo Socola, a native of Genoa, improved rice-growing techniques and set up processing plants that launched the industry as a mainstay of Louisiana's economy. Another leading Italian resident of the early years was artist Achille Perilli, who had fought with Garibaldi during Italy's revolutionary period of 1848 to 1860. Tired of war and bloodshed, Perilli eventually made his way to New Orleans and established his gallery at 464 Dumaine Street. By the time he died in 1891, many of New Orleans's upper class had at least one of his colorful paintings hanging in their homes.

Italians were also noted within the city's glamorous theater and music hall world. In 1860, the French Opera House was a gilded homebase for the noted diva Adelina Patti, a soprano whose golden voice thrilled the highly critical New Orleans audiences. Names of other Italian entertainers and businesspeople were commonplace in newspapers of the era: Vaccaro, Guarisco, La Rocca, Gulotta, and many more.

Yet, as with many nationalities, numerous Italian names eventually became "Francophiled" as the arrivals eventually blended into the general New Orleans potpourri and such initially obvious Italian connections disappeared.

New York eventually won the census race over New Orleans as the flood of Italian émigrés increased. After 1870, the majority of arrivals to New Orleans were laborers from Sicily's smaller villages, while most urban Neapolitans preferred the bustle of New York. Between 1850 and 1900, the direct sea route from Palermo to New Orleans was busy with steam packets ferrying eager Italians to the New World, where there were plenty of challenges. Farmers made up the first wave, eager to grow cotton, rice, and vegetables. They were happy to till the rich Delta soil, which was a far cry from the rocky slopes of their home. Many of the newcomers also came from the island of Ustica, thirty-six miles northwest of Palermo, according to Peter Bertucci, President of the San Bartolomeo Society and head of the Greater New Orleans Italian Cultural Society. Bertuccli's grandfather came to the Crescent City in 1859, one of the thousands of young newcomers ready to carve out a niche for themselves. Now retired, Bertuccli was a manager at Sears for forty years.

The patroon system was in full swing wherever the Italians settled, whereby an early arrival who spoke fluent English and knew his way around would then bring over eight to ten additional strong-backed men to work in factories or on construction sites. The patroon would receive upwards of $1 per head for each body "delivered in working condition," as the contracts stated. Even with wages as minimal as 50¢ a day, a frugal Italian laborer still saved enough to bring his family to America within a few years of his emigration. Upon their arrival in New Orleans, 90 percent of the newcomers settled in the always-crowded French Quarter, which became known both as Little Italy and Little Palermo during that era. Italians subsequently were the primary ethnic group living in the district from 1875 through World War II. In many cases, once their documentation process was completed at the Toulouse Street wharf, they met up with relatives and quickly settled into the bustling social and business whirl that was New Orleans. After World War II, as with other ethnics, the well-established Italians moved to the suburbs and more upscale neighborhoods of Greater New Orleans.

Even in the beginning days of immigration, after a short stay in the city to become acclimatized to America's ways, other Italian newcomers boarded a train or boat and worked their way upcountry to Memphis and St. Louis. Some went to cities throughout Texas and Kansas or to Italian centers in Pittsburgh, Tampa, and Atlanta. Subsequently, the New Orleans Italian-Sicilian influence spread throughout the Southwestern and the Midwestern states. Many young men worked on the railroads in the summer, sweating under the blazing sun as far away as Nebraska, returning home in the winter. Others labored in the sugar and cotton plantations of muggy upstate Louisiana.

Establishing schools and day-care centers during the late 1880s, Lombardy-born Mother Cabrini (who became the first American citizen to become canonized a Catholic saint) spent many of her early years in the United States living and working in the French Quarter before spreading her good works to additional cities. The city's **Cabrini High School** (1400 Moss Street, 504-482-1193) is named in her honor.

Antonio Monteleone was a cobbler from Contessa who bought the old Commercial Hotel in 1888 soon after he arrived in New Orleans. He proudly put his name on the building while upgrading the structure and adding rooms. By the time Monteleone died in 1913, the hotel, at 214 Royal Street (504-523-3341), had become one of the top lodgings in the country. His son Frank ran the Monteleone Hotel from 1892 to 1958. It was the first hotel in New Orleans to have air conditioning, a forty-ton monster piece of equipment installed in 1930 to cool the public areas. Of course, it was an immediate hit. Monteleone's grandson William, who died on November 5, 1993, was the next manager. His children, Billy, Jr. and his brother David and their sister Ann Burr Monteleone now manage the property. The hotel, with enough marble and crystal on its interior to decorate a palace, remains one of the most fashionable in the French Quarter.

For all the Italians, whether saintly nuns or farm workers, cobblers or fruit vendors, the New Orleans port was an important entry point to the New World and its opportunities.

Over the next generations, especially between 1884 and 1924, an estimated 299,000 Italians came to Louisiana to settle. In 1901, one in three New Orleanians was originally from Italy or was a descendant of an Italian emigrant, a total of about 300,000 persons, according to local historian Evans J. Casso. Currently at least one-sixth of New Orleans' million-plus residents have an Italian heritage, historian Casso points out.

Initially the Italian immigrant explosion was met with curiosity, but there was more and more resistance to the arrivals. They looked, acted, and spoke different, raising the eyebrows of other ethnics who had arrived earlier, especially the Irish who had a twenty-five-year jump on the first big influx of Italians. While other ethnic groups moved quickly in becoming "American," the Italians were more cautious at first in integrating with their neighbors. Yet where they mixed with the Irish, especially in the low-income neighborhood of the Irish Channel, love often blossomed and there were many resulting marriages, albeit fiery.

Yet an undercurrent of unrest was never far from the surface, especially as one nationality confronted the other over jobs on the waterfront, security, homes, schools, and living space. The problems burst to the surface in 1890 when Police Chief David Hennessy was gunned down on October 15 in front of his French Quarter home on Girod Street. Although it was never officially corroborated, the dying Hennessy allegedly said that Italian assassins had shot him. The statement was plausible because the chief had arrested several prominent New Orleanian Sicilians who supposedly were members of a secret crime organization. He was also trying to negotiate a truce between the Provenza and Matranga families in an argument over which would control the city's produce business. Earlier Hennessy had also helped in the deportation of a Sicilian bandit named Esposito who had sworn revenge on everyone involved in his case. So the chief had several Italians who might have been carrying grudges against him as a lawman.

Capitalizing on Hennessy's murder, and probably seeing an opportunity to check the growing Italian economic presence in the city, a powerful

New Orleans businessmen's association, the Committee of Fifty, demanded a swift police response for the so-called good of the community. Subsequently, about one hundred terrified Italian men were arrested in a mass sweep of the French Quarter. Of the nineteen finally held, nine were eventually put on trial. When the verdicts were given on March 13, 1891, six were acquitted and a hung jury resulted for the remaining three. But to fuel the already heated situation, a shipload of Italian immigrants docked in New Orleans on the same day. Rumors spread quickly that this was an armed force about to attack the city and free the imprisoned men. Urged on by the Committee of Fifty, vigilantes assembled near the Henry Clay statue on Canal Street and marched to the prison. The sullen, massive structure was located on Treme Street, just beyond Congo Square (today's Armstrong Park). As the jailers scurried out of the way, the mob broke into the prison and attacked only the eleven Italian inmates. They were shot or hanged on the spot, and their bodies were left dangling from lampposts along St. Anne and Treme streets. The affair became a notorious international incident and President Benjamin Harrison paid a $25,000 indemnity to the Italian government for the murders.

Historians now say that Hennessy was probably killed by one of his many political rivals. New Orleans was a wide-open town between 1850 and the mid-1890s, when elected officials hired their own quickshooting police guards in order to protect their personal business interests. In fact, Hennessy's father and a prominent city official were gunned down a decade earlier, allegedly over some shady business dealings. And several years prior to his death, Hennessy had also shot and killed his own chief of detectives in a squabble over payoffs. Hennessy was acquitted of any charges but was fired as a police officer. However, he was later reappointed by Mayor Joseph A. Shakspeare.

The Irish and Italians have long patched up their feud. In March, the *Italian-American Digest,* the New Orleans Italian newspaper, sometimes runs recipes for corned beef and cabbage and corned beef hash. Another visible aspect of the friendly relations in these contemporary days is the annual Irish-Italian parade on the Sunday closest to St. Patrick's Day (Santo Pasquale's Day), March 17. The event, which originated in 1983, is sponsored by the Irish-Italian Association and includes several days of dinners, awards, programs, and other festivities in addition to the parade. The parade court and parade marshals are presented to the public at a supper dance at the Pontchartrain Center in Kenner, featuring both Irish and Italian food and music. The parade, with an eclectic collection of hybrid Irish and Italian floats and marchers, begins at noon in the Clearview Shopping Center (at Waverly and Houma) in Metairie. The route meanders through the New Orleans suburb along Veterans Boulevard and on side streets. For details, call 504-468-9440.

But the Italians have their own parade on March 19, to celebrate St. Joseph's Day, a New Orleans tradition since 1971. Italian-American personalities such as actress Annette Funicello have been parade marshals.

However, it took years before the communities felt comfortable with each other as a result of the prison attack. In the decade following the mob action, New Orleans Italians grew even closer together, meeting at such safe havens as St. Mary's Catholic Church, 1116 Chartres Street (504-529-3040). A plaque noting the church's historical significance as a cultural, religious, and educational center has been mounted there by the American Italian Renaissance Foundation.

Despite difficulties, the Italians of New Orleans continued to make names for themselves, especially in the produce business. The internationally known Standard Fruit Company was organized by the Vaccaro and D'Antoni families to import bananas from Honduras. To give it a business boost ahead of its competitors during its early years, the firm devised a means by which the usually-quick maturation of the bananas was controlled with ice. Previously the stored fruit quickly spoiled in the muggy New Orleans heat. The Progressive Food Company was formed by the Uddo and Taormino families, which soon began marketing products nationally under the well-known Progresso label. Guiseppe Uddo came to New Orleans in 1908 at age 21 and entered the wholesale produce market. During World War I, he purchased cheese made by Sicilians living in Colorado and California and bought the olives they grew, selling both nationwide. By 1925, the families were too big and the company too small, so numerous relatives fanned out around the country to develop additional canneries and distribution centers. The company was eventually sold to a Canadian firm in 1970.

But the success of Lucas T. Cuccia & Son (500 N. Hennessey Street, 504-488-6616) is just as typical. Now the second largest independent wholesale fruit company in New Orleans, the mid-city firm opens at 5 A.M. to serve its hospital, restaurant, and supermarket customers. Founder Lucas Cuccia retired in the late 1980s at age 87, when the business outgrew his original French Market site. Cuccia was the son of a shoemaker who left Sicily at age seven and showed up on the Mandeville Street wharf to work his way up in the New World by delivering coal until he could establish his produce business.

The Italian influence on New Orleans is pervasive, from music to food to politics to business, with names ringing in Old World flavor: Garafola, Costa, Constanza, Pecoraro, Lamarca, and Genovese were among the many Italian-Americans who prospered in Louisiana. The rhythms produced by Sicilian marching bands, with their hard-driving 1-2-1-2 percussion utilizing horns and drums, are considered among the important influences on New Orleans music. Celebrated cornet player Dominic James "Nick" LaRocca was born in 1881, nineteen years before famed trumpeter Louis ("Satchmo") Armstrong. Satchmo called LaRocca "one of the great pioneers of syncopated music" whose fame "will last a long, long time, as long I think, as American music lives."

LaRocca wrote "Tiger Rag" in 1917, which was followed by "Ostrich Walk," "Livery Stable Blues," and additional tunes. Businessperson Harry James brought LaRocca and his Dixieland "Jass" Band to Chicago where the sound became known as "jazz," an immediate hit as the Roaring Twenties gathered steam. In the 1920s, LaRocca made the first-ever recordings of jazz music, working with the Victor Talking Machine Company.

Trumpter Louis "The Chief" Prima was born December 7, 1912 and died August 24, 1978 in New Orleans. Prima, a noted jazz band leader in the 1940s and 1950s, is now a member of the Music Hall of Fame. His New Orleans-born daughter, Joyce Prima, also made a name for herself by singing with numerous New Orleans bands and at such local clubs as her Uncle Leon's well-known Prima's 500 Club on Bourbon Street. She eventually joined her father in New York and Las Vegas, later winning the top Grammy Award in 1961 with the million-sale hit of "That Old Black Magic." Living for years in Chalmette, a New Orleans suburb, she regularly plays on tour and in her hometown.

Many Italians found their way into law and politics. Today some thirty male and female judges of Italian descent sit on the bench. Judge Pascal F. Calogero, Jr. was the first Italian-American named chief justice of the Louisiana Supreme Court. Receiving the honor in 1990, Calogero had been a judge in New Orleans for eighteen years. On the distaff side of the bench, Robin M. Giarrusso worked for ten years under the tutelage of New Orleans City Attorney Sal Anzelmo and became the city's chief counsel for contract matters and public bid law issues. She became a juvenile court judge and then was named judge on the New Orleans Civil District Court in 1988.

Another thirty mayors out of 150 Louisiana cities proudly proclaim their Italian heritage. New Orleans itself has had several Italian-American mayors. In 1936, Robert Maestri was elected as the city teetered on the brink of bankruptcy. But he put New Orleans on a pay-by-cash system and worked hard to improve public services, ranging from fixing broken-down drainage intakes to building new sidewalks. Maestri was re-elected to a second term in 1942 but lost to a reform candidate in a third bid after charges surfaced of backalley gambling and involvement in prostitution.

Another mayor, Victor H. Schiro, was born of an Italian father who had extensive bank holdings in Latin America. As such, young Schiro spent much of his youth in Honduras, where he became a fluent Spanish speaker. He worked with director Frank Capra in Hollywood after graduating from Tulane University and served in the Coast Guard during World War II. Schiro was elected to the New Orleans City Council in 1950 and was appointed mayor in 1961 when then-mayor Chep Morrison resigned to become ambassador to the Organization of American States. He helped ease integration in the city's schools, appointed the first black executive assistant to the mayor's office, and was active in other black-white causes. Under his administration, the plan to build the Superdome was advanced, Hurricane Betsy struck (September 9, 1965), and federal money was poured into the National Space Administration's Michoud assembly plant in New Orleans.

The New Orleans skyline was substantially changed by Italian-American contractors and developers, in a building boom that started in the 1960s. Seven of the twelve major new office buildings constructed in the Central Business District (CBD) and elsewhere throughout Greater New Orleans since that time have been erected by daring executives of Italian heritage. Overcoming opposition by the city's conservative old guard power brokers who said his buildings would slide into the Mississippi, Sam Recile instituted a process by which foundation pilings were layered on top of each other in clusters, enabling forty- to fifty-story structures to be built. Recile's process provided firm footing for the skyscrapers, previously not considered practical or safe for the city's mushy subsoil. Before Recile's audacious and innovative construction practices, the tallest buildings in the Crescent City never topped twenty stories. The glittering Plaza Tower, 1001 Howard Avenue (504-523-1001), is one of his creations.

Another major New Orleans real estate magnate, Joe Canizaro, became one of the biggest office and shopping center developers in the South. His Canal Place, 365 Canal Place (504-587-0711), is a melange of first-run cinemas, fashionable stores, and fancy and fast-food restaurants. There were others in the building trades as well, including Ray Liuzza, President of International Management Corporation. Liuzza built the International Hotel, now called the **Doubletree Hotel Now Orleans,** at 300 Canal Street, 504-581-1300. He was named 1992 outstanding member of the year of the Contessa Entellina Society, a Crescent City organization formed in 1886 to reunite Albanian immigrants who began arriving in New Orleans in the 1850s. The society's officers operate under the same system of governing by direct male descendants used in fifteenth-century Albania.

A third major contractor is Tommy Lupo, a prominent player in high-rise apartment building. Realtor ® Albert Pappalardo, President of Pappalarado Companies, is chairman of the corporation that oversees the operation of the French Market, the nation's oldest continuously operating public market. The Riverwalk, with its plazas, stores, and entertainment areas, stretching along the Mississippi River waterfront, was developed by Matt DeVito, chairman of the Rouse Corporation. While DeVito is a native of Baltimore, the New Orleans Italian community has always considered him a beloved adopted son for his energy and creativity in sprucing up what was the battered, derelict former dock area.

Some of greatest prize fighters in the nation were born in New Orleans, always a center for the boxing world. Often the young Italians would anglicize their names for better acceptance in the rough-and-rowdy ring. Among them was Pete Herman, the 1919 bantamweight champion whose original family name was Gullota. Other well-known Italian champions with deep New Orleans roots were Willie Pastrano, Tony Canzoneri, and Jimmy LaCava Perrin. The Italian Catholics who made the old St. Mary's Church their home-away-from-home, were strong supporters of the Catholic Youth Organization's (CYO) boxing program headquartered there. From the 1930s to the 1960s, the program turned out dozens of tough knucklebusters who became Amateur Athletic Association (AAU) champions. Two national champs and many regional winners got their start sweating at the punching bags in St. Mary's well-used gym.

The Italian-American community in New Orleans, like other residents of Party City, will throw a ball, host a parade, or hold a picnic for almost any reason. And often a formal reason is not needed at all. The nationally celebrated Italian-American Heritage and Culture Month in October is always a good time in New Orleans to find something hot going on. A weekly check of the local newspaper entertainment sections or a call to the **American Italian Museum and Research Library** (537 S. Peters Street, 504-522-7294) will confirm events, times, dates, and places. During any other given month, the Elenian Club might stage its Ballo Di-Natale to introduce a plethora of delightful debutantes; a Foto family reunion might fill City Park, with the Feraci-Cefalu gathering at Lafreniere Park in Metairie; or the American Italian Federation of the Southeast might hold a membership meeting. The Louisiana Italian-American Sports Hall of Fame dinner is held annually in January. The Miller Light Italian Fishing Rodeo held at Battistella's Empire Marina is a favorite activity at the end of July. But the biggest event of the year is the celebration of **St. Joseph's Day** on March 19.

Since the feast of Italy's patron saint falls within Lent, all the traditional foods that are served during the penitential time are meatless. One of the customs still prevalent in homes is for hosts to give a lucky fava bean to guests in order to bring good fortune in the coming year. The centuries-old tradition honors the lowly fava, the only food that was available during a long-ago famine in Italy. Survivors promised to regularly commemorate their luck by annually bringing representative foods to an altar to thank St. Joseph for answering their prayers to end the starvation. Favas were then given to children to remind them to be grateful to their patron saint for his protection.

To celebrate St. Joseph's Day, the Italian American Marching Club stages a parade throughout the French Quarter on the Saturday closest to the holy day. Starting sites vary from year to year, so check the local papers for the kick-off time and route. The procession usually starts about 6 P.M., with tuxedoed marchers tossing out doubloons, leg garters, paper flowers, and club cups to spectators. Women recipients of the goodies are supposed to award the marchers with kisses. Roaring motorcycle units, thundering Sicilian marching bands, and floats appropriately packed with beautiful princesses complement the meandering Italians. A festive club dinner is also held on the St. Joseph weekend in a local hotel.

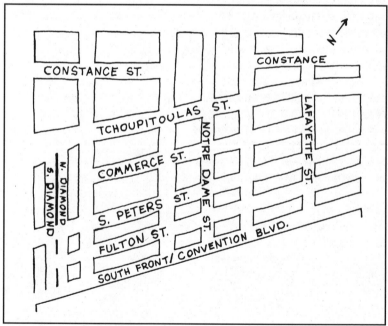

The Warehouse District

Attractions

American Italian Museum and Research Library, *537 S. Peters St. (504-891-1904 or 504-522-7294). Hours are from 10 A.M.–4 P.M., Wednesday though Friday. Admission is free, but donations are accepted.* Established as a museum and research facility in 1985, the center is financed through donations from the Italian-American community in New Orleans. Initially founded in 1973, the museum is a result of the initial modern-day federation of Italian-American societies, the first time in the country that disparate Italian organizations ever joined forces to promote the Italian culture. The museum is a representative of the American Italian Federation of the Southeast. There are thirty-one board members of whom fifteen are at-large and sixteen represent the various member organizations. The three-story museum, library, and research center was founded by Joseph Maselli. It is a tribute to Maselli's organizing abilities that he was able to successfully pull all the disparate groups together for discussion of common issues and to plan public events.

In 1993, Maselli released his *Who's Who Among Italian Americans,* the first national publication listing famous, infamous, and not-so-famous personalities. The directory lists artists, scientists, teachers, public officials, and others around the country. Anyone interested in Maselli's next volume can submit biographies to the *Italian-American Digest* newspaper at the museum address listed above. The current book is available for $35.

Exhibits in the museum include inscribed marble plaques rescued from the old Italian Hall on Esplanade and memorabilia such as mink neckties and diamond-studded cigar holders once owned by the colorful local restaurateur Diamond Jim "Jimmy Brocato" Moran. He used to tip cabbies a silver dollar for every fare they would deliver to his popular French Quarter eatery, a great way to build business. On a more serious side, the museum showcases a collection of photos and memorabilia of the late Dr. Nick J. Accardo, a New Orleanian orthopedic surgeon who developed an artificial knee procedure, and the papers of Dr. John Adriani, a long-time anesthesiologist at New Orleans Charity Hospital who organized an extensive training program there for nurses.

Often used by historians, a library is available for public use with its Italian-American newspapers from around the United States, oral history tapes, Italian phone books, and other archival material. Volunteers such as Zena Valenziano, a retired lieutenant commander in the Navy and one of the service's first high-ranking woman officers, spend hours finding and cataloging subjects that add to the museum's collections. Valenziano's parents were Salvatore and Rose Serio Valenziano of Cefalu, Sicily, who settled in White Castle, Louisiana.

The museum is also headquarters of the **Italian American Sports Hall of Fame,** with rank upon rank of photos, plaques, and artifacts lining the hallways and walls of the parent building. Among the dozens of honored sports figures have been football players Charles Cusimano and Ron Maestri, boxing promoter Angelo Dundee, and baseball players Henry "Zeke" Bonura and Joseph Martina.

Located on the upriver side of the Central Business District, the museum is a short two-block stroll past the area's trendy restaurants, open-air cafes, and high fashion shops. Behind the museum is the Piazza d'Italia, a half-block of columns, stages, and backdrops looking like a Ben Hur film setting or the Roman forum itself. The area used to be the site of the city's Fest d'Italia, last staged in the early 1990s and shuttered for lack of financing. Planners hope to eventually re-establish the weekend cultural event. The interior of the museum is a delightful warren of stylish meeting rooms, art displays, and research facilities. South Peters Street has slipped a bit over the past years, however, with parking lots popping up where storefronts used to be.

Organizations

Italian American Bocce Club, *2340 Severn Ave., Metairie (504-455-8355 or 504-887-2494).*   Purchasing their 5,300-square-foot building in the autumn of 1992, the original twenty-eight members of the club took a big chance that the Italian national game of bocce would grow in the New Orleans area. They needn't have worried. Each September they sponsor the Southern Region Bocce Tournament, with teams from Arkansas, Tennessee, and other states rarin' to go head on head with the New Orleans contingent. The purpose of the game is to toss a small wooden ball (the *pallina*) down a grassy lane, with teams throwing or rolling their own larger bocce balls as close as they can to the *pallina*. Part of the fun is knocking the competitors' balls out of the way. Bob Sagona, Sandro Pieri, Bob Agnelly, Joseph Paternostro, and the other players from New Orleans have racked up impressive reputations throughout the Southland as determined, keen-eyed bocce players who give no quarter. The fun continues after the matches, when every move is analyzed over plates of pasta in a local restaurant.

Italian American Marching Club, *537 S. Peters St. (504-891-1904, 504-522-7294, or 504-833-3794).*   The club will turn out for almost any occasion, with flags and banners proudly proclaiming the Italian colors of red, green, and white. Organizers of the St. Joseph's Day Parade each March in the French Quarter, the club is known for its year-round social activities and enjoyment of good times. Members meet regularly, usually on Wednesdays, at the Airline Lions Club, 3110 Division Street, Metairie. The club also sponsors youth and senior activities and has raised funds to erect the Monument to Immigrants, an eighteen-foot-high white Carrara marble sculpture by Franco Alessandri that is scheduled to be unveiled March 19, 1995 in the French Quarter's Woldenberg Park.

Restaurants

Compagno's, *7839 St. Charles Ave. (504-866-9313). Open for lunch 11 A.M.–2 P.M. and for dinner 5–10 P.M., Tuesday, Wednesday, and Thursday. Open 11 A.M.–10:30 P.M., Friday, Saturday, and Sunday. Closed Monday.*   Compagno's has been a New Orleans tradition since 1929, located where the St. Charles streetcar bends around the Carrollton corner. There's a stop right in front. Tulane University staff, especially law professors, have declared Dominic and Rose Compagno's eatery their home away from home. Married in 1954, the two Compagnos have been cooking together ever since. Well, not exactly. Dominic handles the bar, while Rose whips up dangerous pasta marinara, with its clams, oysters, and shrimp bursting from their smooth red sauce over angel hair pasta. Her ferocious Sicilian arancini is a rice ball the size of a baseball (serves two for $5.25). There's always a surprise inside the concoction, such as a ham filling. Chef Rose is not bad with the bread pudding either. Be sure to get the rum sauce topping.

Both folks are from Ustica, a tiny island about thirty-six miles north of Sicily, as are many other New Orleanian Italian-Americans. Dominic and Rose took over the restaurant from Dominic's parents. You'll be lucky to spend more than $9.50 on a meal here because "lots for little" is the kitchen slogan. And try a glass of Fonta Candida Frascati Superiore with dinner as the crowning touch. A tip: Dominic says he's made a deal with the bank, emphasizing, "They won't serve spaghetti, meatballs, and red wine; and we won't cash personal checks." Credit cards are accepted, however.

Semolina #2, *3242 Magazine St. (504-895-4260), and* **Semolina #3,** *5080 Pontchartrain Blvd. (504-486-5581). Opens for lunch at 11 A.M., closes at 10:30 P.M. weekdays and 11 P.M. weekends.* Praised by *Nation's Restaurant News* magazine, chefs Gary Darling, Greg Reggio, and Hans Limburg have turned their international spotlight on the versatility of pasta. The menu could feature a French pasta or *pad thai,* a Thai stir-fry combo of tofu, shrimp, mushrooms, and rice noodles, just as it might offer muffaletta pasta with Genoa salami, ham, and toasted sesame seeds. You can order *marinara quatro formaggi, spirelli, rotini, linguine, conchiglie, bucatini,* and *rigatoni,* among numerous other Italian pasta dishes. There's even an upscale macaroni and cheese dish that is a signature item developed by Reggio. Entrées range from $4 to $10, with wines ranging between $10 and $20. Takeout is also offered.

Angelo Brocato Ice Cream & Confectionary, *214 N. Carrollton St. (504-486-1465), 9:30 A.M.–10 P.M. daily, except Friday and Saturday when the store closes at 10:30 P.M.; 537 St. Ann St. (504-525-9676). Open daily from mid-morning to late evening depending on the tourist traffic.*   Brocato's has been a tradition in New Orleans since 1905 when Grandpa Angelo emigrated from Palermo where he had been apprenticed to Sicilian ice cream makers since he was twelve years old. His first shop was located on Decatur, prior to moving to 617 Ursuline (where the family name is still in the tile above the front door). Today's two shops carry still the same homemade ice cream and fresh ice fruits, with lemon and strawberry being the most popular of the latter. Italian ice creams include spumoni (lemon, pistachio, and tutti-fruitti); *cassata* (similar to spumoni except with the extra decadent addition of vanilla cake and fruit); *torroncino* (almond cinammon); and *bisquit tortoni* (frozen rum-flavored whipped cream with almonds and pieces of vanilla cake).

Brocato's also adds imported flavors to its more "Yankeefied" ice cream, such as *amaretto, bachi* (chocolate hazelnut) and chestnut. Regardless of the flavor, the cones are all magnificent caloric pillars, perfect on a torrid summer afternoon (or on a cool winter evening, for that matter). Cones ($1.25 for single, $2.18 for double) are served up in true old-fashioned soda-fountain style. There are plenty of napkins available, for any agonizingly slow drips down a chin. Marble-topped tables, wireback chairs, and ceiling fans present a delightfully quaint look in each place.

The shops also make Italian *cannoli* (a deep-fried pastry shell filled with chocolate and vanilla ricotta cream cheese). A one-ounce miniature is merely 50¢ and a three-ounce large is $1.50. Italian cookies are also made on the premises.

The entire Brocato family (six of Angelo's grandkids, plus in-laws) works in the stores. Jolie Brocato merged her Cajun-Dutch background with Italian by marrying Art Brocato and raising a family. She has worked in the firm for twenty-one years. Mickey and Lavenia, Jolie's cousin and her sister-in-law, manage the St. Anne store located on Jackson Square. "I have no idea of the number of cones we serve in a year," says Jolie. "But there is one good thing about working here. You get tired of eating the ice cream, so the hips don't spread so much," she laughs.

Carmine's Italian and Seafood Specialties, *200 Old Hammond Highway (504-833-3004). Hours: lunch Tuesday and Friday, 11:30 A.M.–2:30 P.M.; dinner Tuesday through Thursday, 5–10 P.M., Friday, 5–11 P.M., Saturday, noon–11 P.M., and Sunday, noon–9 P.M.* Carmine's famous seafood stuffed artichoke, an original dish by chef Joe Pacaccio, is worth a stop just for the look and the scent. This appetizer masterpiece (at $12.95) consists of one huge artichoke packed with fried shrimp, fish, and crawfish and topped with heavy dill cream sauce. Other house specialties include fried mushrooms and green onions with angel hair pasta, crawfish pasta, clams tossed in angel hair pasta, and on and on and on. An all-you-can eat family style (just say "when," according to Pacaccio) dinner from appetizer to dessert is $22.

Mama Rosa's Slice of Italy, *616 N. Rampart St. (504-523-5546). Open Tuesday, Wednesday, Thursday, and Sunday, 10:30 A.M.–the last seating at 10:30 P.M.; Friday and Saturday, 10:30 A.M.–the last seating at 11:30 P.M. Closed Monday.* Named by *People* magazine one of the nine best pizza parlors in the country, Mama Rosa's lays out 10- and 14-inch pizzas ranging from simple traditional cheese to a rip-roaring, jalapeno-pepper monster. Prices range from $7.25 to $13.50. Of course there are plenty of other Italian dishes to round out a plate in case pizza is not preferred. A flier at the restaurant lists Mama's famous sayings: "Do I look like a short order cook?"; "If you fall out of a tree and break your leg, don't come running to me."; "If you get separated from me in a crowd, write me."

Pastore's Restaurant, *301 Tchoupitoulas St. (504-524-1122). Open for lunch 11 A.M.–2:30 P.M., Monday through Friday, and for dinner 5:30–11 P.M. daily.* Originally in the French Quarter, Pastore's has been a staple on the New Orleans restaurant scene since 1978. Owned by Roger and Tina Pastori, Uncle Paulo works the kitchen. The family, originally from Venice, are latecomers to the city, arriving in 1950 after a roundabout route through Venezuela. Pastori was a Louisiana State University graduate, working and saving after college with dreams of opening his own place. When the restaurant did open, he emphasized fresh pasta made on the premises. Spaghetti carbonara, mostaccioli in salsa, and ravioli fiorentina are only a few of the specialty dishes offered, along with several veal dishes. The Pastoris offer a complimentary glass of house wine with each entrée. All major credit cards are accepted except Discover. Manager and man-about-the-tables, Gino Atononelli is a third-generation New Orleanian whose family originally came from Rome. Atononelli has been with the Pastoris since they first opened.

Anacapri New Orleans Italian Bar & Grill, *Bieneville House Hotel, 320 Decatur St. (504-834-8583). Validated parking is available at 300 N. Peters, and complimentary chauffeur service is offered from French Quarter hotels to the restaurant. Breakfast, lunch, and dinner are served all week, with banquet space available.*   Owner-chef Andrea Apuzzo was born on Capri, an island that was the favorite of frazzled Roman emperors looking for time away from the office. The restaurant is named after a mountain on the island. Helped in the kitchen by Parma-native Fernando Saracchi, Apuzzo makes his own pasta and breads. There is a wonderful mix of Italian and New Orleans foods on the menu, from hometown turtle soup to Scampi fra Diavolo. Many of their dishes have been awarded a "light and healthy" designation by area health organizations. The patio dining, as well as interior rooms, are presided over by manager Piero Barba, also from Capri. Fernando emphasizes that Italian foods need to be kept simple. A chef should master tomatoes before moving on to more pretentious recipes, he once told local restaurant reviewer Linda Serio.

Louisiana Pizza Kitchen, *2800 Esplanade Ave. (504-488-2800); 95 French Market Pl. (504-522-9500). Open daily for lunch and dinner until 11 P.M.*   The claim to fame at the LPK is the restaurant's wood-fired gourmet pizzas and expansive wine bar. These are definitely touristy hangouts, yet they are the right spots when a craving for anchovies and huge rounds of bread topped with sauces is overpowering.

Vincent's Italian Cuisine, *4411 Chastant St., Metairie (504-885-2984). Open for lunch 11:30 A.M.–2:30 P.M., Tuesday through Friday, and for dinner 5 P.M.–10 P.M., Tuesday through Saturday.*   This is the place where locals go, a fine enough recommendation for any eatery. Owner and chef Vincent Catalanotto has worked in Phoenix and Los

Angeles, as well as New Orleans. A hands-on boss when necessary, he waits tables, washes dishes, and seats guests with equal aplomb. Catalanotto has been awarded numerous prizes for his foods, including several years of the "Best Canneloni in New Orleans" by *New Orleans Magazine,* as well as other honors from *Gambit,* the major New Orleans entertainment magazine, and *Citybusiness.* Catalonotto's grandparents emigrated from Italy to a farm near Lakeview, Louisiana. He keeps his Italian heritage alive by annually constructing a St Joseph's altar in his restaurant. He cooks the food, with mom and aunts baking cookies. Half the day's gross on St. Joseph's Day goes to local charities.

Stores

Central Grocery Co., *923 Decatur St. (504-523-1620). Open daily 8 A.M.–6 P.M., except Sunday.*   You can get anything you want at Central Grocery, to kidnap a line from Arlo Guthrie's famed song "Alice's Restaurant." Featuring a wide variety of Italian food specialities, Central has enough pastas, tomato sauces, olive oils, sweets, and other edibles to put the Italian Boot to shame.

Nor-Joe Imports, *505 Frisco Ave. (504-833-9240). Open 9 A.M.–7 P.M. Monday through Saturday, with Sunday morning hours in the autumn.*   Originally only restaurant food wholesalers, Norma Jean Webb and husband Joe Giglio (hence the name Nor-Joe), now have a public marketplace to augment their other operations. One of the most popular items sold is Webb's homemade mozzarella cheese, which she learned how to make while growing up on her grandparents' farm in Central America. Webb's grandmother was born in Sicily and her grandfather was from Spain. Homemade *caponata,* marinara sauce and pesto are also top sellers. The firm ships virgin olive oils, eight-year-old Colavita wine vinegars, and many brands of pasta to stores and restaurants throughout the South Gulf Coast, as well as catering to the local New Orleans market with Italian coffee, sun-dried tomatoes, and three hundred imported cheeses. Webb and Giglio are considering opening a cafe next to their retail outlet, with homestyle Italian meals.

Publications

Italian American Digest, *1608 S. Salcedo St. (504-891-1904).* Published quarterly, the ten thousand-circulation newspaper covers news from around the South. Domestic subscriptions are $4 a year, and foreign subscriptions are $5. The paper was founded in 1973 by Joseph Maselli, who also heads the American Italian Museum and Research Library. Managing Editor is Bette Caldwell. The newspaper offers calendars of events, book reviews, features on prominent Italian-Americans, historical overviews, crossword puzzles in Italian, columns on Italian issues, and plenty of community coverage. Liberal use of historical and contemporary photos and drawings brightens up the pages in any given issue, with the beaming visages of the Italian American Marching Club Parade Maids, the Flag-Wavers of San Sansepolco, industrialist Lee Iacocca, classic poet Torquato Tasso, and the *Societa Italiana di Mutua Benificenza Maria Immocolata Concezions* (dating from 1904) peering out at the reader. In addition to subscriptions, free copies of the paper can be picked up at numerous locations around the city, including Kenner City Hall, St. Bernard Library, Giovanni's Sausage Company, Tony Moran's Restaurant, Ristorante Carmelo, Venezia's Restaurant, Gambino's Bakery, Frank's Delicatessen, Kwik Kopy Printing, and dozens of other outlets.

chapter six

Jewish New Orleans

══════ History and Settlement ══════

The first recorded New Orleanian of Jewish background was Isaac Monsanto. His family was one of the last to flee Portugal when the Jews were expelled from that country and neighboring Spain in the 1500s. They fled to Brazil, settling in the great commercial and agricultural center of Recife. The city was founded by the Portuguese but occupied by the Dutch, who were inclined to be more religiously tolerant, by the time the Monsanto clan arrived. In fact, the first synagogue in the New World was established in Recife during the Dutch colonization.

The Dutch stayed in Brazil for about one hundred years, until they were deposed by the returning Portuguese, who came storming back with a fiery vengeance to reclaim their colony. With them came the Inquisition, a bloodletting designed to combat whatever the Catholic Church considered heresy. In many instances, the trials, burnings at the stake, and torture were driven by secular jealousy, especially with a slap at the hardworking Jews, many of whom had grown wealthy because of their perseverance. With the advent of the Portuguese crucifix, flame, and sword, the Jewish families who lived in Brazil for generations had to flee for their lives. Most fled to Barbados, Antigua, and the Antilles in the lush, tropical Caribbean. They lived there until the economy soured on the islands a few years later.

Many young people had to seek their fortune elsewhere because family businesses could not support them any longer. However, many left with healthy nest eggs with which to start fresh.

Monsanto's entrepreneurial sense led him to bustling New Orleans, which had established itself by then as one of the Gulf region's key ports. Due to his wealth and trade connections, Monsanto was easily accepted into the Christian business community, despite laws stemming from the Inquisition that prohibited Jews from living in any Spanish colony.

Regardless of what it said in the legal code, Monsanto married a devout Catholic woman in St. Louis Cathedral and was assimilated into New Orleans' ever-growing social hierarchy without a fuss. His children were raised Catholic and disappeared into the mainstream of New Orleans life. As a powerful colonial merchant, Monsanto was a typical businessman of his day, trading in rum, sugar, and slaves.

The *Code Noir* (Black Code) of 1724 regulated treatment of slaves, setting up a rigid system of rules that governed their movements and where they could live. Strangely, the first article of the notorious code decreed that all Jews be expelled from Louisiana, even though there was no tangible evidence that there were any Jews in the colony at that time. Why the rule was placed in a set of laws affecting slaves can be attributed to the city's founder, Bienville, who said that it "was out of missionary concern" for the blacks. Actually, most historians agree that the French actually feared allowing Jews into the colony because of their savvy business acumen. They didn't want any aggressive competition for their own commercial endeavors.

But all rules can be bent, if not broken. Such was the case even with that onerous stricture. In 1758, Governor Kerlerec allowed the docking of a heavily laden merchant vessel whose captain was a Jew. Commerce won out over intolerance.

The biggest wave of Jews came to New Orleans in the late 1700s and early 1800s. Again they were of a Spanish-Portuguese background whose ancestors three generations earlier had fled their homeland. They had sought refuge in the lush countryside of Alsace-Lorraine for the same reason the Monsanto family had escaped to Brazil. These Jews arrived in New Orleans in a flood of Christian émigrés from that same region, all of whom wanted to set up new lives in a French-speaking community. Quickly becoming part of the bustling New Orleans marketplace, they held religious services for several years in their homes. In 1828, they were finally able to establish the Gates of Loving Kindness, the first synagogue in New Orleans.

The next synagogue was located at the busy corner of Canal and Bourbon streets in what was originally Christ Church, the seat of the

Episcopal diocese. Since the Sephardic Spanish Jews were already successful merchants and had extensive business contacts, they were also friends with Christian laypeople of similar social standing. Subsequently, when the Christ Church congregation grew too large and left the Canal Street building for its current St. Charles Street address in the Uptown neighborhood, Jewish businessman Judah Touro knew that it was for sale and bought the building. The new congregation was called the Dispersed of Judah (*Nefutsot Yehudah*) and became the precursor of the current Touro Reform Congregation.

Touro was the son of the rabbi who founded the oldest synagogue in United States, another Sephardic congregation in Newport, Rhode Island. Touro originally lived in Jamaica, managing family business interests there before coming to New Orleans in 1792 where he set up an apartment at No. 35 Conde Street. The building was popular with other up-and-coming young New Orleans bachelors, such as Jean Baptiste Olivier, a chaplain for the Ursuline convent. Touro established a trading house on the 200 block of Chartres Street, which was a short walk from his home. He sent clipper ships all over the world with rum and sugar from his warehouses in the Caribbean and New Orleans and even imported ice. In 1840, he dispatched one of his ships to the Middle East to bring back Lebanese cedar and North African mahogany with which to build an "ark," the chest to protect the congregation's holy Torah. Local craftworkers, probably slaves, built the cabinet for the sacred manuscripts. The beautifully carved chest is still used at the Touro congregation during regular Sabbath services.

When bachelor Touro died in 1854, his estate totaled $4 million, the largest recorded up to that time in the United States. Half of that fortune went to Raizin Shepherd, a business friend. Shepherd had saved Touro's life when they were both volunteer militiamen defending New Orleans against the attacking British army in 1815.

Shepherd took his $2 million, left New Orleans, and went East where he married a lovely young woman from the prominent Saltonstall family. With his share of Touro's estate and his own financial acumen, Shepherd helped the Saltonstalls become even more well-to-do and better known for their cultural and political activities.

The other half of Touro's largesse was awarded to his beloved New Orleans, with donations to area charities, hospitals, and orphanages. Touro's will made no distinction as to whether the institutions served Christian or Jewish families.

In 1870, the two original congregations, Gates of Loving Kindness and Dispersed of Judah, merged to become Touro Congregation in honor of the great philanthropist. In 1880, Touro officially became part of the Jewish Reform movement and took that as part of its name.

Currently, there are about 11,000 Jews living throughout the five Greater New Orleans parishes. Every Jewish house of worship in New Orleans emphasizes that it has open doors to visitors. However, during certain holy days, some services are limited to congregation members. It is best to call ahead to ask.

A general spirit of cooperation continues today between the the city's Christian and Jewish communities, especially around the end-of-year holidays. For Creole Christmas, a program highlighting the melting pot of ethnic traditions throughout New Orleans, a Chanukah Candelight Ceremony is held at St. Louis Cathedral.

The observance includes the traditional lighting of the menorah by the Sinai Temple Youth Group, along with singing carols and welcoming comments by a priest from the cathedral staff and a rabbi from Sinai Temple. The free service begins at 7:30 P.M., usually held on the first Saturday in December. For information, call **St. Louis Cathedral** (504-525-9585), **Temple Sinai,** (504-861-3693) or **French Quarter Festivals** (504-522-5730 or 800-673-5725). The colorful blend of sacred rites would have made Monsanto proud.

Prior to the late 1960s, there were two distinct Jewish communities in the city. One was the affluent, longer-established Alsatian Reform, liberal movement. The other was a more middle- and lower-class Eastern European Orthodox community that arrived early in the twentieth century along with a rush of other émigrés. Until about a decade ago, the Jewish community was divided concerning social mores and cultural attitudes, depending primarily on their financial status. Generally the wealthier were the more liberal. Today most of those differences have disappeared. Many old-family Jews from Alsace-Lorraine have swung back to their Conservative heritage, with younger Jews from an Eastern European heritage favoring the Reform movement.

As such, orthodoxy lines have blurred with the resulting crossover in all aspects of life. Today's Jewish residents of New Orleans are active in the arts, the restaurant world, business, real estate, banking, education, and similar highly visible careers.

Among the newest generation are Doug Gitter, who has one of the nation's largest collections of American primitive artwork displayed at his **Doug's Steaks,** 748 Camp Street (504-527-5433); Steve Latter, owner of the popular **Tujague Restaurant,** 831 Decatur Street (504-525-8676); and attorney Donald Mintz, past president of Touro Congregation, who ran several times for mayor in the mid-1990s. Mintz's family, when they emigrated from Eastern Europe, became prominent furniture dealers.

Other noted Jewish names in New Orleans include the Kullmans, a large Alsatian family who at one time had one family member as president of Touro Congregation and another as president of Temple Sinai. The Woldenbergs are liquor distributors who gave tracts of prime downriver land near the aquarium to the city for a park. They also spearheaded a drive to develop a housing complex for independent, empty-nest seniors called the **Woldenberg Villas,** 3663 Behrman Place (504-367-7288).

The Goldrings, also active in liquor wholesaling, as well as the Besthoffs, owners of the K&B drugstore chain, are long-time supporters of the arts. For years, both families have collected art and shared their passion for the beautiful with the broader New Orleans community.

Monumental permanent outdoor sculptures by noted international artists such as Noguchi, Lipschitz, Henry Moore, and George Siegal are mounted outside K&B Plaza, the Bestoff firm's headquarters on Lee Memorial Circle. One of the pieces by Clevelander Frank McGuire incorporates a metal stool on the Downtown side and two stools on the Uptown side of the St. Charles streetcar stop there. Commuters often perch on the works while waiting for a ride, never dreaming that they are sitting on art.

Special arrangements for tours of the museum-quality collection throughout the seven-story K&B Plaza Building can be arranged through curator Patricia Chandler (504-586-1234). The tours are free, but donations are requested to the **Contemporary Art Center,** 900 Camp Street (504-523-1216). A flier available in the lobby helps with self-guided tours of the office's public areas. While the plaza is open twenty-four hours a day, the building itself is only open from 8 A.M. to 5 P.M. weekdays.

Another prominent art benefactor is Mrs. T. R. Norman, whose oilman husband was active in business throughout southwest Louisiana, has often loaned some of her postimpressionist art for exciting gallery exhibitions.

Over the years, there have been many noted Jewish citizens of New Orleans, including businessman Samuel Hermann who was the original resident of the 1830s-era **Hermann-Grima Historic House,** now a national landmark at 820 St. Louis Street (504-525-5661). The house is open for forty-minute tours from 10 A.M. to 4 P.M. Monday through Saturday. It is closed Sunday, major holidays, and Mardi Gras. Creole cooking demonstrations are held in Hermann's home on Thursdays, from October through May.

Another famous Jewish resident of the city was Judah Benjamin, the Confederate secretary of war who was exiled to London after the Civil War. In England, he became known for his legal skills and earned a well-deserved reputation as an international lawyer. There was also Martin Behrman, who came from hometown New York to seek his fortune in New Orleans and made his way into the rough and sometimes murky world of the city's political scene. He baffled his way, up through the door-knocking and leaflet-passing ranks to become the city's mayor in

1904, a post he held until 1920. He was re-elected in 1925 and died in office. His record seventeen years in office has yet to be broken by any subsequent Crescent City mayor.

It's a matter of obvious record that Jewish money and energy has long been prominent in the city's opera, symphony, and library circles, as well as other secular civic activities.

Synagogues and Prayer Facilities

Beth Israel Congregation, *7000 Canal Blvd. (504-283-4366).* This congregation is primarily Orthodox, of Polish and other Eastern European extraction.

Chabad House-Lubavitch, *7037 Freret St. (504-866-5164).* Located on the Tulane University campus, just around the corner from the anthropology department and a block from the main library, the Chabad House attracts numerous students, as well as the faithful from around the community.

A day-care center on the premises accommodates children from the Lubavitch Hasidic movement, so there are plenty of small feet stampeding around the play rooms. Pictures of prominent rabbis, or teachers, in the movement hang above the fireplace in the foyer of the old multistory home. In 1993, Rabbi Zelig Rivkin purchased a second location in Metairie to accommodate the expanding community: **Chabad of Metairie,** *4141 W. Esplanade Ave., Metairie (504-887-6997).*

Congregation Anshe Stard Synagogue, *2230 Carondelet St. (504-522-4714).* This was one of the original Orthodox congregations in the city, now in a mostly African-American neighborhood. The small Jewish community here still holds Sabbath services.

Congregation Gates of Prayer, *4000 Esplanade Ave., Metairie (504-885-2600).* Reform services are held at 8 P.M. Gates of Prayer remains one of the largest and most influential synagogues in New Orleans.

Hillel Foundation, *912 Broadway St. (504-866-7060).* This facility is located in the Tulane University neighborhood, where it can easily serve nearby students, in addition to accommodating the religious needs of the greater New Orleans Jewish community.

Temple Sinai Reform Congregation, *6227 St. Charles Ave. (504-861-3693).*

Tikvat Shalom Congregation, *3737 W. Esplanade Ave., Metairie (504-889-1144).* This is a conservative congregation.

Touro Synagogue Reform Congregation, *1051 General Pershing St. (504-895-4843).* Touro is located on the St. Charles streetcar line in the heart of the Garden District. As solid looking as its heritage, the synagogue anchors almost the entire block. Dan Lincove, the synagogue's executive director, was born in Shreveport, a philosophically Texas city mistakenly placed in Louisiana, he points out. Lincove is a first-generation American whose family came from Eastern Poland in 1923, from a village eighteen miles west of the old Soviet border province of Byelorussia.

Associations

Jewish Community Center, *6121 W. Esplanade Ave., Metairie (504-887-5158); 5342 St. Charles Ave. (504-897-0143).* Typical of others around the country, the center provides a friendly gathering place for its members and guests. The main JCC facility is located Uptown at St. Charles, while a primarily suburban community utilizes the Metairie site.

Both units accommodate some fourteen hundred primarily Jewish families, although membership is open to anyone. The JCC buildings host an extensive array of activities, from sock hops for kids to lectures by Holocaust survivors to comic routines by Bob Alper, a Connecticut rabbi. Both JCCs also provide day care, nursery school, and camps. All extra programs are usually covered by a separate fee. The membership rate for the Uptown facility is $495 a year, with a $100 joining fee. Membership at the Metairie facility is $395 ($100).

Tours are available at both properties, and guests who belong to other community centers around the country can use the facilities by showing their hometown membership card. However, they must be accompanied by a local member. Outdoor swimming pools are located at both locations along with a gym and health club/fitness center. The Uptown building was built in the 1940s and is expected to be renovated sometime in the next few years. No full-service restaurant facilities are available on-site, but a kosher snack bar is open during the swimming season from May through September.

A monthly newsletter for members called *The Center Life* outlines what is happening at the centers.

Jewish Federation of Greater New Orleans, *1539 Jackson Ave. (504-525-0673). Open Monday through Friday, 9 A.M.–5 P.M.* This umbrella organization raises funds for other Jewish organizations and agencies under its aegis and serves as central coordinating body for the Jewish community. The federation's mission "is to build and sustain a vibrant Jewish community in the greater New Orleans area and in accordance with Jewish tradition to ensure the continuity of the Jewish people in America, Israel, and throughout the Diaspora."

In addition to the B'nai B'rith Hillel Foundation at Tulane University, agencies helped by the federation include:

Communal Hebrew School, *6121 W. Esplanade Ave., Metairie (504-887-3633).* A school through sixth grade is run under the guidance of director Sharon Brown.

Jewish Family Service Agency, *2026 St. Charles Ave. (504-524-8475).* Executive Director Julanne Isaacson and her social worker staff perform counseling and family life education, as well as provide seniors with assistance. The agency also has an adolescent suicide prevention program. The agency is open to the public.

Touro Infirmary, *1401 Foucher St. (504-897-8246).* This is one of the major hospitals in New Orleans, named after Jewish philanthropist Judah Touro.

Woldenberg Village, *3701 Behrman Pl. (504-567-5640).* This living center is available to Jewish seniors and those from the public. It is supported by the Woldenberg Family Foundation.

Anti-Defamation League, *925 Common St., Suite 975 (504-522-9534).* While New Orleans has long been relatively free of anti-Jewish bias over the years (except for colonial times), Executive Director Jerry Himmelstein researches anti-Semitic acts locally, regionally, and nationally and prepares responses to such problems.

Jewish Children's Regional Service, *Jewish Community Center, 5342 St. Charles Ave. (504-899-1595).* The organization sends children to camp for summer and directs other youth activities. Ned Goldberg is the energetic executive director.

Jewish Welfare Fund of New Orleans, *1539 Jackson Ave. (504-525-0673).*

Newspapers

The Jewish Voice, *1539 Jackson Ave., Suite 323 (504-525-0673).* The only Jewish newspaper in New Orleans is published at the beginning and middle of each month. The newspaper is distributed free to all members of the Jewish community and is available at the Jewish Federation offices. Anyone not a member of the Jewish community can subscribe to *The Jewish Voice* for $25 a year. Publisher Abner Tritt, a graduate of the University of Alabama in 1954, started the old *Jewish News* shortly after getting out of school. The paper underwent several name changes and joined the Jewish Federation of Greater New Orleans five years later. It then became *The Jewish Voice,* the official publication of the federation.

Editor Roberta Brunstetter says the paper is always seeking unaffiliated members of the Jewish community who would be interested in receiving the publication. The paper publishes local, regional, national, and international news.

Kosher Shopping

Kosher Cajun Deli & Grocery *3520 N. Hullen St., Metairie (504-888-2010). Open Monday–Thursday, 10–7 P.M., Friday and Sunday, 10 A.M.–3 P.M.; closed Saturday. FAX for deliveries: 504-888-2014.*   New York deli sandwiches, falafel, and other kosher foods are prepared under rabbinical supervision in this, the only kosher deli restaurant in Louisiana. Opened in 1986, the Kosher Cajun restaurant seats forty people, with a small attached grocery store. Dried, frozen, and refrigerated food items are available, along with the largest kosher wine selection in the state. The store has 60 international labels, including Baron Rothschild, Baron Herzog, Gamla, and Kedem. For breakfast, bagels, lox, and Pareve cream cheese are popular.

Typical deli sandwich fare, plus matzo ball soup and knishes like Mama used to make are top-rated. Since there are no kosher hotel kitchens in the city, Kosher Cajun Deli delivers to hotel rooms and caters major functions, such as bar mitzvahs, weddings, and other social occasions.

Owners Joel Brown and his wife Natalie, are native New Orleanians. The couple's two-year-old daughter, Ruth Michelle, attends Gates of

Prayer Temple School. Joel Brown's father moved to the city in the early 1960s as an engineer in the Apollo space program and met his mother, whose family was from a small town in Mississippi. Mrs. Brown's family was originally from Russia, while Mr. Brown's grandparents came from Hungary and Austria, settling first in Philadelphia. Joel and Natalie met and married in New Orleans. Growing up Conservative, Joel Brown studied at Dallas' Yeshiva High School and attended Yeshiva University in New York, before moving to Israel for a few years. He launched his deli when he returned to New Orleans and realized it was devoid of easily accessible kosher products.

"It was my personal need and want to have such products, since I prepare kosher at home. Being in a southern community makes people stronger in religious belief and actions. In New York, you have kosher delis, stores, and temples everywhere. It's a lot easier to be Jewish and religious in a place like that, so it's a bigger challenge here. But it makes people stronger," he emphasizes.

A large sign fronting Hullen Street identifies the Kosher Cajun Deli, located behind the Lakeside Shopping Center. Brown advertises his facility in Jewish newspapers in New York and New Jersey, as well as in Jewish travel guides, so that Jewish business and vacation travelers from around the country know where to purchase kosher products.

African-American
New Orleans

History and Settlement

New Orleans is a modern African-American city, reflecting all the vibrancy, excitement, pain, and challenge of the African experience in the New World. The city, now about 62 percent African-American, has a special place in the nation's Soul. And that's a deliberate capital *S*.

From its birth, New Orleans has had a black presence. In 1720, five hundred black slaves were purchased on Africa's west coast, the Senegambia, and shipped to the new French settlement. Over the next generations, today's coastal nations of Senegal, Guinea, the Ivory Coast, Togo, and Benin continually gave up the flower of their ancestors to the Americas, most notably to New Orleans. Due to the proximity of their geographical homelands, these slaves could more easily relate to one another. This created a strong cultural bonding when they arrived in the colony, allowing a continuation of tradition and cross-fertilization of cultures, a process unlike any other experienced by slaves in the other American slave-holding areas.

According to the whites, this "forced immigration" was based on the ridiculous and tragic notion among whites that only blacks were "naturally equipped" to work in the sticky climate of Louisiana. Many of these men and women were already highly skilled at the time of their enslavement. They were fishermen, cooks, cattlebreeders, furnituremakers, and skilled craftworkers. These enslaved peoples brought their skills to the New

World and improved on them. They became integral in building New Orleans, literally from the ground up.

In the city's first census in 1720, there were 14 white men, 65 white women, 38 white children, 29 indentured white servants, 172 black slaves, and 21 Indian slaves. According to the tally, three times as many whites and ten times as many slaves lived near the struggling city and labored in the nearby indigo plantations. In 1721, there were 684 whites and 514 blacks. And over the years, as the numbers of both races increased, there were numerous instances of racial intermingling, although marriage was not allowed. In the early 1720s, the first recorded emancipation of an African slave was that of Louis Congo, who became the colony's executioner in exchange for his freedom.

A "Black Code" was established in 1724 to set social norms for the African population. With the Code, Catholicism was established as the official religion, no Jews were allowed in New Orleans, and movement around the colony was restricted for people of color. Slaves needed to carry a pass from their masters.

Between 1809 and 1810, more then ten thousand French-speaking refugees arrived from the war-ravaged island of Saint-Domingue (now the Dominican Republic and Haiti). The émigrés were fleeing a bloody slave rebellion, led by Toussaint L'Ouverture. The sudden influx affixed a definite Latin-Caribbean stamp on the city that is obvious today. The newcomers brought even more talents. Louisiana was the first state to commission a military officer of African descent when it made Joseph Savary a major and allowed him to form the Second Battalion, a black volunteer militia company during the War of 1812. Savary had been an officer in the French Army and recruited his troops from the free émigrés from Saint-Domingue and others from Cuba.

Another noted African-American of the period was Jordan Noble, the drummer who beat the long roll at the outset of the Battle of New Orleans. After the war, he became a popular musician in the city and went on to organize free black militia units that fought on behalf of the Confederacy early in the Civil War. When the Union troops occupied southern Louisiana, Noble switched sides and formed the Native Guards, which served under Yankee General Benjamin Butler. Noble eventually went on to become a captain in the 7th Louisiana Volunteers.

By 1808, the annual importation of African slaves soared to 112,000, many of whom were "sold upriver," the euphemism for being sent on to plantations throughout the South. Those "lucky" enough to remain in New Orleans were the metalworkers who produced the intricate balcony grillwork that became the French Quarter's architectural trademark. Others worked in the kitchens where they combined their knowledge of the Old

World with the bounty of the New, with resulting culinary wonders still enjoyed in the city's fantastic array of restaurants. They looked after their masters' children, as well as their own. They groomed the race horses. They roofed the homes. They provided the music. They made the bricks.

The Spanish and French colonizers often allowed slaves to buy their way to freedom or granted them their liberty because of their services. In 1803, there were some 1,355 free people of color out of a total black population of 10,000. Free people of color owned their own successful businesses, often as shoemakers, cigarmakers, and lithographers. Wearing their colorful cloth *tigons,* those distinctive Caribbean headdresses, free black women managed shops and sold goods in the markets.

One of the most famous free persons of color from this era was Santiago Derom (James Durham), a former slave whose master had been a Scottish doctor. Derom eventually purchased his freedom and became a distinguished physician in New Orleans. Derom was one of the earliest known African-American doctors in America's colonial period. Speaking French, Spanish, and English, he developed a large practice among both whites and blacks.

Later on, another well-known African-American was Marie Laveau, who was born a free mulatto and became a legendary practitioner of voodoo. Supposedly her father was a white planter and her mother was part African and Native American. She began her voodoo "services" in 1826, working for fifty years out of her home at 1020 St. Anne Street. She is buried in St. Louis Cemetery No. 1, with a simple inscription on the plain gravesite located near the Basin Street entrance. Look for Veuve (widow) Paris, her married name. True to her heritage, the **Voodoo Museum** at 724 Dumaine Street (504-523-7685), still offers incense, love potions, alligator claws, healing powders, and all sorts of other paraphernalia. It's commercial, but the clutter is fun to explore.

Voodoo, or *vodu,* originated in Dahomey, now the Republic of Benin on Africa's west coast. Slaves who came from the region brought their cult with them and integrated parts of the Catholic religion into the traditional beliefs, without the Christian aspects. The first recorded voodoo ceremonies in New Orleans took place in an old brickyard on Dumaine Street in the late 1700s and early 1800s, presided over by a free black woman named Sanite Dede. However, in 1817, the city's Municipal Council was afraid of the growing influence of voodoo, concerned that it would spark a slave uprising. Subsequently, voodoo gatherings were outlawed, and followers found safe havens elsewhere in places along the shore of Lake Pontchartrain and deep inside the Bayou St. John. Yet as Marie Laveau's influence grew, the authorities did not harass her. She seemed to know what everyone in the city was doing, from the mightiest

politician to the lowest slave, by using a network of followers and inform-
ers who told her the latest juicy tidbits. She "retired" in 1868 and died in
1881.

Concubinage between white men and black or mulatto women was
common in early New Orleans. The custom, in which a single man and
woman would live together, was called *placage*, meaning *to place*. The
mothers of eligible girls would work out financial arrangements with the
men's families whereby the girl would get a home, slaves, and money if
the man married another after the couple had been living together. Many
of the large houses seen today in Faubourg Marigny and along Rampart
Street were owned by women who were once mistresses of well-known
New Orleans businessmen. Many of their offspring became prominent.

Among them were Norbert Rillieux, who discovered the evaporation
process of making sugar, a method that revolutionized the industry; Henriette Delille, who founded the Sisters of the Holy Family; and distinguished portrait painter Julien Hudson.

In the early 1800s, New Orleans's slave owners allowed some time on
Sundays for their people to take a break and relax. An open grassy plot,
just on the other side of today's Rampart and Orleans streets, was The
Place Congo or Place Negre, usually called Congo Square. Slaves could
go there to dance, sing, socialize, and seek out members of their tribe. The
field had been used by Oumas Indians to celebrate festivals and, as New
Orleans expanded, the Native Americans eventually went elsewhere for
their corn ceremony and other dances. Located near the old Carondelet
Canal, where many of the black laborers worked, the square had long been
a gathering spot.

But the site kept its tradition as a hallowed meeting place. There the
slaves could converse and reminisce. Every week, other New Orleanians—both whites and free people of color—would picnic there. Crowds
gathered to listen and clap along to the intricate percussion rhythms,
which would eventually form the rudimentary roots of jazz. Native instruments such as the bamboulla, chauta, babouille, and counjaille drove back
the heat and laid the groundwork for the music of Anthony Jackson, King
Oliver's Creole Jazz Band, Sam Morgan, and, of course, Louis "Satchmo"
Armstrong. Even the banjo can trace some of its ancestry back to the basic
stringed instruments played at Congo Square.

One of jazz's premier saxophonists, Sidney Bechet always said his love
of music probably dated back to an ancestor who danced at Congo Square.
The Square was also celebrated by jazz impresario Duke Ellington in his
famous "A Drum Is a Woman" composition.

However, as the popularity of Congo Square increased, many whites
became nervous as the crowds of slaves grew and grew. Overseers were

told to break up the exuberant gatherings that often stretched on for two or more days. Subsequently, from 1817 to 1837, the New Orleans City Council limited the festivities only to Sundays. The neighborhood was subdivided in 1812, with portions of the Square becoming the homesite for many Creole families who moved into the vicinity. By the 1840s, the rules restricting the gathering of blacks were relaxed for the remainder of the Square, and slaves were again given more opportunity to assemble, a practice that continued until the Civil War.

Historians point out that New Orleans was the only American city that allowed the Africans to sing in their native tongues and perform music and dances from their homelands. Subsequently, black New Orleanians retain a special place in their hearts for the park, which is now a national historic site. As pointed out by contemporary local African-American leaders, it was the first example of black cultural self-determination and artistic expression on a mass level in the United States. Keeping in touch with that heritage, a local group of musicians, Percussion, Inc., holds weekly weekend drum and dance workshops at Congo Square during the summer. Check the local entertainment publications for times.

In 1969, the community felt it appropriate to use Congo Square to announce the founding of the internationally renowned New Orleans Jazz & Heritage Festival, still held each spring at sites throughout the city.

Armstrong Park, which now encompasses Congo Square, was named in honor of the famed Satchmo. The park memorializes all those indigenous musicians and their multitudinous contributions to the New Orleans beat. The rectangular park stretches along Rampart Street, bounded by Basin on the left, St. Phillip on the right, and Villere. A wide white metal archway leads visitors into the park, with its fountains and massive shade oaks. The hallowed ground was dedicated on April 15, 1980. Concerts and art shows are regularly held there. Walking along the pathways, visitors can feel the drumming and chanting of two hundred years ago rise up through their toes, along the spine, and into the heart.

A bronze statue of a beaming Armstrong, trademark handkerchief in his right hand and trumpet in the left, stands proudly in the heart of the park. Surrounded by holly plants, he smiles out over the expanse of trees and park benches. Outside the park, green and white "Renaissance on Rampart" banners hang from the balconies along shopfronts, signifying a battlecry in the ongoing attempt to keep the surrounding neighborhood upbeat and economically viable.

The park can still be considered the heart of black New Orleans. The French Quarter is just across Rampart, at one time the fortress side of the city. Subsequently, it was easy for the early residents to leave their homes, cross the dividing line, and escape the close living quarters. Eventually the adolescent New Orleans flexed its growth muscles, expanding beyond Rampart and swallowing the groves where the slaves danced. So the establishment of the park brings back the gift of repose and rural quiet to the urban rush. The calm is especially appreciated in the summer's pre-dawn or on those sensuous evenings when breezes whisper their own cool, secret rhythm.

By 1860, twenty-five thousand blacks lived in New Orleans. Of these, at least eleven thousand were slaves who were owned both by whites and free blacks. The auction blocks at the Cabildo and Maspero's Exchange on Chartres Street (now a restaurant) were always busy, with new shipments of slaves who came into the city's port or with those who had been "sold downriver" from slave markets in the North. Despite the oppressive social condition of slavery, not all the masters were cruel. In the 1840s, Scotsman John McDonogh owned a plantation in Algiers and was a frequent visitor to the New Orleans slave sales. However, he educated his workers, trained them in a craft, and then freed them all, providing everything they needed to set themselves up in a trade, a home, or a farm. More than eighty of them eventually returned to Africa.

African-Americans from New Orleans fought on both sides during the Civil War, but most signed up for the Union and were among the first black troops to fight against the Confederacy. Many of the city's men of color were among units battling white soldiers at Port Hudson and the Milliken's Bend. After the war, the city served as a prime testing ground for the new order of race relations, when blacks began to vote and take more control over their lives. Many of New Orleans' rising new black leaders had already been free before the war broke out and some even owned their own slaves. During the Reconstruction era, they generally turned their talents toward making the city a better place for people of all colors. One leader in the education field was William G. Brown, who served as the first black state superintendent of education in Louisiana between 1872 and 1876. Born in Trenton, New Jersey, and educated in the West Indies, Brown became a member of the board of trustees at New Orleans University and was editor of the *New Orleans Louisianian* newspaper.

Fanatical white supremacy groups, however, gained a toehold in the city's political sphere and, as elsewhere in the South, gradually regained the ascendancy. After 1877, segregation returned to the state, and blacks were effectively edged into poorer school programs. The only bright light was the role parochial schools played in educating young blacks even beyond Reconstruction and on into the next century.

The strict control under the "separate but equal" provisions that were reinstituted on the minority population lasted until challenged by the civil rights movement of the 1960s. Based on the social victories of those turbulent times, African-Americans have retaken their rightful positions in politics, business, culture, and education. Among the most visible of this new leadership has been Sidney Barthelemy, who won the mayor's race in 1986 with the biggest landslide in the city's history for a nonincumbent. After studying for the priesthood, he became director of city development and the first black state senator since Reconstruction prior to running for mayor. After his stint as mayor of New Orleans, Barthelemy finally returned to private business in 1994.

The new mayor is Marc Morial, elected at age thirty-six. He is the son of Ernest "Dutch" Morial, who served two terms as the first black mayor of the city from 1978 to 1986. The elder Morial had also been the first black in the state legislature since Reconstruction, being elected in 1967. He was also a juvenile court judge and was the first black elected to the state's circuit court of appeals. The younger Morial has a degree in economics from the University of Pennsylvania and is a graduate of Georgetown Law School. Before his election as mayor, Morial served as a Louisiana state senator and was a partner in a law firm.

Basing his election on what he called "The Gumbo Coalition," Morial's inauguration included a free multiracial party to which the entire city was invited, featuring such national entertainers as Lionel Hampton, Wynton Marsalis, and Wanda Rousan. Much of the extravaganza was held in the Ernest N. Morial Convention Center, named after his father, of course. There were also appearances by jazz bands, a thirty-thousand student youth celebration choir in the Superdome, and a parade of all the combined Mardi Gras Indian troupes. It was the first time in the history of the city that the Indians marched in an event other than Mardi Gras festivities.

Morial called the party "a celebration of our city's resources and the new direction and change that is our city's future."

There are many sites in the city important to African-American heritage. They range from public buildings to private homes, small businesses to neighborhoods. As with any large urban area, the ebb and flow of history has dramatically changed the face of New Orleans. Many historical structures and entire districts have disappeared under the wrecker's ball. Urban renewal madness and trendy facelifting has pockmarked and physically divided New Orleans between yesterday and today. Such was the case of legendary Storyville, where legalized red light hanky-panky made naughtiness nice from the turn of the century until the 1940s.

Storyville was named after Councilman Sydney Story, who first proposed the ordinance that set aside a twelve-block playground in the hopes of controlling access to "the pleasures of the flesh." The area was wide open: gambling, drinking, and assorted other vices attracted eager dandies. Extending from Basin to Claiborne and Iberville to St. Louis, plush bordellos bumped shoulders with sleazy cribs where black, white, and mulatto ladies of the evening pitched their delicate wares. In his old age, poor Story admitted that he was never happy that his name would be forever remembered in such a way. The only color recognized in Story-ville was green—the green of cash.

The heartbeat of the district was jazz. From ricky-tick to trombone slides, music made the lights go round and round. Dozens of well-known performers got their start in Storyville's houses of ill repute. Among the African-American musicians who launched their careers there was the great "Jelly Roll" Morton, who played in Emma Johnson's fabled bordello at 331 Basin. A victim of changing times and sensibilities, Storyville was razed in 1947, and the land was utilized for a housing project,

Now, other than the memories, music, and legends, all that is left of Storyville is a stained-glass window plucked from Lulu White's plush Mahogany Hall, which had been a landmark at 225 Basin. The fragile glass is displayed in the Jazz Museum at the nearby old **United States Mint** (400 Esplanade Avenue, 504-568-6968; open from 10 A.M.–5 P.M., Tuesday through Sunday). The mint is now owned by the Louisiana State Museum.

Also exhibited at the Mint, 400 Esplanade Avenue, are paintings depicting Storyville scenes by New Orleans artists. Among them is a scene showing a gunfight on March 24, 1913, in which Bill Phillips, owner of the 102 Ranch, killed a rival, Harry Parker, owner of the Tuxedo Dance Hall. The floor-to-ceiling painting was executed by New Orleans' adopted son Tony Crew, born in Naples, Italy, in 1954. Crew came to the city to play banjo and guitar, in addition to continuing his painting.

The New Orleans Jazz Club Collection also has its home in the old Mint. Allow several hours for roaming while looking over the instruments, photographs, sheet music, and other memorabilia used by the city's famous music makers—many of whom were African-American.

Yet, as with any journey, there must be a starting point, one for reference. A check-in with the Greater New Orleans Black Tourism Network, located in the **Superdome,** 1520 Sugar Bowl Drive (800-725-5652), will open plenty of doors to keener insights into what makes the African-American milieu tick in this town.

Visitors wishing to experience the City with Soul need a copy of the Network's official free guide. The twenty-three-page annual is useful for finding city sites with a black connection, as well as providing a calendar and plenty of historical data on famous and not-so-famous locations. A free pocket-sized synopsis flier is available as well.

Both publications can be found at hotels, information centers, and attractions around town. They contain helpful maps; however, the street names on them are hard to read because of their small size. Anyone needing glasses. and standing in the glare of Louisiana's brilliant sunshine will have a difficult time. Devoting a full page or two to larger maps with more readable type would have made them easier on visitors unused to the maze of avenues that meander Uptown and Midcity in the local patois, rather than east or west.

But there's nothing small about the enthusiasm of African-American tourism officials.

"New Orleans is possibly the only city in North America that has not only retained its rich African, Caribbean, and Native American ancestry, but also revels in it. Every facet of this city, including its churches, schools, architecture, folklore, music, and food has been touched and gilded by the peoples of the African diaspora," says Zenete Austin, president of the Network.

In true Crescent City enthusiasm, Austin invites visitors to "loosen your tie, lace up the tennis shoes, leave your problems behind, and let the good times roll. After all, this is the Soul of New Orleans."

Using the Network's pamphlets and its descriptive materials, start a walking or driving tour of black New Orleans at the massive Customs House, anchoring the downtown area at 423 Canal Street. Built during Reconstruction, each side is a duplicate of the other because its builders wanted to be sure that all entrances would be facing important streets. Numerous black Republican leaders who entered the political arena after the Civil War had their offices in the Customs House, and it became a major employer for a growing black middle class over the years. Among the well-known African-Americans working there were Walter L. Cohen, comptroller of customs in the 1920s, and A. P. Tureaud, a noted civil rights attorney. Undergoing renovation in 1993 and 1994, most of the building has been closed to the public, but a stroll around the block puts the bulky dimensions of the place in perspective.

The heart of the French Quarter is Jackson Square, about a five-minute brisk walk downriver from the Customs House. Named in honor of General (and eventual President) Andrew Jackson, the square is home to pigeons, street performers, and thousands of schoolkids on holiday. Hundreds of free blacks and slaves fought with Jackson at the Battle of New Orleans, including drummer Noble who beat the assembly for the American troops as the battle began.

The Pontalba Buildings, completed in 1851, ring Jackson Square. Considered the oldest apartment complexes in the country, they were built by both black and white craftspeople. Rene C. Metoyer, a respected African-American attorney and notary public, had his offices in the complex.

St. Louis Cathedral, 700 Chartres Street, backs the Square. In the past century, black businessman and philanthropist Thorny Lafon and even voodoo priestess Marie Laveau made extensive donations to the cathedral. They extended their largesse to other church institutions, such as schools and orphanages, around the city.

The Cabildo, at the corner of Chartres and St. Peter streets, now houses the Louisiana State Museum and has a large collection of African-American items. Where slaves were once sold, exhibits now depict the important role of the blacks in the community. Extensive displays trace the history of the free and enslaved blacks, weaving their heritage into the city's history.

In the days before supermarkets, shoppers flocked to the open-air markets to purchase everything from food staples to pots. Today's touristy **French Market** remains the most famous, extending along Decatur Street between the Cafe du Monde and St. Ann Street. Black workers and vendors have kept the open-air facility humming for generations. A century ago, Treme Market, the neutral ground running down the center of Orleans Avenue between N. Robertson and Marais streets, was as big as the French Market. Here, just across from North Villere, black entrepreneurs were busy catering to cost-conscious customers of all colors. That area is now quiet, and no one risks the rush of traffic to set up shop. Another neighborhood shopping square in the old days, one that now has a contemporary twist, was the St. Bernard Market at St. Bernard and North Claiborne avenues. The city enlarged the site in 1958 and erected a landmark bell tower. However, most of the land eventually became a site for a Circle Food Store. So St. Bernard's has retained its shopping heritage.

At the corner of Orleans and North Claiborne avenues, the LaBranche Pharmacy was a gathering place for the community from the 1920s through the 1940s. Many returning soldiers from World Wars I and II would say, "Meet me at LaBranche's after the war." And they did, making it the hub of the black social whirl during its heyday.

The national headquarters of the **Knights of St. Peter Claver,** 1825 Orleans Avenue, are just up the street from the site of the old drugstore, almost under the looming shadow of the overhead ramps of Interstate 10. The Urban League and other civil rights organizations had been headquartered in the fraternal society's adjacent administration offices at 1821 Orleans Avenue.

St. Louis Cemetery No. 1 at Basin and St. Louis was the fourth "City of the Dead" in New Orleans. The cemetery was originally laid out in two sections, one for whites and one for blacks. Today section No. 3 of the site is now the final resting place for Marie Laveau and many other African-American notables. Visits to the cemetery are conducted daily by the National Park Service (504-589-2636). Solitary visitors are warned to be careful entering the walled site because of the potential for muggings. Robberies have taken place amid the towering tombs, in spite of the fact that the First District police station is across the street. Just be smart.

The **City Hall Annex,** 2400 Canal Street, was once Straight University, founded by the American Missionary Association. Hundreds of black New Orleanians attended grade school through college there. The school eventually merged with New Orleans University to form Dillard University.

New Zion Baptist Church, 2319 Third Street (504-899-2519), is proud of the fact that the Southern Christian Leadership Conference, one of the nation's premier civil rights organizations, was established here on February 14, 1956. Reverend A. L. Davis, pastor at the time, was New Orleans' first black council member. A park in Davis' honor is located at the corner of LaSalle Street and Washington Avenue. The grassy, tree-shaded area was the launching point for many voters' rights marches during the 1960s. The first demonstration was held there on September 10, 1960, when the Citizens Committee of New Orleans marched on City Hall. Both the church and the park are in the Uptown area.

New Orleans has memorialized civil rights leader and Nobel Prize winner Dr. Martin Luther King, Jr. with two prominent statues. One can be found on the neutral ground at Martin Luther King Boulevard and South Claiborne Avenue, and the other is along the boulevard at Dryades Street. Ceremonies celebrating King's birthday are held around the first piece, dedicated on January 15, 1981.

For more than eighty years, black New Orleanians found the **Dryades YMCA** a haven for learning and fun. Located at 2220 Dryades Street, the battered old brick building was originally called the Colored Young Men's Christian Association. Tucked into one of the oldest business and residential districts of New Orleans, the "Y" has offered technical training programs to the community's brightest and most hardworking young people for at least fifty years. From here, young African-Americans were launched into the raw world of politics, business, science, education, and a host of other disciplines.

The **Amistad Research Center** in Tulane University, 6823 St. Charles Avenue (504-865-5535; FAX: 504-865-5580) was founded in 1966. After hopscotching around town, it found a home at the university, easily accessible from the St. Charles streetcar line. Located in Tilton Hall, the first building on the left at the campus entrance, the Amistad holds hundreds of thousands of documents from the American Missionary Association, as well as those from other African-American organizations and important personages. More than 250,000 photographs, video- and audio-tapes, microfilm, artworks, and news clippings round out the collection, which is open to scholars and researchers. The materials date from the 1700s to modern times.

The Amistad was named after a ship carrying a group of Africans illegally abducted from their homeland in 1839. They mutinied but were eventually captured and initially sentenced to death. The group was defended by former President John Quincy Adams and others. The case went all the way to the U.S. Supreme Court, which ruled in favor of the Africans.

The research center is open Monday through Friday, 8:30 A.M. to 5 P.M. and Saturday from 1 to 5 P.M.

Sports lovers should enjoy the rolling greens and tough roughs of the Joseph Bartholomew Memorial Park golf course in **Pontchartrain Park,** 6514 Congress Drive. Bartholomew was a black architect who designed and built City Golf Courses No. 1 and No. 2, the Audubon Park course, and the New Orleans Country Club course in Metairie.

The convent of the **Sisters of the Holy Family,** 6901 Chef Menteur Highway, is the provincial house of the order of black nuns founded in 1842 by New Orleanian Henriette Delille. One of the first buildings used by the order was once the plush Orleans Ballroom where extravagant quadroon balls where held. White and Creole dandies attended the parties in search of mistresses. That site is now occupied by the Bourbon-Orleans Hotel, 717 Orleans Avenue.

Tourism

Greater New Orleans Black Tourism Network, *Louisiana Super-dome, 1520 Sugar Bowl Dr., New Orleans, LA 70112 (504-523-5652; FAX 504-522-0785; toll fee: 800-725-5652).* Recognized by the U.S. Department of Commerce as a model for African-American tourism promotion, the Greater New Orleans Black Tourism Network (GNOBTN) works out of offices adjacent to the Greater New Orleans Tourist and Convention Commission (504-566-5045). The GNOBTN helps groups arrange hotel accommodations and meeting space; plans seminars, reunions, and parties; and suggests activities for family adventurers on vacation. The organization also offers up-to-date lists of minority-owned businesses experienced in convention and special event planning, promotions, catering, and related technical operations.

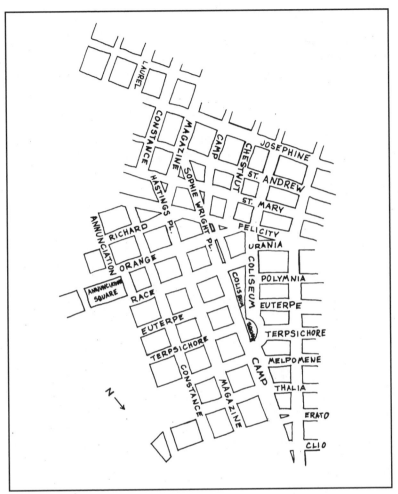

The Lower Garden District

— Black Tourism Summit —

Each July since 1990, international tourist bureaus, travel companies, guides, minority convention and meeting planners, and public relations executives get together at the New Orleans Convention Center. They participate in training sessions to discover how to highlight and promote their hometown's African-American ethnicity. Of course, New Orleans rolls out the red carpet for the guests with its own special emphasis on the black travel experience. Black boat crews, caterers, and entertainers highlight the arts and cultural aspects of the city. Theater productions during the summit focus on black drama. The summit and trade show coincide with the city's Minority Tourism Month.

Tour Companies

Le'ob's Tours and Transportation Service, *4635 Touro St. (504-288-3478, FAX 504-288-8517).*   Black heritage tours are offered daily at 9 A.M. and noon. They run from two to three hours depending on traffic, costing $30/person (without lunch), with group, senior, and child rates available. Vans, minibuses, or motor coaches are used, depending on the size of the party. Reservations should be made the day before the request so hotel pickup can be arranged. Owner Lucille Le'ob organized her tour company in 1986, offering general city tours, as well as charter service. Several years ago, she started the first black heritage tour specifically focusing on the African-American experience in New Orleans.

On the city tour, her guides take visitors past more than fifty black historical sites in Uptown, Midcity, Downtown, the Garden District, and the French Quarter while highlighting the black contribution to New Orleans. "People ask lots of questions," she says. "They are really fascinated about the living background of New Orleans not in the books on the shelves." A native of New Orleans, Le'ob can trace her family back five generations, finding some Choctaw and French blood in the dim past.

Le'ob's tour service also offers a Black Cajun Swamp Tour ($40), which crosses the Mississippi from New Orleans and rolls through the Slidell backwater country. Blacks and Cajuns, descendants of the displaced Canadian Arcadians, often intermarried, Le'ob explains. Their musical styles also melded into the downbeat rhythms of zydeco, which takes the typical cajun sound to a wilder level.

A black plantation tour ($55, including lunch) visits various major plantations in the New Orleans area. On the hour or so drive to get into farm country, tourists learn about the differences between city and country living for the blacks, whether slave, Creole, or freeman. Sites visited might include Melrose Plantation, San Francisco, Houmas House, or Destrehan, all monuments to a long-ago era that was supported by the sweat and blood of the black laboring population. Lunch on this tour is either at the Cabin Restaurant, old slave quarters along the River Road in Burnside, Louisiana, noted for its cajun cooking and seafood, or at the Ormond Plantation. The plantation tour lasts from five to six hours.

Roots Heritage City Tour, *c/o New Orleans Tours, 4220 Howard (504-592-1991).* Arriving on the tour scene in June, 1993, Gwen Carter's Tours subcontracted with New Orleans Tours bus line to develop a black heritage excursion. Regularly scheduled during the week, the tours run Tuesday through Saturday. Six to eight persons are needed before a tour will be run, so it's wise to call ahead because they are subject to cancellation. Pickup at hotels begins at 9 A.M., with the three-hour tour starting at 9:30 A.M. from the Riverwalk. Cost for the morning program, which includes lunch at Dunbar's Restaurant, is $30. Pickup for the two-hour afternoon excursion ($25) begins at 1 P.M. for the 1:30 P.M. departure.

Each tour encompasses many of the noteworthy sites of African-American importance throughout the city. Starting with a short history lesson before the bus pulls away from the curb, the guides put the African-American experience into a New Orleans perspective. Allyson Barthelemy, a former social worker, and the other guides are enthusiastic and knowledgeable about their city. They even pass out Mardi Gras beads to get everyone in the New Orleans mood. Of course, the tourists have to shout, "Throw me something, mister!" in the time-honored festival call before any of the goodies are tossed in their direction.

The tour meanders along Decatur, through the Quarter, up Esplanade, and along Claiborne through what had been the heart of the black business district in the 1930s and 1940s. The construction of Interstate 10 took out the neutral ground on the latter street, splitting the community and resulting in the paralysis of the thriving neighborhood—an example of urban planning that went haywire. After a stop at St. Louis Cemetery No. 1, the tour then rolls back through the Central Business District and out St. Charles Avenue to the Garden District. After lunch you stop at the Amistad Research Center, with about fifteen minutes allotted to tour the art exhibits on the second floor.

Associations

African-American Voters League, *310 S. Broad St. (504-822-2890).*

National Association for the Advancement of Colored People, *1630 Lapeyrouse St. (504-949-1441).*

Urban League of New Orleans, *1929 Bienville Ave. (504-524-4667).*

Shopping

Community Book Store, *1200 Ursuline St. (504-561-0036).*   The shop specializes in reading materials featuring African-Americans, plus ethnic gift items such as jewelry, artwork, and clothing.

Ethnic Traders, *3814 Magazine St. (504-895-8430).*   African masks, pottery, weavings, cloth, baskets, bowls, and other handcrafted items are presented.

Bones Boutique, *3141 Ponce de Leon St. (504-947-9456).*   Located next to the Whole Foods Market, Bones offers imported African tribal crafts, including rugs, statues, and masks.

Colleges

Love of learning has always been valued among most black families in New Orleans. The city has traditionally been a center of study for black youths eager to improve themselves and their families. There have been some changes over the years, however. New Orleans University (NOU), 5300 St. Charles Avenue, is now occupied by De LaSalle High School. The university was supported after the Civil War by the Freedmen's Aid Society of the Methodist Episcopal Church and had the only medical program open to blacks. In the 1930s, NOU joined with Straight University to form Dillard University. LeLand University, 7900 St. Charles Avenue, was supported by the Baptists after the Civil War. It became the site for Gilbert Academy and was a laboratory school for Dillard. The original Southern University, 5116 Magazine Street, was founded in New Orleans in 1879 as the first public college open to blacks in Louisiana. The site is now Xavier Preparatory High School.

Xavier University, *7325 Palmetto St. (504-483-7411).*   The university was founded in 1915, and its first site at 5116 Magazine Street now houses its preparatory school. The modern buildings of Xavier itself, 7325 Palmetto, can be spotted driving into the heart of New Orleans from the airport. The university is proud that, of the 105 black colleges in the country, only Xavier is Catholic. And of the 235 Catholic colleges, only Xavier is black.

Among its distinguished alums have been dozens of educators such as George McKenna, whose tough love discipline at his high school in Los Angeles was made into a movie. At least three graduates are college presidents: Dr. Milton Gordon of Cal State-Fullerton; Dr. Elaine Parker of Northeast College, Houston; and Dr. Tilen Lemell of the University of the District of Columbia. Then there's artist John Scott, former New Orleans mayor Sidney Barthelemy, Air Force General Bernard E. Randolph, Nat "Sweetwater" Clifton of the Harlem Globetrotters, radio news director Janice James, and on and on.

Dillard University, *2601 Gentilly Blvd. (504-283-8822).* The origins of this private, coed liberal arts college date back to 1869. The university itself opened its doors in the early 1930s, when New Orleans University and Straight University merged. The school was named after Dr. James Hardy Dillard, a noted black educator. Dillard has racked up a number of firsts: the first nationally accredited nursing program in Louisiana, the first speech department, the first Japanese studies programs at a black college, and the institution of the National Center for Black-Jewish Relations.

Southern University at New Orleans, *6400 Press Dr. (504-286-5000).* Chancellor Dr. Dolores Spikes is the first black woman to head a major liberal arts college in the country. SUNO, as the school is known, is one of the largest land grant universities with a primarily black enrollment. It is primarily a commuter school, serving the metro New Orleans area. SUNO has a highly regarded Center for African and African-American studies, offering an exchange program with African universities.

Restaurants

There are seemingly countless African-American eateries in this town, where a visitor can pick up a great home-cooked meal for less than $5 or sit down to a top-flight, gourmet dinner where the price is off the charts. The folks in the know always issue the warning that visitors can kill themselves eating. "If you have a health problem, honey, you have to move out of town," is an admonition heard more than once.

Lagniappe is a term used to describe the extra hospitality that everyone dishes up in New Orleans, whether an extra good time or an extra dollop of red beans and rice. This concern about a visitor's well-being is legendary in the black restaurant industry.

There is a strong tradition of keeping family ties in the community. It is common for kids—no matter how old—to make weekly pilgrimages back to mama's house for dinner. Even if not from New Orleans, a single person will be immediately swept up for a holiday dinner or a weekend out. The lucky individual most likely will get more than one invitation. It's easy to be adopted by several families at once.

And remember, it's always okay to ask people to speak slooooowly and d-i-s-t-i-n-c-t-l-y or to spell items on the menu, the name of the street where the restaurant is located, or the family name. The Noo' Awlins' dialect, ya'all know, sometimes takes a few triaaaaals to hear it correctly.

Jaeger Seafood, *1701 Elysian Fields Ave. (504-947-0111). Open Tuesday–Friday, 11:30 A.M.–9 P.M.; Saturday–Sunday, 11:30 A.M.–11 P.M. Closed Monday.*   This well-known seafood restaurant owned by Carlton Charles turns into **Jaeger After 10** on Friday and Saturday, with jazz sets going until 2 to 3 A.M. depending on the exuberance of the crowd. There is usually a small cover charge for the music. The food is hearty, delicious, and plentiful.

Cafe Baquet, *3925 Washington Ave. (504-822-1376). Open Monday–Thursday, 6 A.M.–3 P.M.; Friday, 6 A.M.–8 P.M.; Saturday, 6 A.M.–8 P.M.; Sunday, 7:30 A.M.–1:30 P.M.*   Operated by Kevin Bennett, a cousin of the well-known Baquet family that runs Zachary's and Eddie's Restaurant & Bar, this hopping eatery specializes in gumbo and catfish jourdiane. Ask for the latter dish on Friday. It's a hearty serving, prepared with a shrimp and crabmeat dressing. Cafe Baquet started in 1988 as basically a breakfast and luncheon place but is slowly expanding its nighttime hours—hence the shorter weekday hours. Bennett also runs a catering operation.

Zachary's, *8400 Oak St. (504-865-1559). Open Monday–Thursday, 11 A.M.–2:30 P.M. and 5:30–9:30 P.M.; Friday, 11 A.M.–2:30 P.M. and 5:30–10 P.M.; Saturday, 5:30–10 P.M.; closed Sunday.*   Located in the Uptown district since August of 1993, the place has already become popular among the business set. Owner Wayne Baquet's family also operates several other restaurants around New Orleans. Zachary's features creole and soul food.

Two Sisters Kitchen, *223 N. Derbigny St. (504-524-0056). Open Monday–Thursday, 7:30 A.M.–6:30 P.M.; Friday, 7:30 A.M.–7 P.M.; Saturday, 7:30 A.M.–5:30 P.M.; closed Sunday.*   Two Sisters is a popular neighborhood hideaway, with a wide variety of soul food such as chitlins, fresh fried fish, chicken, greens, and other traditional Southern foods, with a New Orleans touch.

Chez Helene, *1536 N. Robertson (504-947-0111). Open daily, 11:30 A.M.–10 P.M.* Chez Helene really is the "House of Good Food" in New Orleans, having opened in 1964. But the family likes to say the origins of the place started in 1942, when Helen Howard opened her first place at 1108 Perdido Street. Then simply called Howard's Eatery, it catered to the blue-collar workers in the commercial district. Po-boys and down-home creole cooking were the mainstays. After several location shifts, Helen's new husband, Joseph Pollock, encouraged a final move to the current address. The name was upscaled, but the same great cooking style was retained. Nephew, and noted chef, Austin Leslie eventually joined the team and brought years of experience with him. So now there's a great stylistic mix of buttermilk biscuits and frog legs bordelaise at Chez Helene.

Dooky Chase Restaurant, *2301 Orleans Ave. (504-821-0600; 504-822-9506, takeout). Open daily.* This New Orleans landmark started out as a sandwich shop, opening in 1941 as one of the few commercial restaurants serving African-Americans. Edward "Dooky" Chase, Sr. and wife Emily spent their days and nights tending to their patrons—all friends. The rest is history. Their daughter-in-law Leah has run the operation for the past two decades, serving up a great combo of black, Spanish, and French styles in her own way. A breathtaking display of African-American art lines the walls of the dining room for a great insight into the vibrancy of black culture. Many area bookshops carry Mrs. Chase's *The Dooky Chase Cookbook* (1990, Pelican Press, Gretna, $16.95) for those who need a deep-fried-oyster fix à la Chase when they get home. Throughout the book are reproductions of the restaurant's art. Now that is really food for the soul.

Rita's Old French Quarter Restaurant, *945 Chartres St. (504-525-7543). 11 A.M.–10 P.M., daily.* Featuring standard cajun and creole foods, Rita's lays out home cookin' with real style. One of the more popular casual eateries in the city, the restaurant is famous for generous portions of everything. It's a good place to rest weary feet during a French Quarter shopping break. Try the Taste of New Orleans with jambalaya, crayfish pie, vegetables, and other goodies for just $15.95.

The Praline Connection, *542 Frenchman St. (504-943-3934). Monday–Thursday, Sunday, 11 A.M.–10:30 P.M.; Friday–Saturday, 11 A.M.–midnight.* The Praline originally was to be a catering service that also offered home delivery of dinners for working parents stuck late at the office. But Curtis Moore and Cecil Kaigler, who picked up the intricacies of soul cooking at their respective mama's knees, wound up opening a full-fledged restaurant in 1990 because of the immediate demand. Steamed chicken, red beans and rice, yams, and sweet potato pie roll out of the kitchen like the best of a small town church supper. The Praline Connection is at the fringe of the French Quarter in Faubourg Marigny. Plastic tablecloths, artwork, and quick, friendly service complement the scene. Don't forget to stop in the adjoining candy store. This is one of musician Wynton Marsalis's favorite spots. A guest might spot him or any of a number of entertainers, political leaders, and other heavies with cornbread crumbs on their laps. Whoever they are, they fit right in.

Hasan's Restaurant, *300 Monroe St., Gretna (504-362-0200). Tuesday–Thursday, 11 A.M.–8 P.M.; Friday and Saturday, 11 A.M.–10 P.M.; Sunday, 11 A.M.–6 P.M.* Located under the Greater New Orleans Bridge over the Mississippi, Hasan's features the extensive wonders of home-style African-American cooking, with a creole twist. House specialties include shrimp étouffeé, shrimp creole, smothered chicken, candied yams, baked macaroni, beef stew, and red beans and rice with beef smoked sausage. Owner Kahtib Hasan presides over the main dining room, which seats seventy-five. He also has a private dining room for parties. A bar is connected to the restaurant. Prices range from $4 to $10.

Henry's Soul Food, *2501 S. Claiborne Ave. (504-821-7757); 209 N. Broad St. (504-821-8635). Monday through Thursday, 7 A.M.– 6:30 P.M.; Friday and Saturday, 7 A.M.–8:30 P.M.* Henry's serves up red beans, white beans, chicken, catfish, shrimp, okra, and just about everything else that home cookin' symbolizes. Diners get a full stomach and lots of people-watching opportunities at both of Henry's outlets.

Dunbar's, *4927 Freret St. (504-899-0734). Monday through Saturday, 7 A.M.–9 P.M.; Sunday, 7 A.M.–4 P.M.* Celestine Dunbar perches by the cash register, just to the left of the entrance of her cafe. For the past ten years, she has ruled this corner with a spatula in hand and a smile on her face. Chef Frank Jones keeps the chicken and red beans coming, serving a mixed bag of guests, which range from Uptown businesspeople to locals who appreciate the zesty style of home cooking.

Breakfast is served until 11 A.M. daily. Manager Peggy Hendesen will often lead a group out of the upstairs dining area with a flowery parasol and light-steppin' jazz. "Doin' the second line," she says. (The second line is the lively music played by a band coming back from the cemetery after a funeral.) Try the greens and turkey necks.

Eddie's Restaurant & Bar, *2119 Law St., Gentilly (504-945-2207). Weekdays, 11 A.M.–10 P.M.; Friday–Saturday, 11 A.M.–11 P.M.; closed Sunday.* Owned by Wayne Baquet, Eddie's is one of the few real old-time creole restaurants in New Orleans. Go for the pork chops with oyster dressing or the fried seafood. Nobody goes wrong at Eddie's.

Olivier's Famous Creole Restaurant, *2519 Dreux Ave. (504-282-2314). Monday–Thursday, 11 A.M.–9 P.M.; Friday, 11 A.M.–11 P.M.; Saturday, 5–11 P.M.; Sunday, 5–9 P.M.* Armand Olivier has been serving gumbo, homemade bread pudding, and peach cobbler, plus all those other New Orleans delicacies, since he opened in 1979. Ask for the catfish Orleans, which is smothered with crabmeat or shrimp. Olivier's seats thirty-six guests.

Palmers Restaurant, *135 N. Carrollton Ave. (504-482-3658). Tuesday–Saturday, 6–10:30 P.M. Closed Sunday and Monday.* Jamaican Cecil Palmer rules the roost in the city's only real Caribbean restaurant. Others might dabble in a few dishes but Palmer pulls out the island-stoppers with everything from rice and beans to goat.

Riverside Cafe, *1 Poydras St. Riverwalk (504-522-2061). Sunday, 10:30 A.M.–7 P.M.; Monday–Thursday, 10:30 A.M.–9 P.M.; Friday–Saturday, 10:30 A.M.–10 P.M.* Ah, that sweet potato pie! This is the place for all the best in Southern desserts, such as chocolate bourbon pecan tarts and numerous other fattening wonders. Seating 140 guests, this casual restaurant has recipes dating back three generations. Sitting directly on the Mighty Mississippi, paddlewheelers dock close by. Paintings of New Orleans decorate the interior, and artifacts dangle from the ceiling. Just watch out for the toasters and ice picks hanging up there. Delectable bell peppers, shrimp, and seafood-stuffed eggplant turn the mind to better thoughts.

Catering

Heavenly Dishes, *3914 Perrier St. (504-899-4542).* When Cheryl Black isn't singing with the L. L. Reed Ensemble at the New Zion Baptist Church, she's cooking up a storm for weddings, conventions, shut-ins, and neighborhood celebrations. Having learned her cooking from mom, Doris Morris Black forgoes recipes, adding a pinch of this and that to crayfish or shrimp pies, gumbo, turkey, and other home-cooked delicacies. Prices range from $4.95 to $12.95. "In this town, we eat, sing, and work, in that order," she laughs.

Marie's Sugar Dumplings, *6108 Singleton Dr., Marrero (504-348-2546).* Owner Yolanda Casby has a well-deserved, citywide reputation for her fantastic pies and wonderful banana bread.

Omar's Pies, *4637 New Orleans St. (504-283-4700).* Nicknamed The Pie Man, Omar Aziz's father, Omar, Sr., founded the company thirty years ago. Now one of the top catering bakers in the city, Aziz sell his pies at the Jazz & Heritage Festival and to many of the major restaurants around town. Special offerings include sweet potato, custard, lemon, and pecan.

Publications

New Orleans had the first black newspaper in the South, the *New Orleans Tribune,* which began publication following the Civil War. Over the years, publications came and went. However, there are now a number of strong newspapers and magazines still serving the African-American market.

Style, 650 S. Pierce St., Suite 350 (504-947-0007). This upscale, four-color monthly focuses on the key African-American cultural events in New Orleans. *Style* is distributed free at hotels, newsstands, coffeeshops, drugstores, colleges and universities, and retail outlets on the fifth of each month. Editor Sandra M. Gunner focuses on festivals, fashion, art, and the general social scene.

Louisiana Weekly, 616 Baronne St. (504-524-5563). Covering the state's black scene, the *Louisiana Weekly* is a standard newspaper, coming out on Wednesdays. It can be purchased at newsstands throughout the city.

New Orleans Tribune, 2335 Esplanade Ave. (504-945-0772). The monthly *New Orleans Tribune* covers the New Orleans African-American scene in depth, with articles on business leaders, political happenings, events, and local personalities. Costing 50¢, the paper can be found in most black-owned businesses, as well as on newsstands. Publisher Beverly McKenna produces insightful commentary in regular columns, aided by a staff of full- and part-timers.

Arts

A pre-Civil War newspaper commentary claimed that while blacks aspired to artistic notions, it wasn't in their nature to be creative. A placard reads to that effect in a stairwell at the Amistad Research Center at Tulane University. Burying that ill-conceived notion, at the top of the steps is a vibrant, colorful collection of artwork by noted African-American painters. And with the display, any archaic idea of blacks lacking creative fulfillment flies the way of Jim Crow. The New Orleans African-American art world is among the liveliest of any large city.

New Orleans both consciously and subtly incubates the arts. This is a city where residents feel comfortable dancing in the streets, whether on Bourbon Street, at a funeral procession, or at a street fair. Carrying on the tradition in more professional venues are several troupes, including Kumbuka; N'Kfau; the Lula Elzy Dance Company; a children's African dance company called Culu; FAME, a brainchild of the New Orleans Creative Center of Arts; and the San Jacinto Dance Theater, 3623 Canal Street (504-486-4433).

High stepping is the password during Mardi Gras for the Zulu Krewe, among the most famous of the groups staging one of the wild pre-Lenten parades. Made up of black businesspeople and other African-American leaders from around the city, the krewe holds its own ball at the convention center, where thousands turn out to celebrate. Formed as a direct parody of the white krewes, the Zulu began parading in 1909, tossing out real coconuts to the enthusiastic crowd. Films of Zulu coronation balls from 1955, 1956, 1971, and 1972 can be found in the Lillie Mae Green Papers at the Amistad Research Center. The Mardi Gras Indians came about even earlier, starting as an "outlaw" organization in the 1890s and staging their own second-line parades despite objections from the New Orleans power structure. Wearing colorful costumes patterned after Native American clothing, the Indians keep on doing their own thing and are now considered among the most popular groups performing during Mardi Gras. The Amistad is currently assembling artifacts for a major museum on the Indians, working with the Mardi Gras Indian Coalition. Also during that era, more mainline blacks formed the Original Illinois Club to present their own debutantes and stage elaborate dances and tableaux rather than parading.

In 1993, the Ashanti Crewe was organized by Kalamu y Salaam and Bill Rouselle, who had been friends for twenty-five years. The two are partners in their own advertising and public relations agency, Bright Moments Public Relations, 2218 Brainerd Avenue (504-523-4443). Salaam is a New Oleans playwright, as well as a special events impresario. Rouselle was the first black news reporter on WDSU-TV in 1968, covering civil rights issues. In addition to their Mardi Gras work in 1993, they designed the program for the U.S. Olympic track and field trials and the official program and poster for the New Orleans Jazz & Heritage Festival.

Love of flamboyant color is a fact of life here. New Orleanians are in touch with their need for vibrant music, literature, drama, painting, dance, poetry, or any other art form. Black arts leaders emphasize that the city is blessed with residents who have a love of art from almost the day they are born, adding that New Orleans' cultural scene is an essential part of who the people are.

New Orleans' African-Americans actively participate in National African-American Cultural Arts Month each October with choral concerts, Rejoicing in Parks art exhibits, a theater festival, and numerous other arts activities. Organized by the Black Arts National Diaspora, an ecumenical service is held at **Christian Unity Baptist Church,** 1700 Conti Street (504-522-3493). A prayer program is followed by a march to the river for a blessing of the site where, according to tradition, the first chained African slaves were brought ashore. The program usually begins at 3 P.M. on the first Sunday of the month, with the procession moving the sixteen blocks up Conti Street to the slowly rolling Mississippi. Water is poured from a wooden cup onto the ground, while the names of ancestors are called out. For more information on this spiritual journey into the past, with its call to the future, contact Diaspora Director Dr. G. Jeannette Hodge (504-282-7975).

Music

The heart and soul of New Orleans is its music. Everywhere one turns, there's jazz, blues, brass, and everything in between and beyond. New Orleans is the home of the famed Marsalis brothers, Wynton and Branford, gospel great Mahalia Jackson, and hundreds more. There are well-known tourist clubs in the French Quarter, institutions such as **Preservation Hall,** 726 St. Peters Street (504-522-2841), and plenty of holes-in-the-wall where musicians drop by to jam. Most of the latter are funky down-home snugs, replete with red plush and twinkle lights, and are probably not listed in the travel guides. Some aren't even listed in the phone book, and many don't drop a date in the local entertainment publications because their managers probably aren't sure who might show up. Most of the really good music doesn't start cooking until 11 P.M. or later, running on tobacco, wine, and vibes until dawn.

The Babylonian All-Stars, a collection of veteran blues musicians who normally back up marquee stars, could show up anytime unannounced in a corner tap. Or Big Al Carson & The Rap Connexion might strut down to Joe's Cozy Corner on Roberts and Ursuline to blow down the door with music. Big Al, by the way, shows his gentle giant side by doubling as a singing Santa Claus at civic events during the Christmas holidays.

Clubs change their musical faces with regularity. For instance, many places have separate nights for blues and jazz. Witness the Tuesday and Thursday Jamaican dance lessons at **Chesterfield's,** 3213 Kingman, Metairie (504-888-9898), followed on Wednesdays with cha-cha, then with the big-band rhythms of Bobby Lonero and the New Orleans Express on occasional weekends. Or visit **Melvin's,** 1500 block of St. Anne Street, for blues and jazz on alternate nights, and **Gino's,** at Claiborne and Orleans avenues, for just good, solid musical riffs.

Dropping by a place is serendipitous, enough for most New Orleanians who know the scene. Music in this city knows neither time nor geographical constraints. The following clubs are primarily African-American, providing some of the best music New Orleans has to offer. But whether white, black, green, fuchsia, yellow, or brown, anyone is welcome.

Flabor's, *2512 St. Bernard Ave. (504-947-6581).*   Flabor's caters to the forty-somethings and above crowd who appreciate the excellent jukebox here with its Delta-sized jazz, blues, soul, and oldies selections.

Jaeger Seafood, *1701 Elysian Fields Ave. (504-947-0111).*   This well-known seafood restaurant turns into **Jaeger After 10** on Friday and Saturday, with jazz sets going until at 2 or 3 A.M., depending on the crowd. There is a small cover charge.

4th Edition, *2613 Jasmine St. (504-947-1145).*

New Flynn's Den, *8001 Chef Menteur Highway (504-241-9333).*

Muddy Water's, *8301 Oak St. (504-866-7174).*

Jelly Roll's, *501 Bourbon St. (504-568-0501).*

Treme Music Hall, *1601 Ursuline St. (504-596-6942).*

Pampys Tight Squeeze Restaurant and Bar, *2005 Broad St. (504-949-7970).*

Winnaha's Circle, *2169 Aubry St. (504-948-2212).*

Maple Leaf Club, *8316 Oak (504-866-9359).*

Star's, *6200 Elysian Fields Ave. (504-282-9053).*

Whisper's, *8700 Lake Forest Blvd. (504-245-1059).*

Joe's Cozy Corner, *1030 N. Robertson St. (unlisted).*

C&C Club, *1501 St. Philip St. (unlisted).* Music performed only from Friday to Sunday. This is a hard-to-beat blues mecca for the city's top artists of the mournful sound.

Trombone Shorty's, *1533 St. Philip St. (504-523-1481).*

Adeaux's Lounge & Nightclub, *5824 Hayne Blvd. (504-241-3948).*

The Bottom Line, *2101 N. Claiborne Ave. (504-947-9297).*

Charlie B's, *829 Convention Center Blvd. (504-523-9028).*

Club VIP, *9200 I-10 Service Rd. (504-245-1512).* Best Top-Forty dance music rocks 'n' rolls out here.

Festivals

Street festivals are held periodically throughout the year, combining the vibrancy and downhome appeal of talented neighborhood groups with the headliner stage presence of name performers. Three of the best events are coordinated by the New Orleans Jazz & Heritage Foundation, which also produces the internationally known New Orleans Jazz & Heritage Festival each spring. For these neighborhood carnivals, streets are blocked off, and stages and tents are set up in school playgrounds. Food vendors and entertainers who live in the respective neighborhoods are asked to do their "thang." Festival dates each year are always open-ended because the shows are booked around the availability of entertainers. For up-to-date information, contact Jackie Harris at the Jazz Foundation, 1205 N. Rampart Street (504-522-4786).

Programs run from 11 A.M. to 6 P.M. on the Saturday and Sunday of each festival weekend. The Dirty Dozen-Treme Brass Festival is usually staged either at the end of September or in early November on the streets around St. Augustine Church, 1100 St. Claude Avenue. The Uptown Street Festival is held in early spring, whenever the famous New Orleans musical family, the Neville Brothers, can perform there. The Uptown Street fest is held in a bustling corner of Lawrence Square Park, 624 Louisiana Avenue. The third event put together by the jazz foundation organizers is the Carrollton Street Festival, held each summer in Palmer Park at the corner of Carrollton and Claiborne, where the St. Charles streetcar line ends.

Another major New Orleans street fair is the Treme Community Street Festival in April, held a week prior to the opening of the Jazz Festival. The People's Institute, St. Mark's Methodist Community Center, and Covenant House are among the fifteen groups in the Greater Treme Consortium that sponsor this giant blowout of music and frivolity. Treme, consisting of 202 square blocks, is one of the more historic neighborhoods in New Orleans, with Armstrong Park marking the heart of the community. Visitors can hear the likes of the Dirty Dozen Brass Band, Rebirth Brass Band, Trombone Shorty Nelson, and Big Al Carson & The Rap Connexion, among numerous other musicians who spill out from their neighborhood clubs for a chance in the sun.

For information, contact the consortium at 704 N. Claiborne Avenue (504-524-7586). The brainstorm behind the street festival was to pull the neighborhood together, according to director Jim Hayes, who has headed the association since the 1960s.

Today's Treme Street festival planted its roots in 1969 when several local organizations planned a weekend of music in historic Congo Square, across from the French Quarter. The event has metamorphosed over the years, now taking up the entire 1300 block of St. Philips Street near Armstrong Park. The weekend fun runs from 11 A.M. to 6 P.M. on the chosen Saturday and Sunday. Folks cook spectacular pots of steaming gumbo and jambalaya in their home kitchens, bringing the goodies out to share and sell. With prices hovering generally under $5, it's the best food anyone's mama can concoct. One local lady even makes homemade ice cream to tantalize tastebuds.

Black Bridal Fair *(504-488-6852).*   Held in January at the Clarion Hotel, the bridal fair is sponsored by Hallmark Cards, K&B Drugstores, and clothing outlets, with lectures on customs. A fashion show, with plenty of frills and white lace, and an exhibit expo for service providers, such as the caterers and florists, are popular parts of the program. Program director Caroline Hardesty can answer your questions.

Black Heritage Festival *(504-483-6691).* This week-long event culminates in two days at the Audubon Zoo, attended by upwards of thirty thousand people. The week's events include exhibits by black artists at galleries throughout city and a major formal gala, held either at the aquarium or the museum of art. The zoo program features continuous music, with national acts performing on two stages. There's also a gospel tent and arts and crafts displays. For more information, contact Louadrian Reed.

Reggae Fest, *Box 6156, New Orleans, LA 70174-6156 (504-367-3554 or 367-1313).* The Caribbean comes to town the second weekend of each June for a full weekend of programming at City Park, kicked off on Friday with a free show in the square adjacent to City Hall. In addition to local groups, bands are brought in from Africa and the Caribbean to put hot New Orleans on upbeat island time. The festival was the brainchild of accountant Ernest Kelly, who visited Jamaica's SunSplash Festival in 1984. He came home exploding with ideas and capitalized on his experience by booking shows and organizing special events and concerts while still a student at Louisiana Tech. Other than having a fierce love of reggae, Kelly doesn't have a connection with islands. He says he's gone back several times, "stealing the ambience and getting new ideas."

Since Reggae Fest started in 1985, performers have included the Steel Pulse, a European-based band; South Africa's Lucky Dube and Arrow and Mighty Sparrow, both from Trinidad; Yellow Man; Inner Circle; Marcia Griffith; Sophia George; and Julian Marley. The well-known Uptown All-Stars, rockin' locals who blend reggae and a bouncy second-line beat, derives its soul from New Orleans.

Ringing the festival site at City Park's Marconi Meadow are fruitstands, where nimble demonstrators chop coconuts with machetes. Pungent scents of curried and jerked chicken, among other spicy Caribbean delicacies, waft through the summer air. Arts, crafts, clothing, and jewelry from the Caribbean and Africa are sold from booths near the stage. Kids scurry between legs, oldsters on lawn chairs hunker down for a day of talk and music, teens make eyes at each other, and life spins happily around for everyone involved.

The fest attracts upwards of twenty-five thousand visitors from around the country, according to Kelly. "Our festival best reflects the best of the community with whites, blacks, and Hispanics getting together for a great time. I feel good about that," he says.

Two-day passes, which allow ticket holders to mix and mingle backstage with the performers, are available for $30. A one-day pass is $10. Kids under twelve get in free. Marconi Meadow is easily accessible by driving up City Park Avenue to Marconi Drive. Free parking is available in the park. Music, under the supervision of production manager Kahlid Hafiz (504-522-4786), runs from noon to 9 P.M. Blankets and lawn chairs are encouraged for a day of lounging in front of the forty-by-sixty-foot stage.

A free preview is offered in Duncan Plaza, at Loyola and Perdido next to City Hall and the State Office Building, on the first day of the festival. Held during the lunch hour, the sampling of sounds offers the curious a chance to hear what Reggae Fest is all about.

There are some twenty to thirty thousand residents of Jamaica, Trinidad, and the Virgin Islands in New Orleans, tagging the city as the Northern Capital of the Caribbean. "There is a definite connection with the islands," Kelly points out. "There's the people, the music, and the food. We like red beans and rice, and so do they. We like spicy food and so do they. These are certainly cultural links."

But Kelly admits that his festival doesn't attract a great number of homegrown island residents, who feel that the event is too commercial. Consequently, many locals attend their own unpublicized picnics elsewhere in the city. One favorite holiday is Marcus Garvey Day in August. Garvey was a noted preacher, civil rights leader, and political sounding board in the 1920s. He was born in St. Ann's Bay, Jamaica, on August 17, 1887 and founded the Universal Negro Association, the *Negro World* newspaper, and the Black Star Line steamship line.

Reggae

When there isn't a festival to attend, the reggae fan needn't despair. There are a few sunshine spots in which tropical dreams come true:

Oasis Nightclub, *2285 N. Bayou Rd. (504-944-2000). Open only Thursday, Friday, and Saturday.*

Tipitina's, *501 Napoleon Ave. (504-897-3943).* International reggae artists appear at various times, so call the club's Concert Line to find out who's on stage.

Whisper's Nightclub, *8700 Lake Forest Blvd. (504-245-1059).* Local reggae bands such as Cecile Neville, Irie (Good Feeling) Vibrations, and Ben Hunter & The Plantation Posse perform regularly.

Holiday Offerings

While there's no need to find an excuse for a party in New Orleans, the end-of-year holidays are always fabulous fun. A popular presentation is the *Nutcracker Swing,* a Duke Ellington adaptation of the fabled Nutcracker Suite, in which the noted entertainer builds his story around jazz. The city's premier musicians, such as Elston Marsalis, always enter into the fun. Performances are usually held the first weekend of December at the glittering **Orpheum Theater,** 129 University Place. The theater was refurbished in 1993. For information, call the theater (504-524-3285).

Another New Orleans tradition-in-the-making is the production of *Where There's a Will/The Living Christmas Tree.* Performances are traditionally held the first week of December at noon and 7 P.M. on Saturday; at 3 P.M. on Sunday; at 10 A.M. on Monday; at 10 A.M. and 7 P.M. on Tuesday; and at 10 A.M. and 8 P.M. on Wednesday. Tickets are $10 for adults and $5 for children, students, and seniors. For information, call 504-866-5201.

The lavish production, which started in 1992, features African-American theater, dance, and gospel. Held originally at the Municipal Auditorum for two years, prior to the building being transformed into a gambling casino, the shows are now presented at various sites around the city, so check the local entertainment columns for locale. The show's central theme is the contemporary telling of the story of the prodigal son. A 157-voice choir stands on a 15-tier, 37-foot-tall Christmas tree structure ablaze with pulsating lights. The performers have included nationally known singer Aubrey Bryan, the Blessed Melody Choir, the Urhuru Dancers of St. Francis de Sales Choir, Christian Unity Baptist Church, and Judy Leigier's Sacred Dance Ministry.

The show is staged by the nonprofit YICI Productions (Youth Inspiration Choir Inc.), which originated as a youth group that peformed around the country and in Europe. Although members are now adults, they continue to perform because it is so much fun. YICI also hosts the Rejoicing in the Park celebration each October in Armstrong Park.

Reverend Lois Dejean, the show's producer, conceived the Living Christmas Tree idea several years ago. "It is something to involve young people from the area churches and from the neighborhoods on a positive level," says Dejean.

Visual Arts

Painters from New Orleans, such as Louise Mouton, Clifton Webb, and Martin Payton are nationally known for their fantastic stylization and sweeping vision. Works by John Scott, a professor of art at Xavier University, appear in offices, banks, galleries, private collections, schools, and government buildings around the country. His brilliantly colored posters were among the most popular created by local artists for the 1984 New Orleans World's Fair and are still sold at the Amistad Research Center for fund-raising purposes ($3 each). Under Scott's keen tutelage, dozens of other exceptional young black artists have received a jump start in the art world.

For a display by black artists, although not all from New Orleans, the Amistad Collection has more than three million dollars worth of artwork, including Henry Ossawatanne's "The Laundress" and Ellis Wilson's "The Funeral Procession." The latter painting was featured prominently in many episodes of the Bill Cosby television show. The Amistad, by the way, is the exclusive distributor of posters and reproductions of that famed painting. Other artists on display include Jacob Lawrence, George Ridley, Edward Mitchell Bannister, Aaron Doylan, Hale Woodruff, and Romare Bearden.

A minigallery on the second floor of the center's three-story building (the university's original library) provides a snug viewing area for these eye-openers. A revolving collection of African art is also displayed in the first floor research room at the Amistad. Pieces are often loaned from the collection for gallery and museum displays throughout the country.

The Amistad is also the country's largest and most comprehensive repository of material pertaining to civil rights for African-Americans. The more than ten million documents are from the early 1700s to the present day, with an emphasis on the past four decades.

Richard Thomas Gallery *(504-822-7501).*   In late 1994, Thomas was in the process of moving his gallery from his Claude Avenue address to a new location. Thomas's own art and that of his students provide excellent examples of a fantastic New Orleans African-American art scene. Thomas, as the dean of the city's painters, takes kids in tow and frees their minds in an explosion of the creative process. His latest project, painting garbage cans and refuse bins in neighborhoods along Lake Pontchartrain, was commissioned by the New Orleans Levee Board. The riot of color on such prosaic items snazzes up street corners and alleyways.

Neighborhood Gallery, *2135 Soniat St. (504-891-5573).*   A delightful oasis of sound, color, and fun, the Neighborhood Gallery is a constant bustle of creative disciplines, whether drama, art, or music. Managed by Sandra Berry, who seems to be able to juggle troupes of toddlers, elderly poets, and teen artists with equal aplomb, the Neighborhood Gallery has received national recognition for its service to the community. While primarily African-American in orientation, the Neighborhood Galley reaches out to others, as well, with over one hundred artist members. The philosophy of the Neighborhood Gallery is to nurture and showcase New Orleans talent, regardless of race. Opening receptions are usually held on the first Sunday of the month for regularly changing exhibitions. The shows are well attended by the city's cultural elite, who rub shoulders with neighborhood residents.

The Neighborhood Gallery itself is a series of houses turned into artspace. All the adjoining courtyards are connected to make an interesting maze of rooms whose walls are covered with paintings. Sculpture peeks from hidden corners. International in scope, the Gallery recently opened an extension in London.

Theater

African-American theater is regularly presented at Xavier, Dillard, and other universities in New Orleans. Church halls and high school auditoriums also provide forums. In fact, the upbeat attitude is that anywhere an audience can collect is ripe for a staging. Many companies are made up of young volunteer performers eager to display their talents and showcase the depth of the black cultural experience. The city's broad community theater base seeks to bolster touring or professional repertory productions that present the African-American experience. Local theater also offers insight into accomplishing social change, according to Carol BeBelle, Director of the **Contemporary Arts Center,** 300 Camp Street (504-861-4969).

Bebelle points out that New Orleans has a rich pool of talent from which to draw. She describes, among others, author Tom Dent's writings about the civil rights period. In his "Southern Journey," Dent relates what it was like traveling with his middle-class family and learning about the United States from a Southern perspective. Kalamu ya Salaam, a New Orleans public relations executive and special events producer, also has a string of successful, locally staged productions. Then there is the **Kingsley House Community Center,** 914 Richard (504-523-6221), which annually sponsors an amateur drama festival in its Irish Channel neighborhood, usually in September or October. For specific details, contact director Valarie Maurice.

The Black Theater Festival is held annually during the first two weekends of October in the two hundred-seat theater of the Contemporary Arts

Center, presenting original works by local writers and those by other established black playwrights from around the country. In past productions, works by Langston Hughes, California Cooper, and Bill Harris have received critical acclaim. Originating in 1981, the Black Theater Festival is the only annual black theatrical festival in the country. Others are biannual.

Some hometown actors in the festival also use existing narrative, poetry, and music to weave intricate productions highlighting the African-American living experience. For instance, C.A.S.T. (Creative Artists Striving Together) has addressed male-female relationships with presentations from black authors and poets. They have also presented a history piece on resistance oratory by noted black leader Frederick Douglass.

Troupes of young peformers also offer productions during the festival. Among the best are Kids in the Act (with performers 10 and under) and Legacy and Somewhere Off Broadway (both with teens). The young people do their own staging, writing, and set development in what is called *kuji* (from the root word *kuji-chajulia,* which means *self-determination,* one of the seven principles of the Kwanza holiday, a festive time between Christmas and New Year's).

Performances are juried by a panel of judges, which bestow awards for best production, actor, actress, supporting actor, and supporting actress. A reception, dinner, and awards program is held the week after the festival's closing.

The Contemporary Arts Center is seeking technical support to increase its sound and lighting capabilities for its productions, which often feature traveling companies. Among them have been The Children of Selma Theater Company, made up of young adults of high school and college age from Selma, Alabama. The musical group is under the direction of attorney and composer Rose Sanders.

Festival director BeBelle is an admitted educational hybrid, with an undergraduate degree in political science from Loyola and a master's in education from Tulane. She has written a play, "Class Reunion," and numerous poems. Director for the past three years, she has her own planning and development and grant writing firm, working with cultural arts groups in the city and in other Southern states. In addition, she produces local theater presentations throughout the year. A local New Orleanian, BeBelle's granddad was a Baptist minister. Other relatives were active in creative ventures; among them was an aunt in fashion design and an uncle who was a composer.

Tickets for the entire series and for individual productions are available. Prices are $10 at the door and $5 in advance for children, students, and seniors. A $6.50 group rate is also available; matinees are $5. Productions are generally staged at 8 P.M. on Friday and at 6 and at 8 P.M. on Saturday and Sunday. Remember that New Orleans is a church city where worship services are of prime importance, so check with the *Times Picayne* and the alternative newspapers for definitive weekend times. For reservations, call 504-861-4969.

Broadcasting

WYLD-FM, *228 Gravier St. (504-827-6000, business office). The WYLD-AM request line is 504-260-9494. The WYLD-FM request line is 504-260-3698.* Gospel is heard primarily on the AM-940 station, with urban contemporary holding sway on the FM-98. The station broadcasts twenty-four hours a day. The Midday Lunch Buffet (10 A.M. to 1 P.M.), hosted by Neeche Thomas on the FM dial, is a popular request line. Featuring adult contemporary with an urban focus, the station has been operating for more than forty-five years. A lot of people grew up with it in New Orleans, says Cheryl Charles, General Sales Manager. The Program Director is Skip Dillard, who hosts an afternoon drive show. Affectionately called the "hero of the station" for his longevity on air is Greg "Papa Smurf" Vigne. The golden-throated announcer has been on the air more than eleven years with his show, "Mellow Moods," airing from 9 P.M. to midnight on FM-98. Vigne's extensive love ballad playlist includes the likes of Aretha Franklin and her ilk. The word around town is that a lot of kids were born because of "Mellow Moods." Papa Smurf Vigne also hosts "Sunday Morning Jazz" (10 A.M. to 1 P.M.). Recording artists who come to town are often interviewed on the air. On the AM side, "Jammin' for Jesus" with Walter Ross (6 A.M. to 10 P.M.) features contemporary gospel musicians, such as Vicki Winans, John P. Kee, and the Mississippi Mass Choir. WYLD-AM broadcasts live from the gospel tent at the Jazz & Heritage Festival each year. Both AM and FM outlets are active in other community affairs, with radio personalities appearing at schools, festivals, and clubs; helping at benefits; and assisting in other activities.

WWL-TV, *1024 Rampart St. (504-529-4444).* Called the "Spirit of Louisiana," WWL-TV (Channel 4) is a CBS affiliate that airs "Perspectives in Black" at 10:30 A.M. on Saturday. The half-hour news/features/talk show, hosted by Mary Beal, focuses on issues of interest to the New Orleans African-American community.

Hispanic/Caribbean New Orleans

History and Settlement

Perhaps the French Quarter should have been called the Spanish Quarter, at least based on physical appearance. Architecturally, the most famous district in the Crescent City is the result of an aggressive building program launched by the Spaniards after they inherited Louisiana, or what they called New Iberia, in the mid-1760s. Although the original New Orleans was plotted by French engineer Adrien de Pauger in 1721, haphazard construction of the first buildings presented a dilapidated, scruffy look even before the city was a year old. It took the hurricane of September 11, 1722 to literally clean house, destroying two-thirds of the existing buildings and damaging the rest. As one resident remarked after the storm, "There would not have been any great misfortune in this disaster except that we must act to put all the people in shelter."

So the French builders went back to work, filling in the Vieux Carre (the French Quarter) with more sturdy structures. However, the Spanish completed the job, adding their own Mediterranean touches. By the time the French returned in the early 1800s, the look was solidly that of a Spanish town, with tile roofs, stucco, wrought iron balcony railings, and Spanish street names. The Cabildo, the seat of Spanish power (and also the term applied to the city's governing council at the time), became one of the dominant buildings on the *Plaza de Armas*. The plaza became the *Place d'Armes* for the French, and today's Jackson Square. Flanking St. Louis Cathedral, the Cabildo and the Presbyter on the other side of the church still present the graceful lines and archways typical of Spanish building styles. Compounding the hammer, nails, and masonry fervor of the Spanish, two fires in the eighteenth century eventually cleaned out most of the remaining French architectural influence. Subsequently, only one authentic, original French colonial building remains in contemporary New Orleans: the Ursuline Convent at 1114 Chartres Street, completed in 1751 and now believed to be the oldest building in the lower Mississippi Valley.

Despite the changes that took place throughout the Spaniards' forty-one-year rule (1762 to 1803), this city fiercely retained its French mindset. There was never a Spanish-language newspaper, nor was Spanish the language of commerce. Yet the relative political stability during the Spanish tenure ensured that New Orleans could peacefully develop as one of the region's mightiest ports, ensuring unprecedented economic muscle and fat bank accounts for its entreprenurial residents.

The Spanish administrators and military personnel stationed in New Orleans were primarily single men, unlike the French who had settled in the city with their families. Subsequently, there was little generational Spanish influence. Many of the love-struck Spanish married Creole girls, learned to speak French so they could get along with their mothers-in-law, and were subsequently slowly absorbed into the mainstream of French New Orleans life. Today the only Southern Louisianans who can trace their direct heritage to Spain are the remaining descendants of a contingent of Canary Island fishermen who settled in nearby St. Bernard Parish in 1778. Tourists wishing to visit their only remaining community can take the St. Bernard city bus along Perez Avenue for the six-mile ride from downtown New Orleans. Several small grocery stores and a cluster of houses are all that remain there.

How did the Spanish arrive in New Orleans in the first place? Actually it was mixture of politics and benign confusion, cemented by blood. The transfer of Louisiana from France to Spain was made official by a secret treaty signed at the French royal place of Fontainbleau on November 23, 1762. The pact intended to compensate ally Spain for the staggering losses it suffered in the Seven Years' War. This was to be done by ceding to Spain all French colonies west of the Mississippi. Everything to the east of the river went to England. But the Spanish felt that they needed a stronger military presence in their new acquisition before they could govern and protect it adequately.

In 1764, Louis XV told Jean-Jacques Blaise D'Abbadie, the governor of Louisiana, that he was out of a job. It was even agreed that French soldiers in the colony would enlist in the Spanish army, thereby saving the Spaniards the expensive aggravation of raising extra troops at home and shipping them overseas.

However, the independent-minded colonists in New Orleans objected to the entire plan and petitioned Louis to revoke the orders. Their complaints were rejected, and the king told them they were no longer his concern. On March 5, 1766, Don Antonio de Ulloa, the new Spanish governor, arrived in town. He expected a warm greeting and rapid enlistment of French troops into his new force. He received neither.

In fact, de Ulloa immediately got off on the wrong foot by enforcing commercial restrictions that required Louisiana to trade henceforth only with Spain, a long-standing rule that had always applied to his country's colonies. Another sore point with the New Orleanians was de Ulloa's proposal to exchange the old French currency for Spanish money at only 75 percent of its standing value. The city's freewheeling business community, long accustomed to doing what it wanted as long as it was profitable, was furious.

Their hostility eventually flowered into open rebellion in 1768, with armed colonists (including disgruntled Acadians and Germans) marching into the outskirts of New Orleans. De Ulloa, fearing for his safety, scurried aboard the Spanish frigate, *El Volante,* which was anchored in the harbor. Somehow during the night, the ship was set adrift, and de Ulloa disappeared into the mist. Wisely, he just kept going. According to local legend, the ship's anchor rope was cut by revelers returning from a wedding party in New Orleans. They supposedly saw a great chance to have some fun, as well as strut their stuff as patriots.

Shortly thereafter, the city's Supreme Council drew up a letter that reaffirmed its allegiance to France. But the Spaniards had had enough. In 1769, the Spanish king dispatched Don Alejandro O'Reilly, an Irish-born soldier-of-fortune, to put down the rebellion. O'Reilly, who fought for the Spanish crown in the Seven Years' War and in Cuba, was considered tough enough to handle any emergency. To make sure there would be no problems, he was backed up by twenty ships of war, more than two thousand battle-hardened veterans, and dozens of cannons and mortars. The show of force demonstrated to most of the 3,100 free citizens of New Orleans that O'Reilly meant business. In ensuing negotiations, however, holdout civic leaders still outlined their objections to any form of Spanish administration and its economic restrictions. O'Reilly promised to see what he could do. Everyone was relieved, figuring that this, indeed, was a reasonable man. After all he was Irish and Catholic, they told each other. But what the Gaelic don eventually did was not quite what the citizens expected.

During the night of August 16, O'Reilly's troops entered the sleeping city and began arresting the more vocal opponents of the Spanish presence. A leader of the German rebels, Joseph Villere, was bayoneted to death when he resisted. A number of other prominent personalities were tried for treason and eventually shot by firing squad or imprisoned. The rest of the populace quickly lost heart as the rebellion was crushed. From then on, the Irishman-turned-Spaniard was known as Bloody O'Reilly.

As the saying goes, "Sticks and stones may break my bones, but names will never harm me." Unfazed by the charges of brutality, O'Reilly abolished what was left of the Supreme Council and substituted a *cabildo,* a governing body of six *regidores* (councilmen) and *alcaldes* (mayors), plus other office-holders. Spanish laws were substituted for those of France.

Historians have argued for years about whether O'Reilly's actions to protect Spanish interests were justified. Yet his heavy-handed administration had certain merit. He abolished Indian slavery, permitted many low-ranking French officials to remain in office, and even set up a homesteading act for settlers, in which they received land if they promised to clear it and live on the property for three years. He built roads and public buildings and even made sure the streets were "clean" in an era in which contents of chamberpots were often launched from upstairs windows.

O'Reilly left New Orleans in 1770, much to the delight of the populace. There are no records of anyone throwing him a bon voyage party, and there are still no statues dedicated to him in New Orleans. O'Reilly was replaced by Don Luis de Unzaga y Amezaga, who set a trend for the next three decades of Spanish rule. Unzaga was a gentle fellow who married a Creole beauty, turned a blind eye to smuggling, and let the locals trade with anyone they desired. All three factors endeared him to his fellow New Orleanians.

During this period, Don Andrés Almonester y Roxas immigrated to New Orleans and became Unzaga's right-hand man as clerk and notary. He became well known for his real estate dealings, as well as for his charity, distributing much of his fortune to the poor. But history notes Almonester primarily because he was the father of the legendary New Orleans society matron Baroness Pontalba, who built the fabled Pontalba apartments around what became Jackson Square.

Don Bernardo de Galvez took over as Spanish governor in 1777. Like his predecessor, he married a Creole maiden and lackadaisically enforced the economic regulations. Galvez openly aided the embattled American colonists in the Revolutionary War and, when Spain declared war on England in 1779, he personally led Louisiana troops. Soldiers from New

Orleans fought with him in battles at Baton Rouge, Natchez, Mobile, and Pensacola. His actions and those of his fellow Spanish military helped divert the attention of the English war machine and probably can be credited with playing a major role in ensuring the success of the American Revolution.

The Treaty of Paris in 1783, which officially ended the war, also delineated the southern boundaries of the new United States at thirty-one degrees latitude. The line was important because it marked the border with the Spanish colonies in the South and West. In 1785, Galvez was named Captain-General of Louisiana, Cuba, and Florida, as well as Viceroy of Mexico. A statue of him, striking a suitably heroic poise, stands at the foot of Canal Street.

Another five thousand Acadians arrived during the tenure of Don Esteban Rodríguez Miró, the next governor, who welcomed them with open arms. Many of the Acadians, swelling the ranks of those who had begun moving to Louisiana in the 1750s after being exiled by the English from their Canadian homes, ventured into outlying parishes near New Orleans. Their outback culture eventually evolved into what today is called "Cajun." Miró also married a Creole woman, Marie Celeste Elenore de McCarty, whose name alone demonstrated the mixed heritage of the local populace.

Disastrous fires in 1788 and 1794 swept New Orleans during Miró's tenure. As a result, new building codes were enforced. They utilized solid, fireproof construction materials, providing the solid look that permeates the French Quarter today. The Spanish *patios,* or inner courtyards of the homes, were popular features, as were shady arcades and cooling fountains, which were blessings in the muggy Delta summers.

Francisco Luis Hector, Baron de Carondelet, was the next governor. He developed the city's first lighting system and a bilingual, night police force. Carondelet also instituted a tax on every chimney to help pay for these municipal benefits. However, the crafty New Orleanians avoided paying extra by using the same chimney for all floors of their newly built houses, thereby giving another distinctive look to many buildings that can still be seen today. Several other Spanish governors marched through New Orleans on their way into the history books, but the only Spanish administrator buried in the city is General Manuel Luis Gayoso de Lemos, who died of yellow fever on July 18, 1799. His burial site is supposedly in St. Louis Cathedral but no plaque marks the spot and the records are hazy on the exact location.

One book says Gayoso de Lemos was buried under the altar, but church historians say they don't have any evidence of that possibility. Other references indicate that the governor might have been buried in a plot behind the cathedral. The fires that swept New Orleans in the 1800s left the cathedral heavily damaged, so any definitive evidence of the governor's last resting place may be permanently lost. You might try asking his ghost.

Spanish rule ended in 1800 when Louisiana was re-ceded to France in the Treaty of Ildefonso. Napoleon Bonaparte, wishing to revive France's overseas empire after victoriously sweeping most of central Europe into his vest pocket, pressured Spanish King Charles IV to give New Iberia back to France. Charles, nervously eyeing the mighty French armies near his country's borders, decided to comply. By 1803, the formalities were concluded and France again had possession of New Orleans. But later in the same year the Louisiana Purchase was made, and the city wound up as part of the United States. It is no wonder that citizens of the era were a bit politically confused. In that one year, the colorful flags of Spain, France, and the United States were routinely hoisted, then removed, from poles in the central plaza by somebody wearing a different uniform.

By the time the city passed over to the brash Americans, New Orleans was indisputably the paramount Southern city. Hospitals, canals, docks, and marketplaces had been built under Spanish rule. Exports had increased. The population had tripled. The steady hand of the Spanish on the helm obviously played an important role in ensuring the city's preeminence.

Yet Spanish influence in New Orleans has weakened in the twentieth century. For instance, Spanish Fort was a popular amusement park along Lake Pontchartrain between 1883 and 1906. The site, at the mouth of the Bayou St. John, was originally that of a French rampart dating from 1701 that had been rebuilt and expanded by the Spanish in 1799; hence, the name. In its heyday, the park had a casino, a restaurant, and amusement rides. When its buildings burned down, Spanish Fort was taken over by the New Orleans Railway and Light Company, which put up a ferris wheel and installed bathing facilities in 1909. In 1928, the lakefront was further developed into grassy parkland, and the bayou was filled in. The amusement concessions were moved eastward to the end of Elysian Avenue and renamed Pontchartrain Park. The facility finally closed in 1983, and the memory of Spanish Fort faded away.

For contemporary sightseeing, Spanish Plaza along the Riverwalk between Aquarium of the Americas and the Jackson Brewery features a sunken fountain and pool ringed by bench seating and a bank of mosaics bearing the crests of provinces in Spain. Erected during the adminstration of Mayor Maurice "Moon" Landrieu in the mid-1960s, the fountain stones and artwork were brought to New Orleans by the Lykes Brothers shipping line. Today, however, weather has taken its toll on the richly colored designs. Many have crumbled away, leaving blank spots in the rank of patterns. While the initial impression is eye-pleasing, closer examination points out the need for repair and preservation of the pieces, something apparently not in anyone's civic budget. When walking around the fountain, be aware that the slick surface of the paving stones can be slippery when wet. Rain or wind-driven fountain water can make simple strolling somewhat treacherous. The plaza remains a gathering place, however, with the fountain a pleasant background for various activities throughout the year, including multiethnic choral concerts during Creole Christmas.

There are other individual Spanish touches as well. **Brennan's** popular restaurant in the French Quarter used to be the home of Alfonso Murphy, a world chess champion in the 1800s whose family included Spanish and Irish ancestors. Brennan's is located at 417 Royal Street (504-525-9711). Keeping the Irish connection alive, the restaurant was founded by Owen Brennan, Sr., and is now run by his three sons: Owen, Jr., Jimmy, and Ted.

Yet even with the overriding architectural presence and faint remembrances of Old Spain that give old New Orleans a Latin look, the contemporary Hispanic population of New Orleans is fairly small. After the Spanish administrators departed, it was not until the late nineteenth century, when Hondurans were recruited to administer the banana warehouses for the United Fruit Company, that Spanish was again heard regularly on the streets. The largest influx of Latins came as a result of the anti-Castro Cuban exodus and mid-1960s immigration law changes. Although the numbers of Hispanics have mushroomed since that time, only about 4 percent of the city's population traces its ancestry to Latin lands, primarily those of Central America. Barely a hundred or so current New Orleans residents are from Spain itself, according to the Spanish consulate at the **International Trade Mart,** 2 Canal Street (504-525-4951).

A visitor will be hard-pressed to find much visible Hispanic nightlife in New Orleans proper, although one or the other of the French Quarter clubs might do a Latin revue for the tourist crowd once in a while. The city's only authentic Spanish restaurant, the **Altamira,** 701 Convention Center Boulevard, was shuttered in late 1993 as convention business slumped in the city. The closing was disappointing because Ángel Miranda, the Seville-born owner, had learned cooking from his mother and served the best *paella* (a Spanish rice dish) in the South. He also presented regular flamenco dancing and folk guitar sessions.

Yet all is not lost. There are two popular nightclubs catering to the younger Hispanics of numerous nationalities located in suburban

Metairie: the Silver Palace and Boccacio 2000. Of course, anyone who enjoys the driving beat of salsa, marimba, and cha-cha is invited to dance the night away.

New Orleans is unique in the Hispanic world, according to observers of the city's ethnic scene, because it does not have the *barrios,* or highly visible concentrations of Latinos, that are found in Los Angeles and Miami. In fact, even in Midcity, the most "Latin" of New Orleans neighborhoods (the tract betwen Tulane Avenue to Bienville, just past Canal and on to Carrollton and Broad) barely 19 percent of the locals claim Hispanic heritage, according to census reports. There are a few grocery stores scattered around town and in suburban Kenner, especially along Williams Avenue, that serve as focal points for those of Latin heritage, primarily because their proprietors are Spanish-speaking.

However, not much else is obviously Mexican, Cuban, Honduran, or any other Latin nationality, at least to the casual observer, demonstrating that the population has melded well with the rest of the community, according to scholars such as Dr. Karen Bracken of the Center for Latin American Studies at Tulane University. "You can't point to where Hispanics live because of the fluidity of each group, demonstrating that they live everywhere. Neither are they concentrated in any one industry," she emphasizes.

New Orleans Hispanics are a very multiclass group, without the salsa flash of a city such as Miami. Hondurans comprise by far the largest native grouping. Most were brought to work in New Orleans for the banana companies, serving as managers and highly trained workers. These basically middle-class families have since moved to New Orleans' suburbs, especially Kenner in Jefferson Parish, which now has about a 20 percent Latin population. However, there remains a large number of Hondurans living in parts of Faubourg Marigny, Bywater and the 7th Ward, and along Esplanade Avenue near Broad Street, according to a survey done by the Louisiana AFL-CIO.

The study also indicated that Hispanics in the Greater New Orleans area share similar economic, citizenship, and language concerns. However, the Spanish-speaking arrivals didn't think they had much in common, especially in politics, because they came to the United States for varying reasons, according to Maxime Lowy, Director of the Louisiana AFL-CIO, which financed the survey in the early 1990s.

The next largest group are the Cubans, a tightly knit community united in their distrust (no, make that hatred) of the Castro regime in Cuba. While there are many Cuban blue-collar workers, as in many enclaves in New York and New Jersey, many second-generation Cubans have become white-collar professionals. In fact, several of the city's prestigious law firms have at least one to two partners of Cuban descent.

Many well-known Hispanic business, cultural, and professional leaders live in New Orleans. Cuban Sam Levi is general manager of Schegman's Supermarkets, a well-known chain of stores that employs numerous Spanish-speaking natives. Guatemalan Roberto Forster is a senior vice president of Pan American Life Insurance. A fellow Guatemalan, Ernesto Schweikert III, is owner/manager of the Spanish-language WGLA-AM radio station and owner of ABA Travel, a specialist in Latin American tours. Schweikert, who came to New Orleans in 1970 as a Loyola University student, had a Cajun great-grandfather who moved to Guatemala in the last century.

Realizing the growing importance of the city as a bilingual community, the New Orleans City Hall has a Spanish Answer Desk to assist individuals needing translations for housing and other issues. Call 504-565-7115.

An *Ethnicity in New Orleans* study series, with an emphasis on the Hispanic connection, was published by Professor Ruperto Chávarri in the 1970s by the University of New Orleans' department of international economic development. For more information, contact the UNO library humanities reference desk at 504-286-6549.

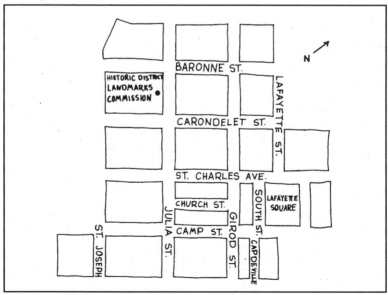

The Lafayette Square District

Business and Professional Associations

The Hispanic community prides itself on its diversity but is strongly committed to advancing the cause of the entire Latin world. Leading Hispanic men and women in many fields regularly meet to talk over common issues, plan promotions that highlight Hispanic culture, and simply socialize. Among the major business organizations are **Cámara de Comercio Hispana Internacional del Golfo,** 3501 Chateau Boulevard, Suite C-114, Kenner (504-466-1315) and **Unidad Hispanoamericana,** 3353 Coliseum Street (504-891-7165). Others are:

Asociación de Abogados Hispanos de Louisiana, *4500 One Shell Square (504-581-3234).* The President of the Hispanic lawyers association is Cuban-born Salvador Longoria of Gaudin & Longoira, 614 Tchoupitoulas Street, (504-524-7727). An estimated fifty lawyers from all Hispanic nationalities belong to the organization.

Hispanic Medical Doctors of Louisiana, *4204 Teuton St. (504-888-4297).* Dr. Gustavo Colón, a Puerto Rican who has been in New Orleans since the 1970s, is president of the 150-member society. The group meets irregularly at Doctor's Hospital of Jefferson, 4320 Houma Boulevard, Metairie (504-456-5800) to discuss medical questions.

Cámara de Comercio Hispana Louisiana, *Box 5985, Metairie, 70009-5985 (504-834-3217; FAX 504-566-0546).* The Hispanic Chamber of Commerce, formed in 1983, emphasizes commercial networking and providing business support for its members in New Orleans and Jefferson parishes. The chamber presents a regular series of forums on banking, business loans, and related international financial issues. Its executive committee meets the first Monday of each month, with a public meeting from 6:30 to 8:30 P.M. every fourth Thursday at a member restaurant or business. Attorney Louis R. Koerner, Jr. laughs that he became president by working hard for the association, whose membership is open to Hispanic businesses, any firm interested in targeting the Hispanic market, or large companies wishing to expand in the Latin field. Two hundred members belong to the association, ranging from large oil companies and South Central Bell to smaller but growing firms, such as Paige Communications and Enplanar, Inc.

President Koerner is a native New Orleanian who laughs about his German-Welsh heritage. "I'm a German who likes to have fun and a Welshman with concentration," he says, explaining the cross-culturalization that comes naturally with many city residents. Koerner came by his

Hispanic connections legitimately as well. His Welsh grandfather was a commodore for the Standard Fruit Company steamship line on the Central American banana run. Koerner visited Cuba as a youth and is a regular business visitor to Hispanic countries. He hopes to use the chamber as a sparkplug for Hispanically oriented cultural and political affairs, from event sponsorship to get-out-the-vote drives of the Latin electorate.

He and Nicaraguan business acquaintances, Jack Balonos and Nora Fine, formed the Hispanic Cultural Coalition of New Orleans in 1994. The coalition is thinking of promoting a regular series of festivals that have economic outreach, aiming to attract from twenty-five to seventy-five thousand guests. "Job fairs are dull and boring," Koerner says, so he hopes that the fests demonstrate the Latin economic potential. The coalition's first event was Fiesta Americana in October 1994. The program incorporated music and dance from twenty-five Central and South American Spanish-speaking organizations.

Arts and Entertainment

Cervantes Foundation of Hispanic Art, *5519 Elysian Fields Ave. (504-469-7190).*   Cervantes was founded in 1980 with the intention of bringing art, theater, and conferences with artists and authors to New Orleans. The founder of the group is Dr. Guillermo de Bango, a Cuban actor who came to the New Orleans in 1979, after serving nine years as a political prisoner. In the first year, Cervantes (drawing its name from the Spanish author of *Don Quixote*) hosted a troupe from Miami for a production of "My Fair Lady" in Spanish. The organization grew from that point. Over the years, plays and actors were brought in from Argentina, Spain, Puerto Rico, Venezuela, and other Latin nations. Beginning in 1985, homegrown Hispanic talent was used for all aspects of the productions, from directing to set construction.

In 1993, de Bango founded a school of art, a nonprofit organization funded by grants. The school focuses on many different arts, ranging from oil and pastel painting to music and drama. It is currently housed in an old, red brick building in Kenner that de Bango cleaned and renovated himself. Located at 3521 Florida Street (504-469-6237), the school occupies the second story of the two-story structure. The first floor is used as a Sunday bible school.

De Bango's school is free to any student of Hispanic background, with well-known Latin art teachers volunteering their time. The staff includes Julián Touceda from Honduras, a painter of abstract art; Heidi Domenici, a Cuban specializing in sketching and life drawings; Alma Moncada, a Nicaraguan still life painter; Julia Quiral from Cuba who teaches drawing; Dr. Raquel Cortina of Cuba, who teaches voice and is director of the opera school at the University of New Orleans; and de Bango himself, who teaches drama, voice, and the history of theater.

Adult classes are held from 7 to 10 P.M. Monday through Saturday and from 10 A.M. to 1 P.M. Saturday. On May 13, 1994, the Kenner city council declared a Day of the Hispanic Arts to celebrate the one-year anniversary of the school. Two weekends of art exhibitions and a festival with food from different Latin countries, plus folkloric dancing and singing, were featured.

The foundation still stages Spanish-language plays each September. Productions are held in the fourteenth floor auditorium of the **Masonic Temple,** 333 St. Charles Avenue (504-523-4382). Schedules are run in the *Times Picayune* newspaper and on Spanish radio. Taped for television, the plays are then shown on the Cox Cable public access cultural station.

In 1987, de Bango founded Hispanidad, an organization that brought Latin organizations together to prepare for the Columbus Day anniversary in 1992. Every year while the group functioned, each Hispanic club in the city selected a girl who best represented their culture. She would then participate in a Miss Hispanidad competition. Many of the contestants eventually went on to professional jobs. For instance, Puerto Rican-born Suzanne Bray, the 1992 winner, starred in a UNO production of *Agnes of God.* The play was presented in 1994 by the Cervantes Foundation.

For several years, Hispanidad also hosted a parade on the weekend closest to Columbus Day (October 12), with floats, high school bands, and other pageantry. After the parade, a Festival of the Americas was staged at Spanish Plaza at the foot of the river.

Dance Studios

Both Anglos and Hispanic locals take lessons in the numerous varieties of Latin dancing. To brush up on the latest steps, try the following schools:

Escuela de Danzas Españolas, *Metairie (504-455-0069).*   Instructor Maria Aliberti offers private gypsy-style flamenco and similar traditional dance instruction. Aliberti came to New Orleans from New York in 1985 with her husband, a designer of nuclear power plants. Born in Messina, Sicily, she teaches such regional Spanish dances as the *jota,* akin to a wild aerobic workout, as well as the more staid *seguidilla.* Her lessons for the traditional *bolero* and court dances are based on ballet movements, done to music by de Falla and Albéniz, composers from the early 1900s. Remember that these dances are not like the Cuban *bolero*-style ballroom dancing. Nor will a visitor learn a *mambo* from Aliberti, who studied with classical Spanish teachers at their studios in Carnegie Hall.

Jasime School of Dance, *631 N. Alexander St. (504-482-3412 or 835-0246).* Featuring master teacher Paco del Puerto, a native of Seville, the school is one of the prime flamenco schools in the South. Its troupe of adults performs throughout the area at university functions, folk programs, and conventions. Del Puerto spends part of the year in Spain, so be sure to call for information about when his lessons are offered.

Myra Mier Escuela de Ballet, *3621 Florida Ave., Kenner (504-486-1231 or 443-2252).*

Nightclubs

Boccaccio 2000, *4609 Airline Highway, Metairie (504-887-1307). Friday–Sunday, 9 P.M.–5 A.M.* Get the total Latin beat at Boccaccio 2000 as Super Luis mans the DJ console to rock the night away. Super Luis, from Honduras, is morning man on WGLA-AM/Radio Tropical, switching to the late, late slot for the weekend show. Glittering lights, a huge dance area, and lots of room for conversation make for a swinging Latin scene. The club is owned by Ramos Victoria of the Dominican Republic and Eduardo Rey, also from Honduras. If lost, look for bumper stickers proclaiming "Follow Me to Boccaccio," which are seen everywhere in New Orleans.

Silver Palace, *2726 N. Causeway Blvd., Metairie (504-834-9432). Friday–Sunday, 9 P.M.–5 A.M.* Latin and South America's most popular bands often play the Palace on the long weekend slots when dancing goes on for hours. A large open floor space ensures plenty of room to rumba, salsa, and generally glide around. Friends come from around the Greater New Orleans area to meet and talk.

Media

Radio Stations

WGLA-AM (1540 AM), *Box 428, Marrero (504-347-1540 or 504-347-8491). Broadcasting from 6 A.M.–10 P.M.* Guatemalan Ernesto Schweikert III purchased the twenty-seven-year-old station in 1991, after being one of its principal advertisers for a number of years as owner of

ABA Travel. Schweikert, although from the village of Tecpan, is no stranger to New Orleans. He attended high school, Loyola University, and the University of New Orleans, graduating with a degree in business administration. With unrest in his home country several years ago, his parents convinced him to stay in the United States. In addition to almost nonstop music, the station broadcasts Spanish-language news from CNN and is the official Spanish station of the New Orleans Saints football team. From 6 A.M. to noon, you can listen to Honduran Super Luis with his "Good Morning, My Love" show, featuring musicians Moises Cando, Eddy Herrera, Jossie Esteban, Tony Rivera, and others from throughout the Latin world.

From noon to 6 P.M., Darío, another Honduran, doubles as sports director and afternoon jock. María Dip, the Honduran news director, and Nestor Julián, from the Dominican Republic, complete the on-air staff.

The station is active in community affairs, helping sponsor Christmas Tropical, a Latin holiday revue held along Poydras and Convention Boulevard in December, and other local activities. In December 1993, *Radio Música* magazine judged WGLA-AM to be the number one Spanish station in the under-$300,000 market-share category. Its hot music mix earned the honor.

Station receptionist Sylvia Medina is from El Salvador, coming to New Orleans with her husband and two children to be near other family members who emigrated more than twenty years ago.

WADU-AM (830 AM), *1500 E. Airline Highway, Louisiana Place (504-469-4660). Broadcasting in Spanish from 6 A.M. to midnight.* WADU-AM started broadcasting in Spanish in 1992, complementing an English format on the FM-band. Cuban Manager Guillermo Guichale has been in local New Orleans radio for thirty-one years, working for different radio stations. Call-ins to the five thousand-watt station come from throughout the four hundred thousand-person market, with listeners in Mississippi, Alabama, Georgia, and Florida, in addition to Louisiana. On-air staff make a veritable Pan-American conference of nationalities. Among them are Costa Ricans José Hidalgo and Alberto Carrillo; Alicia Harris and Andrea Santana from Colombia; and Eddie Ávila and Marta Merella from Guatemala. UPI news is aired every hour.

Publications

¿Qué Pasa New Orleans?, 901 Veterans Memorial Blvd., Metairie (504-822-8861). Published monthly and distributed free at area Hispanic shops, restaurants, and other gathering places, *¿Quéx Pasa?* covers

events, personality features, and general news. Editor José R. Cosio and his wife, Ada, are Cuban. Cosio also publishes an annual free *Directory of Hispanic Businesses for New Orleans,* covering a range of services, from hairdressers to dentists. Some Anglo law and insurance firms with Spanish-speaking staff or partners are also included. There is also a general listing of local, state, and federal offices that cater to the health and educational needs of the Latin community.

Aquí New Orleans, 4324 Veterans Blvd., Suite 205, Metairie (504-456-6122). *Aquí* is published the first Friday of each month by Cuban-born Imara Arredondo. Some 20,000 copies are distributed free in Hispanic businesses, at the airport, in doctors' offices, and similar sites from the West Bank through Metairie, Kenner, and New Orleans, as well as at the World Trade Center. The paper features general news and lifestyle stories from the Hispanic community. A column called *Aquí Noticas* is a great source for events coverage. Ten writers from several Latin countries make up the staff.

Enlace (Embrace), 1354 Madrid St. (504-283-6384). Published monthly in Spanish, *Enlace* covers the Latin American scene with stories from south of the border, as well as the Greater New Orleans area. Free distribution blankets New Orleans, Miami, Houston, and Central America (mainly in Honduras). Local and Central American stringers provide the latest coverage of entertainment, culture, politics, and sports, with the four-color printing done in Honduras to hold down costs. Copies are available at Latin supermarkets, doctors' offices, and restaurants, as well as in the New Orleans public library. *Enlace,* with a circulation of 8,000, was started in 1992, according to Pedro Milla, Marketing Director for New Orleans. Like most of the staff, Milla is Honduran, living in New Orleans since 1983. Founder and editor Sigfrido Pineda Green, also from Honduras, spends half his time in New Orleans and the other half in his home country. Green has written five books and was formerly a professor of sociology at University of Honduras.

Mensaje (Message), 3645 Williams Blvd., Kenner (504-443-4612). This bimonthly religious magazine is distributed throughout the country and published by the communications office of the Archdiocese of New Orleans. It has a circulation of 5,000 and contains news of interest to the Catholic Hispanic community. On the alternate month, the office publishes a newspaper also called *Mensaje,* distributed free around the Greater New Orleans area. This has a circulation of about 12,000. Father Pedro Núñez, director of the Hispanic communications ministry for the archdiocese, is Cuban-born. He and his brother came to the United States as children, attending boarding school for a few years until their parents could join them. He also presents a religious television broadcast in Spanish on Tuesday at 10:30 P.M. on local cable television.

Times Picayune, *3800 Howard Ave. (504-826-3300).* A weekly Hispanic column called *Nuestro Pueblo* is written by stringer Ana Gershanik, an Argentinian of Germanic background. The column is printed on Sunday in the *Times Picayune,* New Orleans' major daily newspaper.

Shopping

There are no Spanish-only stores in New Orleans because the community is so varied and dispersed. The following, however, cater to Hispanics of all nationalites:

Castellón Discount Pharmacy, *8232 Oak St. (504-866-3784). Sunday, 9 A.M.–4 P.M.; Monday–Saturday, 9 A.M.–6 P.M.*

Speciality Shops

Beaucoup Books, *5414 Magazine St. (504-895-2663). Sunday, noon–5 P.M.; Monday through Saturday, 10 A.M.–6 P.M.* The store has a wide selection of adult and childen's books in Spanish, as well as Spanish-language newspapers from Central and Latin America.

Música Latina, *4237 Magazine St. (504-895-4227). Monday–Saturday, 10:30 A.M.–7 P.M.; Sunday, 1–6 P.M.* The only Latin music store in New Orleans features top recording artists from around the Caribbean and Americas, such as Cuban Rolando Laserie and Mexican performers Ricardo Arjona and Laura León. Racks of Puerto Rican salsa line up next to bins of Colombian and Santo Domingo sounds. Owners are Cuban Juan Suárez and his wife Yolanda, a Honduran. Mail orders are taken for customers throughout the country.

The Mayan Stall, *1200 N. St. Peters St. (504-738-0107 or 522-7835). Daily, French Market.* Guatemalan Roberto Carrasco has been in New Orleans since 1991, working for his sister Sylvia Asturias, who sends handmade hats, headbands, shirts, rugs, shoes, belts, and other craft items northward. The stall (No. 81-83-85c) has been in the French Market since the late 1980s, with imports from Honduras, Guatemala, and other

Central American nations. Sylvia's husband, Juan, sells their crafts at craft shows around the country. Among the more popular items they sell are colorful ribbons used to decorate the waterproof palm-frond hats. Their stall is a rainbow of fluttering hues as the breeze up from the Mississippi flutters the ribbons, making it easy to find. Carrasco wares can also be found at the Tropical Christmas Festival.

Supermarkets/Food Stores

Los Latinos Super Market, *3507 Williams Blvd., Kenner (504-443-1029); 3501 Division St.; Metairie (504-455-5972).* For general Latin merchandise and food items, either shop has it all.

El Palceno Grocery, *2301 Dauphine St. (504-944-7606).* For the best in chicharrones, fruit, and baked goods, try El Palceno.

Union Supermarket, *4129 S. Carrollton Ave. (504-482-5390).* Noted for its fresh meats, the Union has spices, fruit, tortillas, and other items favored by the Hispanic palette. The *pandería* (bakery) at the Union is favored by hungry shoppers seeking *cakes de bodas, cumpleaños,* and *bautizos,* as well as other baked sweets with a Latin touch.

Pineda Supermarket, *837 Barataria Blvd., Marrero (504-348-1779); 1163 Temy Parkway, Gretna (504-392-3250).*

Centroamericana Mini Market, *3507 Hessmer Ave., Metairie (504-455-7722).* The best place in town for Nicaraguan cheese and other imports, this small market also has a restaurant attached. The owner is Máximo González, who came to New Orleans from Nicaragua in the late 1970s.

United Supermarket, *3750 Williams Blvd., Kenner (504-443-3770).*

Vázquez Supermarket, *6215 Franklin Ave. (504-283-2515).* In addition to foodstuffs, Cuban sandwiches and other deli items are available.

Tortilla el Sol, *1514 Monroe St., Gretna (504-362-6888). Monday–Friday, 8 A.M.–5 P.M.* This is primarily a wholesale outlet for Hispanic restaurants and grocery stores in Louisiana, Mississippi, and Alabama. However, visitors can drop by and get fresh flour or corn tortillas, nacho chips, and tamales straight from the oven. Opened in 1971 by Bella Torres, of Honduras, the factory employs twenty people to churn out six hundred pounds of nacho chips an hour and thousands of tortillas a day. Torres worked for eleven years in a clothing factory before branching out on her own. The facility is the only such manufacturer in its tristate market area.

Tour Companies

The proximity of Latin America and the Caribbean has made New Orleans a major entry and egress point for thousands of business and vacation travelers each year. All the area travel agencies service the Hispanic and island markets, but some concentrate more heavily on this important travel niche. Ground tours around New Orleans are also available from many of them, and the major tour lines can provide interpreters as needed for their motor coach meanderings around the Crescent City. Combining both travel agency and local tour service are:

ABA Tours & Travel, *444 St. Charles Ave. (504-525-8585).* ABA was started in 1976 by Ernesto Schweikert III, a native of Guatemala whose great-grandfather incidentally was a Cajun Louisianan who worked in Guatemala and married a local beauty. ABA Tours & Travel was the first in the city catering to the Spanish market. In college, Schweikert had been a guide for Gray Line Tours and knew of the need for a firm to present Spanish-language tours. He saw New Orleans losing out to Miami and Houston as a destination for Latin tourists, so he launched his bilingual firm with immediate success. Two-and-a-half-hour daily van tours of Orleans Parish, with an emphasis on Spanish history, are offered at 10:30 A.M. Pickup at guests' hotels is available by making a reservation. Tours also are offered in Portuguese, catering to Brazilians and Portuguese guests. ABA is located on the first floor of the glittering Inter-Continental Hotel.

Latin Tours, *2 Canal St., Suite 1147 (504-524-1157 or 524-4732).* Tours are offered daily, with hotel pickup between 9:30 and 10 A.M. via chartered van service. Tours require at least four persons for confirmed departures. The tour is a leisurely and informative drive through the city and the French Quarter, along St. Charles Avenue, and over to the lake. Latin Tours was started in 1972 by Emilio Medina, a Colombian who has lived in New Orleans since 1965. He was attracted to the city because it was unique, quiet, and peaceful, he says. "After you live in some other crazy cities, you look for a place like this," according to Medina. But Medina's tours, given in either Spanish or Portuguese, don't compare New Orleans with other communities. "We simply show off what New Orleans has to offer and explain the history," he adds. Group rates are available. No lunch is served.

Spiritualists

There always seems to be another dimension to life in New Orleans—literally. Religious life is very important in all walks of life, and sometimes spiritual activity takes a different twist. *Santería,* a mixture of Catholicism and Afro-spiritualism with a Hispanic flavor, has a number of devotees in New Orleans. Emphasizing folk medicine and use of talismans, practitioners blend the various creeds in their daily lives. For instance, using the Do As I Say brand of soap for washing the kitchen supposedly puts a visitor under a homeowner's spell. Carrying a certain kind of root to a courtroom hearing will make the judge rule in your favor. *Santería* is commonly practiced throughout Latin America; even deposed Panamanian dictator Manuel Noriega supposedly was a devotee. Several small groceries in the city, mostly in the Elysian Fields Avenue neighborhood east of the French Quarter, used to carry a supply of the charms, powders, and statues that are also sometimes used by voodoo followers. The shops are shuttered now, and their owners have moved elsewhere.

Anna Maria Adams *(504-488-3688). Call for an appointment.* Spritual healings, tarot cards, and palm readings are the stock in trade for Anna Maria Adams, whose father is Mexican and mother is Cherokee. Her husband, Georgio, is Greek and Mexican, making for a true multiethnic family. They have two toddlers at home. Adams says her great-grandmother was a medicine woman born in New Mexico and that her mother always seemed to have psychic powers. That Native American influence, with its openness to the "other world" was influential in drawing her to her trade, she explains. A full palm reading is $25 and a tarot card review is $35. "I can't say how I learned about this. I just knew things," she says. "This is a gift, not anything evil. I believe in God; I go to church. But this can help people in time of need. You just have to be open to the soul and spirit of others," she emphasizes. Adams does not ask her clients any questions, putting to rest any doubts that she receives insights by promoting responses. "I'm always learning," she says.

Festivals

New Orleans Hispanic Heritage Festival, *Canal St. at Riverplace (504-581-2080). Held annually in mid-June; admission is charged.* Since 1986, the festival has attracted both Anglos and Hispanics to a long weekend of music, food, dancing, concerts, and general Latin fun. José Feliciano, Luis Enríquez, Rita Moreno, and other top Latin stars regularly perform. The heritage fest is similar to Miami's Carnival Calle Ocho, which is usually held in March. "We want to show that New Orleans has great Hispanic offerings as well," a festival spokesperson says.

Mensaje Spanish Festival, *St. Jude's Church parking lot at W. Esplanade and Loyola aves. Held annually on a mid- to late-April weekend; times are 7–11 P.M., Friday; noon–11 P.M., Saturday; and noon–10 P.M., Sunday; free.* Homemade food from fifteen Latin countries is sold from booths ringing the festival. Among the delicious dishes are *pupusas,* which are tortillas stuffed with beans and pork. Famous singers from different countries and local bands from around the city perform. Even cajun music is often played. The festival was started in 1970 by Father Pedro Núñez, director of Spanish comunications for the New Orleans archidiocese. In the first year, there was the typical crisis of money, because no income was received from archdiocese or other outside sources. "Just a group of volunteers got together to raise money. And every year, it grows," says the priest. Today some fifty thousand people from around Louisiana attend the event.

Carnival Latino, *at the Old Driving Range in City Park. The Carnival is held annually in mid-June, sponsored by the New Orleans Hispanic Heritage Foundation, World Trade Center, 3 Poydras St. (504-522-9927). Admission is charged.* Carnival President Luis A. Cruz, an electrial engineer from Puerto Rico, oversees a multinational volunteer board representing Mexico, Guatemala, Belize, Argentina, Honduras, and other Hispanic nations. The festival started in 1988 as an offspring of the Mayor's International Council. The council encouraged ethnic communities to hold tourist-oriented events that create awareness of the city's various cultures, as well as promote tourism. Some thirty-five thousand people usually attend the event, which features music from Central and South America, the Caribbean, Portugal, Spain, and the United States. In addition to the entertainment, state and local social service agencies staff information booths, and there are craft exhibits and demonstrations and a children's area with a moon walk, carnival rides, and games. Profits from the carnival are funneled into a scholarship program for Hispanic high school students, according to Ana Chinea, the Carnival's Office Administrator. Chinea came from Puerto Rico in 1987 to attend the University of New Orleans for studies in communications. She married and settled into life in the Crescent City.

Tropical Christmas, *the parking lot across from the Riverfront Convention Center. Held in early December; admission charged.* First held in 1993, organizers hoped to make Tropical Christmas an annual program featuring Latin music, food booths, a fortune teller, and vendors. Salsa, flamenco, a *creche* (nativity scene), treats for kids, and other holiday displays are highlighted to tune into the season. Sponsors include the Spanish-language station KGLB-AM.

Nationalities

Almost all the Central and South American and Caribbean ethnic communities are represented in New Orleans. Most have consuls or honorary consuls based in the city to help with business relations, stranded visitors, questions by school kids, and cultural affairs. Most have their offices in the World Trade Center at 2 Canal Street. Among the nations represented are **Argentina** (504-523-2823); **Barbados** (504-586-1979); **Belize** (504-522-2311); **Chile** (504-528-3235); **Colombia** (504-525-5580); **Ecuador** (504-523-3229); **Panama** (504-525-3458); **Uruguay** (504-525-8354); and **Venezuela** (504-522-3284). The **Costa Rican consulate** is located at 2002 20th Street, Kenner (504-467-1462). Offices for **Peru's** honorary consul Raffaele G. Beltram are located at 333 St. Charles Avenue (504-525-2706).

Social organizations and sports clubs, such as **Club Deportivo Ecuador (Ecuador Sporting Club),** 1325 Veterans Boulevard, Metairie, 504-837-5590, are popular gathering places for their respective nationalities.

Some of the larger Hispanic and Caribbean groups include:

Cubans

There is no definite estimate on the number of Cubans in the Greater New Orleans vicinity, but the arrival of the first émigrés in the 1950s and 1960s set a firm Latin stamp on the city. Reminiscent of the flood of Caribbean refugees after the slave rebellion on Hispaniola in the 1700s, the Cubans who fled the Communist excesses of Fidel Castro's regime were mostly professionals and middle-class. As did other new arrivals, they had to adjust their life-styles upon first arriving stateside. But as they were assimilated into the New Orleans community, they edged back into white-collar careers. Lawyers such as Luis Pérez and Salvador Longoria are both leaders in the Hispanic lawyers' association, and others are teachers and business executives. Attorney George Fowler is president of the **Cuban American Association** (504-523-2600).

Restaurants

Liborio's Cuban Restaurant, *322 Magazine St. (504-581-9680). Monday through Friday, lunch from 1 P.M.–2:30 P.M., dinner from 6–9 P.M. The restaurant is closed Monday evening and all day Sunday.*   Founded by José and Nancy Cortizas in 1980, Liborio is a typical Latin success story. José Cortizas was a soldier in Cuba prior to Castro and fled to the United States in 1961. Settling first in Miami, the couple heard that jobs were plentiful in New Orleans, so after six years in Florida, they moved to the Crescent City, where Cortizas took up welding in the shipping industry. When that business slowed, he opened a doughnut and snowball (snowcone) stand, where he eventually began selling hamburgers and hot dogs. Friends suggested that he serve some easily prepared Cuban foods, and soon business was booming. So José stepped back into the kitchen and learned how to prepare more authentic dishes from his home island. By 1971, he moved into larger quarters. He moved to a larger space in 1975 and again in 1987.

   Son Felipe now manages the front end of the popular facility, with dad in the back, and mom and Felipe's eighty-plus-year-old grandma helping as necessary. Popular with lawyers in the area (the restaurant is near the New Orleans Board of Trade and the courts), it does a brisk lunch business. Evenings are somewhat slower, except during convention time. Meals are always filling and hearty. Lots of chicken, black beans, rice, and fresh vegetables round out the bill of fare. A visitor who enjoys Cuban foods won't go wrong at Liborio's. Ask for the *tamarindo, guanábana,* or *fruta bomba,* all natural fruit drinks that are a great substitute for iced tea on hot, humid days.

Restaurant Garces, *4200 D'Hemecourt (504-488-4734). Open 11 A.M.–3 P.M. and 5:30–9 P.M., Monday, Wednesday, and Thursday, 11 A.M.–3 P.M. and 5:30–10 P.M., Friday; noon–10 P.M., Saturday; and 1–9 P.M., Sunday. Closed Tuesday.*   Chef Carmen Garces came to New Orleans from Cuba in 1958 and opened her restaurant in 1980, specializing in Cuban and Mexican foods, with a hint of creole. Dinner prices range from $7 to $9 at the sixty-seat facility. Sunday is a big dining-out day for Hispanic families, so reservations are a must on weekends. Garces often operates food booths at Latin festivals, operated by other members of her extended family, such as brother Jesús, who fled Cuba in 1980.

Dominican Republic

Dominican Consulate, *333 Julia St., Apt. 218 (504-523-7624). Joaquín Balaguer is the Dominican consul.*

United Dominican Club, *1125 Tensar Dr., Apt. D, Harvey (504-362-1373). The group meets monthly in Gretna. Call for times.* There are few Dominicans in the city, with only about five hundred families belonging to the United Dominican Club. The earliest arrival came as recently as the 1970s. Despite their small numbers, the Dominican community has made its mark on the city. Most are doctors, and Dominican Club President is Attorney Nestor J. Fornes, who came to New Orleans in 1990. In addition to his law practice, Fornes is also an announcer with the Spanish-language Tropical Radio. Another well-known Dominican is Margarita Bergen, who came to New York from Santo Domingo as a teenager and moved to New Orleans in 1975. She opened her **Bergen Gallery,** 730 Royal Street (800-621-6179 or 504-523-7882) in the French Quarter, specializing in graphics and African-American artists, such as William Tolliver. Hours of the shop, one of the largest in the city specializing in poster work, are 9 A.M. to 9 P.M., daily. In 1994, Bergen was the first local New Orleanian named queen of Carnival Latino, an annual Hispanic festival held in mid-June.

In mid-March, the Dominican community stages a Merengue Festival in the **Hyatt Regency Hotel,** 500 Poydras Street (504-561-1234). The *merengue* is the vibrant, colorful national dance of the Dominican Republic. For the festival, which is open to the public, the community hosted a folkloric orchestra and, in past years, children have presented choral arrangements. Discerning diners cluster around the food tables at the program, savoring the lip-smacking *sancocho,* a meat, chicken, and pork dish grilled with vegetables, such as plantain and yucca.

El Salvador

Salvadoran Consulate, *2 Canal St., Suite 1136 (504-522-4266). Consul is Emilio Roberto García Prieto.*

Salvadoran Club of New Orleans, *1626 Taylor St., Kenner (504-467-0856).* Approximately two thousand Salvadorans live in the Greater New Orleans area, with another two thousand scattered around the state. Most came in the 1970s, many originally to Miami or Texas before winding up in New Orleans. The first contingent were not political refugees because the situation in their home country was relatively stable at the time. As with other arrivals to the city, they came seeking better jobs that offered upward economic mobility. They were managers and professionals, including lawyers, engineers, and doctors. A number were students at Tulane or the University of New Orleans who came to study and then stayed, attracted by the life-style and opportunities offered by New Orleans. It didn't take them long to be absorbed into the general community. Arrivals in the 1980s were mostly working-class refugees who were fleeing the civil war that was devastating their homeland.

They formed the Association of Salvadorans Living in Louisiana, actively participating in many Latin activities in the city, including the summertime Hispanic Festival. Their booth is among the most popular there, especially with the serving of exotic foods, such as *pupusas,* traditional Salvadoran tortillas made with pork, along with tamales.

During the first Sunday of August, Salvadorans celebrate their national feast day with a religious procession out of the **Immaculate Conception Church,** 4401 7th Street, Marrero (504-341-9517). Beginning at 12:30 P.M., the congregation walks around the neighborhood carrying a six-foot-tall wooden statue of *El Salvador del Mundo* (The Savior of the World). The image is a replica of a thirty-meter statue greeting visitors to San Salvador, the capital of El Salvador. Six strong men are required to carry the statue around the block. Lunch follows a Mass, with salsa music by a local El Salvadoran band long into the night. A folklorico group of twelve teens also performs. In addition to the church gathering, many families have their own parties at home.

The celebration draws representatives from other Hispanic communities from around New Orleans, according to Father Salvador Galvez, a parish priest at Immaculate Conception. Galvez, coordinator of the Spanish ministry for the New Orleans archdiocese, has been in New Orleans for twelve years.

Restaurants

Pupusería Divino Corazón de Jesús (*Divine Heart of Jesus*), *2300 Belle Chase Highway, Gretna (504-368-5724). Sunday, Monday, Tuesday, and Thursday, 11 A.M.–9 P.M., Wednesday, 11 A.M.–6*

P.M.; Friday and Saturday, 11 A.M.–10 P.M. Specializing in *pupusa,* the traditional Latin "sandwich" of pork cracklins and cheese, regular diners always load up on takeout for extended trips, even to America's Latin capital of Miami. Mexican, Nicaraguan, and Honduran chefs work the kitchen under the supervision of owner Gloria Salmerón, whose devotion to the Sacred Heart gave the restaurant its name when it was opened in 1988. Salmerón is aided by her daughter, Carmen. The tiny restaurant has only twelve tables, but guests come from as far away as Baton Rouge and Mississippi for Salmerón's delicacies.

Guatemalans

Guatemalan Consulate, *2 Canal St., Suite 1532 (504-525-0013). Consul is Jerez A. Mario.*

Asocación de Guatemala en Louisiana, *6417 Nora St. (504-733-5070). Association President is Roberto Villacorta.* The Guatemalan community crowns a queen in November to compete in the next year's Miss Hispanidad contest, in which royalty from all Latin countries and Spain participate. A dance is usually held at **Riverboat Hallelujah Hall,** 3615 Tulane Avenue (504-484-7868).

In addition to participating in community-wide activities, the consulate hosts many events and brings in artists and marimba bands from Guatemala. On the nation's Independence Day, September 15, the consulate sponsors a concert either at a local university or in the lobby of the World Trade Center (WTC). It also features house concerts with opera singers, such as baritone Luis Girón May, pianists, and other Guatemalan musicians. At least twice a year, the association presents exhibits of Guatemalan artwork by leading painters, such as Caesar Fortuny, whose depiction of native landscapes and birds are popular with collectors, and Fernando Oberlin, who paints characters from Latin legends. Hand-woven textiles made by Guatemalan Indians are also occasionally displayed in the WTC lobby. To encourage learning traditional Guatemalan music in the city, the consulate purchased a marimba so the community would have an instrument for practice.

Haitians

Unofficial Haitian Consulate, *416 Commons St. (504-586-8309). The honorary consul is Pierre B. Clemenceau.* Haiti and the Dominican Republic share what was called by the Spanish the island of Hispaniola. The name evolved into Santo Domingo and was eventually changed to Saint-Domingue by the French. Haiti occupies the western third of the island, bounded on the north by the Atlantic Ocean and on the south by the Caribbean Sea. Its location made it perfect as a commercial outpost. The island is one of the most mountainous in the region, but there are several large plateaus that were used for sugar plantations during colonial years. The combination of trade and agriculture in the area brought in vast amounts of wealth to the favored few. With their common backgrounds, New Orleans and the island were always commercially, socially, and culturally linked.

Christopher Columbus is credited for discovering Hispaniola in 1492, but the Arawak Indians who lived there never felt they were lost in the first place. They subsequently wiped out Columbus's first garrison of forty soldiers in 1493. Undaunted, the Spanish came back with a vengeance and heavy-handedly retook control of the island. However, after years of political maneuvering in European courts, compounded by bloodshed on the high seas and raids on Spanish cities on the island, France was eventually ceded the island in 1697 by the Treaty of Ryswick.

Influenced by the lofty promises of the 1789 French Revolution, highly educated free mulattoes on the island attempted to gain representation in the new French national assembly, along with white Creoles. Both races were excluded and unsuccessfully revolted out of frustration and anger. Yet the ideals of freedom had filtered down to the thousands of slaves, who outnumbered the rest of populace by ten to one. Joining black freemen in 1791, some half-million slaves also rebelled, and the island was devastated by the ensuing horror. Toussaint L'Ouverture, a freed slave, emerged as leader of the rebels and set up an independent government. However, Napoleon Bonaparte sent in troops, who crushed the uprising. L'Ouverture eventually died in a French prison. Yet in 1803, fever decimated the French forces and the army abandoned the island. On January 1, 1804, the island was declared independent by survivors of war and plague. No one bothered to question their stand.

Fleeing all this turmoil, surviving white planters, as well as thousands of *gens de couler libres* (free blacks) and a few slaves, escaped to safe havens around the Caribbean. Boatloads made their way to New Orleans, attracted by the French way of life and the familiar culture. In fact, so many free blacks arrived that they doubled the African-heritage population of Louisiana, making the slaveholders nervous. The arrival of the Haitians put a distinct stamp on the city. They immediately felt comfortable in their new environment and were generally welcomed because of their wealth or their skills. Many of the blacks were artisans and craftspeople whose talents were previously unequaled in the colonies. Almost every profession was represented, including sculptors, blacksmiths, carpenters, printers, and chefs. They made the ornate cast-iron balconies still seen in the French Quarter. As early as 1793, a troupe of refugee actors and gorgeous quadroon actresses staged some of the first theater productions in the city.

One of the leaders of the Haitian community today is Dr. Sylvain François, a social worker at the YWCA (504-568-9622, ext. 259) 920 St. Charles Avenue. He also has an office at the New Orleans City Hall, where he helps in a community relations program (504-565-7130).

Hondurans

Honduran Consulate, *2 Canal St., Suite 1641 (504-522-3118). The consul is Carmen Serrera.*

Honduran Association of Louisiana, *3116 N. Arnoult Rd., Metairie (504-456-0900). The president of the association is Mario Zeron, also owner of Destinations Travel.* Among the two hundred thousand-plus New Orleanians who can track their Latin heritage, there are some one hundred twenty thousand Hondurans. They comprise the largest contingent of their nationality outside of Honduras and the largest of any city in the United States. "This is like our second home," says Consul Carmen Serrera. Many came to New Orleans to work for the fruit companies in the 1960s, covering a range of professions from managers to dock workers. Rather than concentrate in one neighborhood, the Hondurans quickly spread throughout the Greater New Orleans vicinity, with many settling in Kenner. There is no single parish with a majority of Hondurans, but Catholic churches that offer Spanish-language services are always full. St. Jerome, 2400 33rd Street, Kenner (504-443-3174), and St. Clement of Rome, 4317 Richard Avenue, Metairie (504-887-7821), are among several churches where Hondurans worship.

In mid-September each year, the Honduran Festival is held in the French Market with stirring traditional music, homemade foods, artisans showing off their handwork, and dance presentations. For specific times and details, local and Hispanic publications carry news and features on the always-popular program.

The consulate also hosts Honduran orchestras, singers, and other entertainers throughout the year.

Mexicans

Mexican Consulate, *2 Canal St., Suite 840 (504-522-3596).*   Consul General Raul Castellano is considered dean of the consular corps in New Orleans, serving in the city since 1990. He is aided by Consul Leonora Rueda.

In contemporary New Orleans, there are only about one thousand Mexicans. Another five thousand are scattered throughout the state, with the majority living in the Shreveport area. While their numbers are small, they have had a long and distinguished history in New Orleans. The first Mexicans came to New Orleans in Spanish colonial days. Since the city was a major port, it was also a prime diplomatic post for other countries ringing the Gulf, especially when Louisiana was the border with Mexico under French rule and under U.S. governance after the Louisiana Purchase. Subsequently, since the early 1800s, there was a Mexican consulate based in New Orleans. After the Treaty of 1847, which ended the Mexican War, Texas was ceded to the United States and the border was pushed back into the southwest.

Yet economic and political ties remained strong between Mexico and New Orleans. From 1853 to 1855, exiled Mexican revolutionary Benito Juárez lived in the city, working for a cigarmaker in the French Quarter until the dictatorship of Santa Ana collapsed in his homeland. Juárez almost died of yellow fever in the city but managed to recover and return in triumph to his country. In 1965, to thank the American people for their hospitality to one of their country's principal heroes, the Mexican government erected a statue of their hero on the neutral ground along Basin Street, across from the Archdiocese of New Orleans' Cemetery No. 1.

Juárez's words were remembered by Vice President Al Gore when he visited Mexico in 1993 after the passage of the North American Free Trade Agreement. "Between the nations and among individuals, the respect for others' rights is peace," Gore recalled, much to the appreciation of his listeners. On Juárez's birthday each March 21, Mexican consular officials and local politicians process to the monument at 11 A.M. to lay a wreath and present time-honored speeches.

New Orleans has also hosted other prominent Mexicans. Since the 1920s, sculptor Enrique Alserez has called the city his home. As a revolutionary, he was forced to flee his Mexico, relocating in New Orleans as did Juárez almost a century earlier. In thanks to his adopted town, Alserez's works can be found in front of the Pan American building and other prominent sites around the city. At Magazine Street is "The Teacher," one of his more famous statues. He also designed sports motifs on the iron gates and fences in City Park. In 1994, the sculptor was still working, although almost ninety-three years old.

For another artistic touch, a wall of colorful decorative tiles can be spotted on the Riverwalk near the Hilton Hotel. The gift was appropriately donated by Merada, the capital of the Mexican province of Yucatan and New Orleans' sister city.

A Mexican Independence Day party is held September 15 to celebrate Latin America's break from Spain. Occasionally a joint celebration, such as a reception or dinner party, is held with the consuls of other Hispanic countries that also gained freedom at that time.

The city's Mexican community also annually celebrates the feast of Our Lady of Guadalupe on December 12. Many other Hispanic nationalities that also honor the Blessed Virgin gather with the Mexicans for a bilingual Mass at **Immaculate Conception Church,** 4401 7th Street, Marrero (504-341-9517). At 5:30 P.M. on December 11, on the vigil of the feast, a mariachi band from San Antonio and nonprofessional dancers called *matachines* (sacred dancers) perform at the church.

On All Souls' Day, October 31, and All Saints' Day, November 1, Mexicans celebrate what they call the Days of the Dead by lighting votive candles in their homes. The ceremony reminds participants of their human frailties and helps them keep their ancestors in mind.

The Mexican community is primarily blue collar, with many workers in the scrap metals industry cutting up decommissioned derelict ships. Others work cleaning petroleum tanks or handling the sleek greyhounds at the New Orleans dog track. Many others work in the restaurant industry as chefs and kitchen help.

Restaurants

Castillo's Mexican Restaurant, *620 Conti St. (504-525-7467). Monday through Friday, lunch from 11:30 A.M.–2 P.M. and dinner from 6–10:30 P.M.; Saturday and Sunday, 6–10:30 P.M.* Established in 1955, Castillo's is the oldest Mexican restaurant in the city. The restaurant is adjacent to the Vieux Carre Police District stationhouse and across the street from the old Supreme Court building in which the movie *JFK* was filmed, starring Kevin Costner. Owner Carlos Castillo Guadiana presents foods from around his native land. While guests can get the typical tacos for lunch, dinner is another matter. His recipe for Spanish *romesco* sauce, liberally applied over fresh fish, dates back to the twelfth century. Castillo's New World *mole poblano* ($9.50) captures contemporary taste buds. The *poblano* is a sauteed chicken breast topped with a *mole* sauce flavored with sesame seeds, cocoa, three kinds of peppers, anise, and raisins.

From the Yucatan, Castillo serves a *chili mole de puerco o pollo* ($12.95), which is either pork or chicken in a sauce of roasted dried peppers, blackened corn, and apasote. Mexican soup, called *caldo tochcil,* is made with vegetables, avocados, and herbs. Guests can finish off with a *flan,* egg custard with nutmeg, rum, and black syrup sauce.

Casa Tequila, *3229 Williams Blvd., Kenner (504-443-5423).*   Live Latin music is offered each Thursday from 6–10 P.M., compliments of Casa Tequila. On Sunday and Monday, margaritas are only 99¢, a deal in any language.

Gustavo's Authenic Mexican Restaurant, *3515 Williams Blvd., Kenner (504-443-2260). Sunday–Thursday, 11 A.M.–9 P.M.; Friday–Saturday, 11 A.M.–10 P.M.*   Another great Mexican eatery, featuring the usual range of easily recognized Mexican dishes done with flair and style.

Country Flame, *620 Iberville St. (504-522-1138). Daily 5:30–10:30 P.M.*   Tucked onto a tight alley corner, adjacent to the French Quarter's Exchange Street where Creole dandies once practiced their fencing, the Country Flame is a casual hole-in-the-wall eatery that lures passersby with delicious cooking scents wafting from the inside. The food brings guests back a second time or more. The Country Flame features both Mexican and Cuban foods. Takeout is available.

Casa García Mexican Restaurant, *8814 Veterans Memorial Highway, Metairie (504-464-0354). Monday–Thursday and Sunday 11 A.M.–10 P.M.; Friday and Saturday, 11 A.M.–11 P.M.*   Casa García serves great Tex-Mex foods, along with steaks and hamburgers.

Nicaraguans

Nicaraguan Consulate, *No. 2 World Trade Center, Suite 1937 (504-523-1507). General consul is Mayra L. Grimaldi.*   There are about fifteen thousand Nicaraguans in Louisiana, with about nine thousand living in New Orleans. While some Nicaraguan professionals have been in the city for several decades, the largest influx came during the Nicaraguan civil war of the late 1970s. Until the early 1990s, the community was scattered and fragmented. But when Consul Mayra L. Grimaldi founded the Nicaraguan Relief Fund in 1991, there was a reason to come together to assist in humanitarian efforts. Since that time, the consulate and community stage public events on a regular basis. Meetings to discuss social issues are regularly held at the consul's home. The community tries to hold a major open-to-the-public activity every three months at such major hotels as the Doubletree or the Holiday Inn Crown Plaza. Such events might include a Tropical Night dance party held in July or a New Year's Eve Party in January.

In August, Nicaraguans celebrate the Santo Domingo feast day in honor of their country's spiritual patron. A fair is held at various locales, the date dependent on when a site is available. Traditional clothing is worn, with plenty of music to add to the fun. Among the traditional dances performed at the holiday celebration are *El Zanatio* (The Blackbird), a marimbalike dance enjoyed by children, and the *torovenado* (in which a "bull" dances with a "deer"). Food is always special, with huge servings of *nacatamales* (tamales with raisins, rice, and tomatoes); *chicharrón con yucca* (a deep-fried pork rinds appetizer); and plantains with refried beans and cheese. And there is always Spanish rice.

Vicki Guiford, President of **Club Social Nicaraguense** (504-524-1329), holds a special party each year for Nicaraguan women in New Orleans. The get-together is considered the highlight of the social season. Guiford also coordinates a beauty pageant for Nicaraguan girls sixteen to twenty-two, whereby the winner goes on to participate in the annual Hispanic Heritage beauty pageant.

The community performs a great deal of humanitarian efforts, with the consulate taking the lead in soliciting donations for its homeland. Working with the Louisiana National Guard, the consulate arranges for trucks and soldiers to pick up medical supplies from area hospitals that are then sent to Nicaraguan health facilities. Guard General Ansel Straud (504-271-6262) has been a tremendous supporter of the project, according to Consul Grimaldi. Supplies are loaded at the Marine base in Chalmette or as far away as Norfolk, Virginia, the headquarters for Operation Smile International, a group of doctors who perform mission work in different countries, including Nicaragua. Working with that organzation, the consulate helped coordinate visits by forty-two technicians and doctors visiting Nicaragua in January of 1993 and 1994, with more trips planned for the future. While in Nicaragua, the team performs more than two hundred operations for children. Doctors and other medical personnel from around Louisiana also donate their private time and effort to work in Nicaragua, in individual efforts directed through the consulate.

Monsignor Gregory Aymond, Director of Missions for the Archdiocese of New Orleans (504-866-3355 or 504-866-7410), has also helped recruit small groups of New Orleans' medical personnel for Nicaraguan relief efforts. Aymond directs the Christ the Healer Foundation, which is equipping a clinic in Nicaragua, as well as performing other humanitarian activities. President of the foundation's board is New Orleans Archbishop Francis B. Schulte.

Restaurants

The Latin American Restaurant, *2604 Magazine St. (504-895-9420). Daily 3 P.M. to midnight.* Ed-Ma Enterprises, owned by Nicaraguans Edgar and María Villanvincio, has operated food booths at numerous Latin church and holiday festivals around the New Orleans area since the late 1980s. Using their restaurant as a base, the Villanvincios are noted for preparing popular finger foods, perfect for munching while roaming around an event. *Carne asada* (beef filets), *tritangas* (a combo plate of various meat and veggies), *gallo pinto* (beans and rice), and *vigoron* (yucca and cracklins) are among the best. For sit-down meals, there's *modongo* (a soup with tripe, yucca, and corn). Carmen Navarrede, María's sister, is head chef, ensuring that family demands for quality continue to be met.

chapter nine

Asian New Orleans

History and Settlement

There has been an Asian presence in New Orleans since the colonial era with the arrival of Spanish-speaking Filipino sailors who jumped ship in Mexico and made their way to the colony in the 1700s. However, there was not a heavy presence of Asians until after the Civil War. A few hardy Chinese led the influx, arriving as contract workers in the 1860s. The 1880 U.S. census indicated that there were 489 Chinese in the entire state of Louisiana. Currently, it is estimated that there are about five thousand in New Orleans alone.

By the 1990s, the Asian and subcontinent population had diversified, with the arrival of Thais, Indians, Pakistanis, Taiwanese, and, after the fall of Vietnam, thousands of Vietnamese. Some of the more established groups, such as the Chinese and Filipinos, are seeing value in "growing public" and are gaining political influence by being more vocal. Harry Lee, a prominent Chinese-American whose family members are well-known restaurant owners, was elected sheriff of neighboring Jefferson Parish in 1980. His penchant for wearing a cowboy hat and boots has earned Lee the friendly nickname Chinese Cowboy.

There are other signs that Asians in New Orleans are being paid more attention to because of their growing voting power. When election time rolls around, candidates meet with the larger Asian national groups and are seen at Asian festivals and other cultural activities focusing on the

Orient. These subtle changes had become more obvious by the late 1980s, as the economic muscle of the international Asian community was flexed on a grander scale. The impact of each group has depended on how long it has been in the New Orleans community. Members of smaller communities from Thailand, Taiwan, and Japan fit in well because they are primarily highly educated professionals.

Asian families are spread throughout the Greater New Orleans area; however, most of the recent arrivals are Southeast Asians who live in eastern New Orleans or on the West Bank. Although relatively poor and in the city for only a short time, they have made extraordinary strides in establishing themselves.

The primary umbrella organization linking most Asian cultures in the New Orleans area is Asian Pacific American Society (APAS). The major communities represented include Bangladesh, China, India, Korea, Japan, Vietnam, the Philippines, Taiwan, Pakistan, and Thailand. Total membership through affiliation with the APAS numbers from forty to fifty thousand throughout Louisiana. They range from a small Korean community of about eight hundred to the fifteen thousand-plus Vietnamese, one of the largest concentrations of Vietnamese new arrivals in the United States. The 1994 President of the APAS was Kiem Do, a Navy captain in charge of a rescue sealift of thirty-five thousand of his fellow South Vietnamese as his country fell to North Vietnam. After several months in refugee camps, Do made his way to New Orleans. He has since received his master's in business administration at UNO and is currently an engineer at a Louisiana Power & Light Company nuclear power plant.

One of the founders of the APAS is Marina Espina, a first-generation Filipino whose husband, Cipriano, is the Filipino consul. The Espinas have been in New Orleans since 1966, when Cipriano was stationed as a diplomat there and then as a commercial representative. He left his country's service during Ferdinand Marcos's rule in the Philippines but was reappointed honorary consul by the new Corazon Acquino regime. Marina had been a librarian at UNO for twenty-seven years before semiretiring in 1994. Involved with the National Association of Asian Pacific Education, which was founded in New Orleans in 1977, she was a delegate to the Asian Pacific Women's Conference in Washington in 1978. At the conference, U.S. President Jimmy Carter proclaimed Asian Pacific American Heritage Week, a national program still celebrated the second week of May. Upon her return from the conference, Marina was fired up with all the possibilities of promoting Asian heritage. She quickly assembled other New Orleanian Asian leaders and formed APAS in 1978.

APAS hosts several public events throughout the year. The most popular is the Heritage Festival, captivating the New Orleans community during the first weekend in June at the **Audubon Park Zoo** (504-861-

2538) with its sounds, scents, and fervor. Food booths and cultural shows, arts and crafts, and a steady stream of performances on a central stage highlight national dances, song, and drama. From ten to twelve thousand people flood the oak-shaded Audubon grounds for the colorful pageant. Admission at the zoo is halved if a guest brings an Asian Pacific flier promoting the festival. The zoo's grassy, shady grounds are easily accessible by the St. Charles streetcar. Get off the streetcar in front of Tulane University and cross Audubon Park to reach the zoo entrance on Magazine Street.

The Asian community also participates in the New Orleans Jazz & Heritage Festival held each the spring, presenting folk music and dance exhibitions. Several Asian restaurants are always selected to represent the community. In 1994, the Ninja Japanese restaurant and the Old Calcutta Indian restaurant were chosen.

Another popular event for those interested in Asia is the APAS Fall Gala, a fund-raising dinner traditionally held at the **Riverside Hilton** (Poydras at the Mississippi River, 504-561-0500) with a music and dance performance by troupes from several nationalities complementing an award presentation for community leaders. A dance band swings out for a full evening of fun. The public is invited to the function, which usually costs about $25 to $30 per person.

Activities more geared to the association include a summer picnic, youth leadership conferences, and sessions designed to help recent arrivals adjust to life in the United States. The main objective is to highlight the Asian-American heritage through various functions and to acclimatize members' children with the national heritage, poetry, and dance of the various Asian countries.

The society serves the needs of first-generation Asians, according to Shameem Choudhury, editor of the APAS newsletter and an English teacher at New Orleans' Delgado Community College. "We are nostalgic for some of these things from our homelands and want to participate in activities that remind us of home. But the younger people are the transitional generation. Most of them are being assimilated into this great melting pot of America, whether they want it or not," he says. "In my view, our association and the different ethnic groups give a sense of where we came from. Yet we older people don't need to stand in the way of the younger ones. They are Americans, although racially Asian. And now they are more American than Asian."

To keep that sense of rootedness, according to Choudhury, several of the Asian associations hold language and culture classes in members' homes. The group has even published an Asian-Cajun cookbook, updated and revised in 1994 with additional recipes from Singapore and Malaysia to augment those from Cambodia, Laos, China, and other Asian nations.

The Louisiana twist comes in with the addition of readily accessible local foods such as soft-shelled crabs. For a copy of the book, send $5 to the APAS, UNO Box 797, New Orleans, LA 70148-0001. For general information about the association, contact secretary Cecil Murphy or newsletter editor Choudhury (504-589-6893).

Demonstrating the ethnic camaraderie of the APAS, Murphy, a native New Orleanian, met his wife, Kiku, while serving in the Marine Corps on Okinawa. As a sergeant-major in a helicopter unit, he was later stationed at the Naval Air Station-New Orleans at Belle Chasse and retired in 1980. Capitalizing on sixteen years of Far Eastern Service (starting as a grunt in the Korean War), Murphy was one of the original members of the New Orleans Japanese Club when it was formed in 1975. To be a member of the club, an applicant must be Japanese or the spouse of an ethnic Japanese. With that background, Murphy was eventually asked to be secretary of the group and then just stayed on to help. He currently is a deputy magistrate for the U.S. District Court in New Orleans.

Another leading contact for information on the Asian community is the Center for the Pacific Rim (CPM), headquartered at the University of New Orleans. The center was founded in 1988 to coordinate and expand undergraduate and public Asian studies at the university. The center is also Louisiana's resource outlet for economic and business information pertaining to the Far East. Its lending library has hundreds of books and reams of statistical material, as well as videos, tapes, and related resources. The center's programs, especially its school outreach, tries to interact with the local community. "Our goals are designed to create greater awareness of the Asian world in New Orleans and Louisiana," says Center Director Edward Lazzerini, a UNO professor of Russian and Asian history.

An APAS/CPM program of guest lecturers and an annual fall film festival featuring Asian producers have been popular. The free movies are shown in the 250-seat UNO auditorium. The center also has an extensive exchange program with People's Republic of China, hosting visiting scholars and artists-in-residence who spend varying lengths of time in New Orleans. The artists demonstrate their crafts at local schools, as well as present their works at galleries, on campuses, and in the wider New Orleans area. Since 1990, the center has also sponsored an annual mid-April workshop for teachers, featuring a full day of programs with academic specialists and cultural representatives from different Asian nations living in New Orleans.

The center can be reached at the **College of Education, UNO,** New Orleans, LA 70148 (504-286-6886). Other details on regular programs can be obtained through the center's semiannual newsletter or by reading Thursday's "On the Rim" column, written by Chinese journalist Tina Soong, in the *Times Picayune* newspaper.

Helping bridge the gap between East and West, at least in the religious sphere, is Abbot Robert Livingston, who presides at the **Zen Buddhist** temple at 748 W. Camp Street (504-523-1213). The temple is above **Doug's Steaks** (504-527-5433), an upscale eatery in the legal and financial district near St. Patrick's Cathedral. Livingston, who lived and worked in the Far East for more than twenty years, returned to New Orleans as a Buddhist missionary. He renovated his 1840s townhouse and attached warehouse, hoping to put in an art gallery on the first floor. When that didn't pan out, restaurateur Doug Gitter moved in with his steak house. Gitter has an extensive collection of American primitive art, which is now hanging at the site. Abbot Livingston got his gallery after all. He is also President of the American Zen Association.

Zen practicing is held at 6:30 A.M. Tuesday–Friday; 12:15 P.M., Monday, Wednesday, and Friday; 7:30 P.M., Tuesday and Thursday; and 10 A.M., Saturday and Sunday.

The **Buddhist Fellowship of Louisiana,** 202 Woodland Highway, Belle Chasse (504-392-0327), and the **NSA Buddhist Church** of New Orleans, 2435 S. Carrollton Avenue (504-866-9479), also cater to the church-going community.

Publications

Times Picayune, 3800 Howard Ave. (newsroom: 504-826-3300). Tina Soong, a part-time journalist born in Shangai, writes a weekly column for the newspaper called "On the Rim." The name refers to the influence of Asian nations around the Pacific shore. For the past five years, she has focused on the New Orleans Asian community in her Thursday report, writing about personalities, trade and cultural delegations, economics, and other subjects pertaining to the growing Asian minority. Soong, a librarian at the University of New Orleans, came to the United States in 1956 and later earned a master's degree in journalism from the University of Missouri. She then moved to New Orleans with her engineer husband. Two of their three children are medical doctors and one is a chemical engineer.

Shopping

The following shops cater to the broad Asian populace and other New Orleanians who need specialty spices, rice by the sack, woks, and cooking utensils.

Asian Food Store, *6051 Woodland Highway (504-394-7440). Daily 9 A.M.–6 P.M.*   Imported noodles, rice, fish, and other Far Eastern delicacies are featured.

Asia Market, *3601 Division St., Metairie (504-885-7531). Monday through Saturday, 9 A.M.–8 P.M.; closed Sunday.*   Korean owner Young Sun Lee serves all Asian nationalities.

Asian Imports, *14349 Chef Mentor Highway (504-254-5219). Daily, 9 A.M.–6 P.M.*   Gifts from China, Taiwan, and Vietnam line the shelves here, catering to the entire Asian community in the Greater New Orleans area. Vietnamese owner Nguyan Sung opened the store in 1988 in a bustling shopping center strip.

Nationalities

Bangladesh

Unofficial Bangladesh Consulate, *321 St. Charles Ave., 10th floor (504-586-1979). Honorary consul is Thomas B. Coleman.* Shameem Choudhury, President of the Bangladesh Society, came to New Orleans in 1967, went to Canada for a time, but soon returned and is now a professor of English at Delgado Community College and Director of its honors program. Mrs. Choudhury is from Bombay.

The community celebrates Language Day on February 21, celebrating when East Pakistan launched a movement to create a national language. March 23 is also feted as the Bangladesh Independence Day, with a dinner and cultural show with songs, music, dance, and drama. The program reenacts the language movement and achievement of independence won through the 1971 civil war.

Bangladesh citizens started coming to New Orleans in the late 1960s. Many arrived as graduate students at local universities, especially Tulane, when the country was still part of Pakistan. When the civil war broke out, a number of the students simply stayed in New Orleans. Currently the Bangledesh community numbers about 150 to 175 in New Orleans, plus another 250 in the Baton Rouge area. They are successful professionals, securing good positions as engineers, doctors, or college professors, often marrying into the Indian community. For instance, Zeeta Rahman, wife of Mac Rahman, the owner of the Old Calcutta Restaurant, is Vice President of the Bangladesh Society. In addition to juggling home affairs and two small children, Mrs. Rahman is an office manager for six doctors at Southern Baptist Hospital.

Chinese

Chinese Association, *3320 Woodlawn, Metairie (504-887-8328).* Like the Asians who came to the West Coast to work the gold fields and railroads, the first Chinese in Louisiana were also contract workers. The laborers, all men, were brought to New Orleans from different cities in the United States, from Cuba, and from Canton, China. They were agricultural laborers in the cotton and sugarcane fields after the Civil War during the rough-and-tumble Reconstruction era of the late 1860s. The plantation owners hoped to replace slaves with cheap Asian labor.

The Chinese workers signed agreements that supposedly outlined the details of their jobs and length of service, prior to setting out for New Orleans. Details varied, but after a certain length of time on the plantation, each worker supposedly was free to leave or stay on.

Not many remained in the fields after they completed their service. A proud and determined people, some even broke the contracts because they did not feel the plantation overseers were treating them properly. Since New Orleans continued as the region's major economic center, the Chinese came to the city to live and work where their "exotic" culture was better tolerated, at least on the surface. A small but lively Chinatown evolved near what is today's Public Library on Loyola Avenue, extending toward the neighborhood around Loews State Theater at Canal and Rampart Streets. Urban renewal over the decades has changed the face of the neighborhood, so no trace of that early Asian community exists. Although there was a strong sense of ethnic cohesion in the blocks of crowded flats that were once there, negatives existed side by side with the good. Several opium dens flourished, where addicts of all races could find refuge before the turn of the century. But most of the Chinese worked hard and set down roots. For years, they ran their network of laundries with an almost endless supply of work. The popularity of starched shirts, despite the muggy New Orleans weather, kept many cleaners working around the clock.

The Chinese Merchants Association still has offices in the French Quarter, located above the K-Creole Kitchen Restaurant, 530 Bourbon Street. Cantonese is often still spoken by the old-time businesspeople who meet there to talk economics and the state of the Asian world.

Over the generations, the Chinese also worked on the docks and in the fishing industry downriver, mostly in the shrimp drying field. Of course, the ubiquitous Chinese restaurant became popular in New Orleans, as it has almost everywhere in the United States.

In the 1940s, a second wave of Chinese immigrants arrived as students and settled into New Orleans life. Third-generation Chinese, today's young Asians, are computer scientists, statisticians, lawyers, and doctors. Tulane, UNO, or Loyola educational backgrounds in international trade and Asian studies are becoming a much-sought-after educational discipline that bridges American and Asian concerns. The West does meet East, at least in New Orleans.

Festivals

Since 1990, New Orleans has celebrated the Chinese New Year with an annual five-kilometer run at the end of January or whenever the lunar calendar decrees the appropriate timing for the new year. The run is followed by a colorful Chinese dragon dance and music from 9 A.M.–4 P.M. in Lafreniere Park, Metairie. The race, held in conjunction with the New Orleans Track Club, offers tickets to members and nonmembers. Advance tickets are available. The money raised is being used to relocate the Chinese Presbyterian Church, currently at 2525 Bienville, to a site it has purchased in Kenner. For information on the festival and race, call chairperson Edward Lee (504-832-0640).

(The Chinese Association also holds a spring dinner, which is limited to members.)

Restaurants

Even New Orleanians become excited when they find a place they can call their own secret hideaway. There are numerous Chinese restaurants in town that fit that bill, many with Vietnamese chefs and kitchen help. The restaurants range from trendy, business-oriented properties to small places in the suburbs with mom and pop and kids and cousins working long hours.

China Doll, *830 Manhattan Blvd., Harvey (504-366-1111 or 504-366-8822). Monday through Thursday, 11 A.M.–10 P.M.; Friday, 11 A.M.–11 P.M.; Saturdays, noon–11 P.M. Dinners only are served Sundays, from 5–10 P.M. Most dinners are $8–$10.* One of the better-known Chinese restaurants in the Greater New Orleans area, the China Doll serves such specialties as Crawfish Cantonese; Empress Lo Mein, delightfully delicious pan-fried noodles with pork, chicken, beef, and mixed vegetables; Wo-ba Sizzler, a mixture of jumbo shrimp, chicken, and pork sautéed with mixed vegetables and served on a sizzlingly hot plate where the food cooks on the dish; crawfish velvet, fresh crawfish or shrimp sautéed with snow peas in white wine sauce and served in the shell in lettuce. The owners, Ping and Agnes Tsang, run a tight kitchen but are always available for a hello. The restaurant, noticeable with its bright red and gold decor, is located in a small shopping center on Manhattan Boulevard. Tables and booths are available, along with a full bar. And, yes, daiquiris are served. Complimentary photos for birthdays and anniversaries are available for an extra party perk.

Chopsticks Restaurant, *216 N. Carrollton St. (504-488-4292). Monday through Thursday, 11 A.M.–9:30 P.M.; Friday through Saturday, 11 A.M.–10 P.M. Closed Sunday.*   Szechuan shrimp, wonton, and vegetable soup are great at this tiny thirty-seater restaurant operated by Vu Chuong and his family. Although Vietnamese, Vu emphasizes more fiery styles of Chinese food. The restaurant was opened in 1984, catering to locals who appreciate its comfortable snugness, as well as its careful food preparation. Prices are in the $4–$10 range.

Fong's Chinese & Cantonese Restaurant, *2101 Williams Blvd., Kenner (504-467-9928 or 504-469-8216).*   Fong's is especially proud of its mandarin chicken and duck, both well worth the order. It is also one of the best locales in the New Orleans suburban area for peppery Hunan and Szechuan heart-thumpers. Fong's touts its "exotic Polynesian drinks" for some extra barside fun.

Great Wall Chinese Restaurant, *930 Canal St. (504-523-3217). Monday through Thursday, 10:30 A.M.–11 P.M.; Friday and Saturday, 10:30 A.M.–midnight; Sunday, 11 A.M.–11 P.M.*   For the quickest Chinese turnaround for takeout along Canal Street, the Great Wall has knocked down all barriers to good food, low cost, and fast takeout. There's nothing fancy about the place, with formica-topped tables and all sorts of wonderful downtown characters dropping by for fried rice, chow mein, and the usual range of Chinese dishes. An army of young people is hard at work in the open kitchen area, visible from over the front counter. Toiling over huge woks, they flip, fry, and stir ingredients with paddles large enough for canoeing. The counter help always seem to be smiling, and there might be a toddler or two peering up with soft almond eyes from the work area—showing that this indeed is a family-style place. Prices are great, with most dishes in the $4–$7 range. Carryouts are available in pints and quarts. There's also an exotically interesting mix of cooking styles. For instance, try the fried chicken gizzards (you get 10) with crab meat and fried rice for only $4.15. And if a guest wants hot and spicy, just say so and be prepared to run for the bomb shelter.

Kung's Dynasty, *1912 St. Charles Ave. (504-525-6669). Daily, 11:30 A.M.–10:30 P.M.* The restaurant, set in a mansion on the St. Charles streetcar stop, looks as if Beijing met *Gone With the Wind*. Snarling Asian lion statues greet guests walking up to the porch, which is framed by towering white columns à la some plantation tour. But don't chicken out. Kung's Dynasty fixes that plebeian bird in numerous styles: plum chicken, chicken with vegetables, fried chicken, and enough other chicken wonders that would make Col. Saunders take up Zen.

Panda Riverview Chinese Restaurant, *600 Decatur St. (504-523-6073). Monday through Friday, 11:30 A.M.–10:30 P.M.; Saturday and Sunday, 11:30 A.M.–11 P.M.; happy hour on weekdays, 3–6 P.M.* Located in the Jackson Brewery Millhouse, the eatery serves Mandarin, Hunan, and Szechuan food. A specialty is soft-shelled crab. Another Panda's is located at 3442 St. Charles, in a skinny pink building reminiscent of a late-night movie set of the 1930s. But food is just as great there as at the Central Business District Riverview site. Try the Dragon and Phoenix, which is lobster and chicken chunks sautéed in a Hunan sauce with vegetables and honey walnut shrimp.

Churches

Chinese Baptist Church, *5701 Veterans Memorial Blvd., Metairie (504-455-0105). Sunday School; 9:45 A.M. and 11 A.M. services in Mandarin and Cantonese.*

Chinese Presbyterian Church, *2525 Bienville Ave. (504-822-7313). Services in Cantonese and English.*

Shopping

The following shops, while emphasizing their specific national origin, cater to the entire New Orleans Asian community, as well as to anyone else seeking goods from the Far East.

Chinese American Food Store, *1474 W. Broad St. (504-948-6856). Daily, 8* A.M.–*6* P.M.

Chinese Market, *2300 8th St., Harvey (504-362-6213). Daily, 8:30* A.M.–*4:30* P.M.

Publications

Hua Fong News, *330 Morgan St. (504-367-3995).* This free four-page newspaper, which comes out on the fifth of each month, is published in English and Chinese by editor Shaie Mei Temple. It features news about the Chinese in New Orleans, mainland China, and Taiwan. Other correspondents with Chinese backgrounds also write for the paper, which has a circulation of about two thousand. The *Hua Fong News* can be picked up at Chinese stores and restaurants throughout the Greater New Orleans area. Temple owns a business and management consulting firm in Atlanta and commutes regularly to her home in New Orleans.

Filipinos

Filpino Consulate, *World Trade Center, Canal St. 70130 (504-525-5225; FAX 504-522-7861). The consul is Cipriano Espina.*

Filipino American Goodwill Society, *931 Touro St. (504-945-3536). Founded in 1946, the organization meets on the second Sunday of the month at 3* P.M. *in the summer and at 2* P.M. *in the winter. The president is Marina Espina.* There are approximately twenty-five thousand Louisianans of Filipino descent, with several thousand living in New Orleans in the oldest Asian community in the city. The first arrivals found their way to the colonial city early on in 1765. They were seapeople from Spanish galleons who had jumped ship in Acapulco, Mexico, and struggled their way northward to escape Spanish law. Ever since Spain had colonized the Philippines in the 1500s, there had been strong commercial links between Manila and Mexican ports, so it was not unusual for large numbers of Filipino sailors to serve before the Spanish mast.

Many of these deserters eventually fled into the bayous around New Orleans, fearing the long reach of the Spanish law. Since they were all men, they intermarried with Cajuns already living there. Many

Louisianans named Martinez or Madrigal can even trace their heritage back at least eight generations to these Filipino-Cajuns, who retained the Spanish-French speech patterns of their ancestors. Other Filipinos married Indians, Spanish, and Irish, further expanding the gumbo of ethnic backgrounds. With this mixture of nationalities, the original fugitive eventually disappeared, assimilated into the general population.

But by then at least seven Filipino villages had been established deep in the swamps closest to the Gulf, just below the city in Orleans, St. Bernard, Jefferson, and Plaquemines parishes. Accessible only by canoe, they felt safe in their new surroundings. All the communities have long since disappeared under the murky backwater, but a mound of mud still remains where St. Malo in St. Bernard Parish was once a thriving fishing village. Pilings also can still be seen where Jefferson Parish's Manila Village was home to descendants of those early refugees. Manila Village was destroyed by Hurricane Betsy in 1965, and the last few residents moved on.

However, once they became established, those first Filipinos introduced to Louisiana their tradition of drying shimp. Historical records note that platforms were built on a field the size of a baseball diamond about thirty miles southeast of New Orleans in the early 1800s where the Filipinos dried their catches (since there was no refrigeration in that era). The picturesque but rugged life of these people was chronicled by New Orleans journalist Lafcadio Hearn, who wrote regularly about St. Malo Village, beginning in 1883. He learned about the community by talking with Italian fishermen who had discovered what they called a "strange population" of Spanish-speaking people in the bayous. Hearn brought a newspaper illustrator with him into the swamps, earned their trust, and was able to preserve much of the community's history. The Filipino villages had even organized a loose association in which they put down all their correspondence in Spanish.

A few of the families sent their children to study in New Orleans, with many of their descendants becoming doctors and other professionals. In 1976, Louisiana's teacher of the year was Isabel Walsh, who was born in Manila Village of Filipino, French, and Italian heritage.

Over the ensuing generations, Filipino families became well established throughout southern Louisiana and in New Orleans, forming one of the country's oldest Filipino associations in 1870. That organization was the precursor of the current Filipino American Goodwill Society.

Filipinos took an active part in the city's activities. In 1935, they won the first grand prize awarded in a Mardi Gras parade put on by Elks Krewe Orleans. This was also the first parade in New Orleans made up entirely of trucks. The Elks procession traditionally is the first parade immediately following the grand Rex parade. The Filipinos also won in 1936, 1937, and 1946, when the Mardi Gras festivities were renewed after World

War II. Since then, the Filipinos have not paraded; but the Elks Krewe Orleans commemorative doubloon is dedicated to that initial Filipino prize-winning contingent. The doubloons, tossed to the parade watchers along the route from St. Charles to Canal Street, are considered by Mardi Gras connoisseurs among the best collectibles at the festivities.

Although the community no longer parades, there is still a Filipino Mardi Gras Ball open to the public, usually held two weeks before Fat Tuesday, the day before Ash Wednesday. The exact date depends on the availability of a hall. Admission is $10, with live Filipino and pop music. Most attendees dress in costume and bring their own food, such as the fabled Mardi Gras King Cakes made by home bakers and bakeries eager to present the best decoration. For information on the ball, contact the Filipino consulate.

Another influx of Filipinos came to New Orleans after 1965, following the relaxation of immigration and naturalization laws. The latest arrivals are primarily medical, engineering, or military professionals.

For more background on the Filipino community in Louisiana, read *Filipinos in Louisiana* by Marina Espina (1988, Laborde Press). Now out of print, this history book is still available in most libraries throughout the state or at other educational institutions (Harvard ordered five). "They went like hotcakes," reports author Espina. "All two thousand copies were gone in a year," she says.

With the aging of the Filipino community and the assimilation of the younger generation into the broader "American" society, few people attend Filipino-only functions. The city's last Filipino restaurant, the award-winning Tahiti Room on Tulane Avenue, closed in the late 1980s when owner, cook, waiter, and dishwasher Roy Campanga retired. Shoppers wanting Asian foods to make Filipino dishes usually shop at Chinese or Vietamese stores.

Yet the community has not rolled over and died. In late April, the Filipino Fiesta is held in the St. Bernard Auditorium, Chalmette. For more information, contact Robert Ormero (504-466-0875), President of the sponsoring Filipino Lions Club of Greater New Orleans. The program of song and dance usually starts at 7 P.M., with an admission charge.

Philippine Independence Day is celebrated June 12 to commemorate the country's break from Spain in 1898. Held along Decatur Street near the French Market's Cafe du Monde, the consulate presents a cultural program of traditional music and dancing, along with martial arts exhibitions and, of course, plenty of food. Among the items to be sampled (usually for under $3) are *lumpia* (an egg roll counterpart to that of the Chinese), *panchit* (fried noodles), and *adobo* (marinated pork and chicken). A local caterer is hired to prepare the traditional dishes, served from stalls and food booths at the festival.

Indians

Fewer than two thousand Indians live in New Orleans, which is considered off the beaten track for émigrés from the subcontinent. Those who have come to the Crescent City are mostly doctors, lawyers, and other professionals. Several hundred students from India attend Tulane, Louisiana State University, and the University of New Orleans.

Restaurants

Old Calcutta, *724 Dublin St (504-861-0565). Monday through Saturday, 5:30–10:30 P.M.; closed Sunday.*   It was a natural thing for owner Mac Rahman to open the Old Calcutta Restaurant after arriving in New Orleans in 1988. After all, he had always loved entertaining and cooking, confides his wife Zeenat, who gave her blessing to the project. The restaurant serves a wide array of standard Indian foods.

Taj Mahal Indian Cuisine, *923 Metairie Rd., Metairie (504-836-6859). Sunday–Saturday, lunch 11:30 A.M.–2:30 P.M.; dinner 5:30–10:30 P.M.; closed Monday.*   The Taj Mahal serves smooth North Indian dishes rather than hot and spicy South Indian food. On the extensive menu are tandoori chicken, lamb, fish, or shrimp cooked in the typical clay pot or in a curry gravy. Vegetarian dinners are also popular, including a creamed spinach dish call *saag paneer. Tikka masala* is tandoori chicken breast in tomato curry. Lamb *roganjosh* is in onion curry. Prices range from $8.95 to $14.95. Owners Har and Anila Keswani from Bombay came to New Orleans twenty-six years ago, when Har was working as a naval architect. When the oil boom went bust, the couple opened their comfortable, casual restaurant. The current location, one of several they've operated over the past fifteen years, seats fifty people. On the wall are Indian paintings depicting folklore and countryside scenes. The restaurant also runs an extensive catering service called **Taj Mahal Ethnic Eats.**

Tandoor Indian Cuisine, *3000 Severn Ave., Metairie (504-887-7414). Daily, 11:30 A.M.–2:30 P.M., 5:30 P.M.–10:30 P.M.*   The word of mouth is right among New Orleanians when they say this is one of the best Indian restaurants in town. Serving seafood, chicken, vegetarian, and lamb entrées, the Tandoor is popular for lunch and dinner. The Tandoor has consistently been awarded excellent ratings by not-easily-swayed local food critics. Tandoor has an all-you-can-eat lunch buffet.

Japanese

Japan Society, *1729 Lark St. (504-283-4890). Tom Akers is president.* Formed in the 1920s, the club is one of the oldest in United States. Reorganized after World War II, the society now consists mostly of European-Americans interested in Japan's culture. Four general meetings are held each year, with lectures by scholars, business executives, and diplomats. The group holds several members-only parties.

Japan Club, *c/o Asian Pacific Society of America (504-589-6893).* To be a member, an applicant must be Japanese or have a Japanese spouse. Formed in 1975, the group holds monthly membership meetings and social activities.

The New Orleans Japanese community numbers between two hundred and five hundred people, depending on the numbers of business executives and foreign students in the city at any one time. One-third of the total number of Japanese nationals are war brides from Okinawa and Japan who married servicemen stationed overseas in the late 1940s and 1950s. Others are *nisei,* or second-generation Japanese-Americans who came from the West Coast, resettling primarily in New Orleans after World War II. Forced from their homes in California, Oregon, and Washington in the era's anti-Japan frenzy, they were sent to one of the ten War Relocation Camps located in Arkansas, Wyoming, Nebraska, and other states. After the war, rather than returning to their former homes, they spread throughout the country. Several families found their way to New Orleans.

Typical of the older generation of Japanese in New Orleans is retired watch maker Hajimi (Jim) Yenari, who came to the city with his parents following World War II and eventually became one of the first presidents of the restructured Japan Society. He met his wife, Katsu Oikawa, a West Bank pediatrician, in New Orleans when she was finishing her internship at New Orleans Charity Hospital. They always laugh that although they were both raised in Seattle, they had to come to New Orleans to meet and marry. Their adopted daughter, Midori, is a research doctor at Stanford University and their adopted son, David, is local deputy sheriff. Most of the Japanese here work either with foreign diplomatic services or as businesspeople.

Restaurants

Ichiban Japanese Restaurant, *1414 Veterans Memorial Blvd., Metairie (504-834-1326.) Daily, 10:30 A.M.–10:30 P.M.*

Hana Japanese Restaurant, *8116 Hamston St. (504-865-1634). Lunch 11:30 A.M.–2:30 P.M., dinner weekdays 5:30–10 P.M., dinner weekends, 5–11 P.M., Sunday 5–10 P.M.*   Offering sushi and other stable Japanese cuisine, lunch and dinner takeout is great for munchies on the run. But a sit-down Japanese-style meal is worth the time in this comfortable establishment that offers a lot of Asian charm.

Ninja, *8115 Jeannette St. (504-866-1119). Daily, 11 A.M.–10:30 P.M.*   The well-known Shigure-Sushi & Such underwent a management and a name change in 1994. The Ninja features some interesting mixes of Japanese and local traditions. The new owner, Ms. Momo, was proud that Ninja was one of two Oriental restaurants chosen to represent the Asian community at the world-renowned New Orleans Jazz & Heritage Festival in 1994. Among the taste temptations that earned her position at the festival were sushi rolls with soft-shelled crab wrapped in a traditional seaweed covering.

Shogun Japanese Restaurant and Steak House, *2325 Veterans Memorial Blvd., Metairie (504-833-7477). Saturday and Sunday, noon–11 P.M.; Friday, 11:30 A.M.–11 P.M.; Monday through Thursday, noon–2 P.M. and 5:30–10 P.M.*   The Shogun supposedly has only a hibachi table, where the chef whips out his flashing utensils and cooking gear for theatrical table-side preparation of steak and seafood. There's also a sushi bar, with tempura, sukiyaki, and kaiseki.

Koreans

Korean Association of Greater New Orleans, *3324 Transcontinental Dr., Metairie 70006 (504-456-1606).*   There is a small but active Korean community scattered around New Orleans, numbering only about eight hundred permanent residents and two hundred businesspeople. The first arrivals came to the city in the early 1960s, primarily to attend universities and for jobs, according to Yup Kim, former Korean association president. Kim came to Atlanta's Georgia Tech in 1971 to earn his master's in computer science and then moved to New Orleans in 1974. Currently he is Manager of Computing Telecommunication for Exxon Oil in New Orleans.

When the United States relaxed immigration laws for Asians in the 1970s, more Asian nationals arrived. Many Koreans who came during those eager early days, however, left the city after several years because of the boom-or-bust economy in New Orleans at the time, which was heavily tied to oil and tourism. Those who remained were primarily professionals, working in the service industry as doctors or teachers. However, some Korean professionals began moving back to New Orleans from Atlanta, Houston, and Los Angeles in the 1990s. This second migration resulted from an improved economy along the Gulf Coast.

The Korean association holds a general membership meeting in early March at the **Airline Lions Club,** 1627 Metairie Road, Metairie, 504-837-4861. Other get-togethers include a traditional year-end party, a spring picnic held on the fourth weekend of April in City Park, and a Moon Harvest Festival, also held at the Airline Lion Club. Timing for the Moon Harvest Festival depends on the lunar calendar, but it is normally held around August 15. The Koreans also participate in the APAS program the first weekend in June at the Audubon Zoo.

Normally only members and their guests attend Korean association functions, but anyone who calls the society in advance is welcome. "They will be more than welcome," asserts Kim.

Much of the Korean social life centers around churches. In their native country, markets open early on Sunday. Subsequently, everyone attends dawn service before going to work, a tradition still practiced. Initially the first Koreans in New Orleans met in homes for worship services; then they rented space from the St. Charles Baptist Church before building their own First Korean Baptist Church, 4836 W. Esplanade in Metairie (504-454-7905). Reverend Kwan Soo Song leads the 11 A.M. Sunday worship. Dawn services begin at 5 A.M.

Korean businesspeople have carved out a niche in the city's dry cleaning and janitorial industry. A number of office and hotel cleaning companies in New Orleans are owned by Koreans. Kyu Cho's **Tidy Co.** is the largest, with cleaning operations in twenty-four cities around the country. Tidy is located at 609 W. William David Parkway, Metairie (504-838-9843). Another major cleaning service, **Ramelli Janitorial Service,** is owned by an American but employs numerous Koreans.

The **Asia Marine and Supply Co.,** 3603 Division, Metairie (504-885-7531), is owned by Lee Young Sun, who started the chandler firm in 1985 after emigrating from Korea. Candles, ropes, metalwear, foodstuffs, and everything else a Korean freighter captain would need is available at his warehouse, which is open from 9 A.M. to 8 P.M., Monday through Saturday.

Ace Camera Repair Service, a major retail and technical repair service that repairs equipment from overseas and stateside firms, is owned by Soon Hong Song. The office is located at 852 Manhattan Boulevard, Harvey (504-367-1310). Song's son, Myoung Chul Song, is one of the city's leading professional photographers and a stringer for the Houston-based *Han Kook Il Bo* **(Korea Times)** daily newspaper.

Young entrepreneurs, such as Sam Yi, aged twenty-one, operate gift and souvenir shops around the Greater New Orleans area. Yi's shop is called **Hot Ochra,** 425 Decatur St. (504-523-7265). Typical of the family self-help ideal prevalent in the Korean community, Yi's mother and father, Hyong and Sang Yi, assisted him in getting his store off the ground. The whole family works the cash register and arranges his stock of Mardi Gras masks, postcards, shirts, and other items on the shelves.

The **Korean Travel Agency,** 110 Orchard Road, New Orleans 70123 (504-737-4235), helps numerous Korean business travelers coming to New Orleans. Owner Ho Sook Lee specializes in greeting Korean guests and providing translations, in addition to offering the general range of agency transportation services. The **Korean Consulate** in Houston covers the New Orleans area, assisting with questions about commercial and emigration issues, among other things. The consulate is located at 1990 Post Oak Boulevard, Suite 1250, Houston, TX 77056 (713-961-0186).

The Koreans enjoy their social connections. The Korean American Association holds an annual New Year's Celebration on December 31 at the **Bayou Plaza Hotel,** 4040 Tulane Avenue (504-486-7144) and celebrates the lunar new year with a party usually at the end of January or early February, depending on the year.

The **Korean Culture and Language Academy of New Orleans,** 7001 Canal Boulevard (504-241-4093), also helps keep Korean traditions alive. Classes in Korean language, history, and culture are held from 10 A.M. to 1 P.M. Saturdays, at the Korean Presbyterian Church, under the careful tutelage of the principal, Mrs. Song (in Korean society, it is impolite to call a woman by her first name, so only the last name is used for introductions). She emphasizes to her small charges, who are children from Korean families and adopted Koreans kids from American households, that to understand their culture they need to know the language. Tuition is $80 for the first child in a family and $60 for the second child. Demonstrating the importance the community places on education, the academy is heavily subsidized by local Korean businesses and individuals.

The academy accommodates preschoolers through high schoolers. Advanced courses for adults are also offered to the general public and several non-Korean students have enrolled in the past.

Restaurants

Genghis Kahn, *4053 Tulane Ave. (504-482-4044). Saturday and Sunday 5:30 P.M.–midnight, Tuesday through Friday 5:30–10 or 11 P.M. (depending on the crowd); closed Monday.*   The Genghis Kahn is one of the premier Korean restaurants in the South, operated since the early 1970s by Henry Lee. In 1989, a People's Choice poll judged it the best ethnic restaurant in Louisiana. Lee, who was born in Korea but studied classical violin at the University of Wisconsin-Milwaukee, moved to New Orleans and brought over two brothers and a sister from Korea. They started the restaurant to provide the entire family with work. He named his facility after the great Mongol chieftain and features open-pit cooking in the Mongolian barbecue style. Drumfish and Shrimp Genghis Kahn are among the most popular dishes. Of couse, there's the explosive *kimchee,* the Korean version of fermented cabbage. True to his love of music, Lee regularly presents classical music performances in the Genghis Kahn, with a violinist and pianist entertaining on Tuesday, Wednesday, and Thursday. Opera singers perform on Friday, Saturday, and Sunday. "Music is an international language," explains Lee. First-time callers seeking phone reservations or takeout are often surprised to hear an Italian operetta being presented in the background. Prices range from $8 to $15.

Seoul Restaurant & Club, *3547 18th St., Metairie (504-888-0654). Monday and Tuesday and Thursday through Saturday, 11:30 A.M.–10 P.M.; Sunday, 5–10 P.M.; closed Wednesday.* There's the usual range of excellent Korean specialties, complemented nightly with live karaoke music for a wild time over the *kim-chee,* a spicy marinated cabbage made with lots of red pepper, garlic, ginger, shallots, and soy sauce. The no-fat dish is praised for its minerals and vitamins. Seoul offers lunch and dinner specials. Takeout is available. The owner is Sang Man Kim.

Korea House, *1011 Veterans Memorial Blvd., Metairie (504-835-2758). Daily, 11 A.M.–10 P.M.* Owner Sun Shil Myoung specializes in Korean barbecue and seafood, with an emphasis on freshly caught Gulf shrimp redfish and black drum. The Korean House is the latest Korean restaurant on the New Orleans scene, opening in 1991.

Churches

First Korean Baptist, *4836 W. Esplanade Ave. (504-454-7905). Services are held on Sunday at 11 A.M. and daily at 5 A.M. The pastor is Reverend Kwan Soo Song.*

Second Korean Presbyterian Church, *7001 Canal Blvd., (504-283-7299). The pastor is Rev. Kwan Jun Park, offering services in*

Korean. Worship is Sunday at 11 a.m. with a children's program at the same time. Services are also offered daily at 6 a.m. and on Wednesday at 7 p.m.

Korean Catholic Church, *140 27th St., Kenner (504-469-3956). Parish president is Paul Kim and the pastor is Father Joseph Kim. (They are not related.) Services are on Saturday at 8 P.M.*

Korean Presbyterian Church of New Orleans, *7001 Canal Blvd. (504-283-7299).*

Korean United Methodist Church, *3900 St. Charles Ave., New Orleans, 70115 (504-897-3060). Pastor is Reverend Chang Kyu Lee. Services are held Sunday at 1 P.M., with Sunday school at the same time.*

Korean Church of New Orleans, *4422 St. Charles Ave., New Orleans 70115 (504-885-7531). Services are held on Sunday at 11 A.M. This church has no specific demonination, with guest pastors visiting in rotation.*

Calvary Korean Baptist Church of New Orleans, *2403 Farragut St., New Orleans 70114 (504-362-3511). The pastor is Reverend Moon Ki Kim. Services are Sunday at 11 A.M., with Sunday school at 10 A.M.; Friday at 10 P.M., with dawn worship Monday through Thursday at 6 A.M.*

Shopping

Korea Market, *3324 Transcontinental Dr., Metairie (504-456-1606); Monday through Saturday, 9:30 A.M.–8 P.M.; Sunday, 10:30 A.M.–7 P.M.*   Just about anything a shopper needs for Korean meals or gift items for the home can be secured at this well-stocked, friendly establishment run by Byung Kwan Hong, the president of the Korean American Association. Rice, noodles, clothing, woks, videotapes, music cassettes, and numerous packets and barrels of wonderful somethings line the shelves. Food items are imported from Korea. Korean newspapers such as the *Korea Times, Dong Ah Il Bo* and *Chosun Il Bo* (*Il* stands for *daily* and *bo* is *newspaper* in Korean) are available for sale.

Asia Market, *3601 Division St., Metairie (504-885-7531).* Owner Young Sun Lee serves many Asian nationalities from his store which is open from 9 A.M. to 8 P.M., Monday through Saturday.

Publications

Han Kook Il Bo (Korea Times), *9355 Long Point, Houston, TX (713-932-6696).* Local New Orleans news is reported by Myoung Chul Song, a photographer and writer. The daily newspaper can be found at the Korean and Asian markets for 30¢. Most readers, however, subscribe for $15 a month. Written in Korean, the sixteen-page daily covers both overseas and U.S. news. The paper has news bureaus in Houston, Los Angeles, New York, and Chicago.

Pakistanis

Pakistan Community Association (PCA) of Greater New Orleans, *1104 Green Ave, Metairie (504-454-2667). Monthly executive committee meetings are hold in French Quarter hotels. President of the association is Syed B. Ali, a local engineer who came to New Orleans in the 1970s.* There are several hundred Pakistanis spread throughout Greater New Orleans, with many living in suburban Metairie, Kenner, and the West Bank. They celebrate Pakistan's Independence Day on August 7 with dinner and a music program, usually held at Tulane University's McAlister Auditorium. The PCA also holds a community-wide picnic early in November in Lafrenier Park. In 1993, the association compiled a directory that contains background about Islam, Pakistan, and Urdu (the Pakistani language); literature; and community addresses and phone numbers. The one hundred-page directory is available through the organization. Primarily Muslims, they celebrate the conclusion of the one-month spring fasting period of Ramadan with a morning prayer service and refreshments at the **Louisiana Nature and Science Center,** 10601 Dwyer Road (504-246-5672). Usually held around 7 A.M. early in March depending on the lunar calendar, a local *imam,* or priest, from one of the ten mosques in the city leads the open-air service. Upwards of a thousand worshippers gather from several different Muslim countries for the service.

To help spread knowledge of their community to the broader public, the Pakistani association sponsors various music and social programs, often held at Tulane and other universities in the city. It sponsors a professional dance troupe from Houston for its presentation at the Jazz & Heritage Festival. The troupe presents the rhythmic *bhangra* and other Pakistani folk dances for the spring event. Contact the association for other community events.

The PCA actively participates in the annual Asian Pacific Heritage Festival held in the Audubon Zoo the first week of June. In addition, the Pakistani Youth Association also helps keep traditional values alive by dancing, singing, and engaging in children's activities at ethnic functions sponsored by the city and at the various Pakistani and Muslim festivals.

For immigration assistance, Pakistanis in New Orleans can use the services of the Consulate General of Pakistan at 12 E. 65th Street, New York, NY 10021 (212-879-5800) or at 10850 Wilshire Boulevard, 11th Floor, Los Angeles, CA 90024 (310-441-5114). The Pakistani embassy also can provide help if required: 2315 Massachusetts Avenue, NW, Washington, DC 20008 (202-939-6200).

Mosques/Places of Worship

Times of worship vary for Pakistani Muslims and others who follow the faith. Their prayer services are tied to the lunar calendar. Five periods of the day are reserved for worship. For instance, in the holy month of Ramadan (choosing Thursday, March 10, 1994, as an example), the times are Fajr (before sunrise, 4:47 A.M.), Zuhr (12:11 P.M.), Asr (3:33 and 4:25 P.M.), Maghrib (at sunset, 6:06 P.M.), and Isha (7:25 P.M.).

Masjid Abu Bakr Al-Siddque, *4425 David Dr., Metairie (504-897-5365).*

Masjid Al-Taubah, *449 Realty Rd., Gretna (504-392-3425).*

Bilal Iban Rabah Islamic Center, *717 Teche St., Algiers (504-362-6758).*

New Orleans Islamic Center, *1911 St. Claude St. (504-944-3758).*

Masjid Al-Shurabaa, *University of New Orleans (504-282-0700).*

Masjid Yaseen, *7527 W. Judge Perez Dr., Arabi (504-277-9222).*

New Orleans Masjid of Al-Islam, *2626-32 Magnolia St. (504-895-6731).*

Masjid-Ur-Rahim, *1238-40 N. Johnson St. (504-827-0017).*

Masjid Al-Rahmah (Tulane University), *7103 Burthe St. (504-866-3879).*

Slidell Masjid of Al-Islam, *37482 Browns Village Rd., Slidell (504-641-3172).*

Thais

New Orleans architect Arthur Q. Davis, Sr., 335 Julia Street (504-522-3400), has been honorary Thai consul since 1981. A regular commercial traveler to Thailand, he helps the twenty-five hundred-family community with its various immigration needs. Most Thais are relatively affluent professionals—mostly doctors, lawyers, and accountants—who live throughout the Greater New Orleans area with a number in Metairie. Filtering into the city over the past two decades, they were attracted to New Orleans because of its similarities to Bangkok. Both low-lying cities are located on the banks of major rivers in the heart of a rice-producing countryside. They also have similar weather patterns—a factor appreciated by the Thai people.

The Thais eagerly celebrate their national holidays and Buddhist religious festivals, even though there is no close-knit neighborhood or separate Thai association. Birthdays for King Bhumibol Adulyadej (Dec. 5), who has been Chief of State since 1946, and Queen Sirikit (Aug. 12) are good reasons for gathering family and friends, as well as for singing and staging folk dances. Usually other Southeast Asian nationals are invited to public programs. Many of the events are also open to the public and are held at parks and area universities. For listings of times and places of these events, check the local New Orleans entertainment newspapers and the *Times Picayune.*

The Asian Pacific Society of America is working toward developing a centralized Asian cultural center for New Orleans, according to consul Davis, so that the Thais and other groups can have a place to celebrate their holidays and display national artifacts. Funds are being solicited from the respective Asian countries and from private donors. Louisiana Senator Bennett Johnson of Shreveport has been helping organize federal support. Three or four potential sites in the city have been evaluated through the National Park Service for possible use.

A Thai newspaper is irregularly published from Biloxi, Mississippi, primarily emphasizing Buddhist news from throughout the South.

Restaurants

Bangkok Cuisine, *349 S. Carrollton Ave. (504-482-3606). Monday through Friday, 10:30* A.M.–*10:30* P.M. *Weekends, 11* A.M.–*10* P.M.

Bangkok Thai Restaurant, *2440 Veterans Blvd. (in the Cinema City 8 Shopping Center), Kenner (504-464-7668). Daily, 11* A.M.–*10:30* P.M. Ask for the pork *satay,* the grass noodle soup, the beef in red curry sauce, the *kan-kai-nor-mia,* or just about anything on the menu and come away with a wonderfully full feeling. Ah, the shrimp with garlic pepper—designed to ward off the evil hungries any time. Bangkok Thai Restaurant has been awarded a three-star rating from *Times-Picayune* food critic Gene Bourg.

Taiwanese

The small Taiwanese community in New Orleans is closely knit, numbering only about two hundred families. One of the community's leaders, Li Schon Shih, a local architect and planner of major institutional and corporate projects such as schools, hospitals, and shopping centers, came to New Orleans from Houston in 1975. Many of his fellow Taiwanese, however, found their way to New Orleans in the early 1960s, mostly to attend school. While not located in any particular neighborhood, many Taiwanese now live throughout the suburb of Metairie. Of all the Asian communities, the Taiwanese are among the most Americanized, according to Schon Shih.

However, many are active in chapters of national groups, such as the Los Angeles-based Taiwan Association, the politically oriented Formosan Association for Public Affairs, and the North American Taiwanese Women's Association. The community gathers eight to ten times a year to celebrate the lunar New Year, Easter and other Christian religious holidays, and a mid-fall Chinese harvest. Most of these events are family- and friend-oriented picnics or small private gatherings. It celebrates a Mid-Autumn Festival in mid-September in Lafreniere Park with food and family games.

Ballroom dancing is a passion with some of the Taiwanese families who meet monthly at one or another of the area's hotels or motels owned by Taiwanese nationals. Held at lunchtime on the last Sunday of the month, they twirl and swirl either at the **Airport TravelLodge,** 2240 Veterans Memorial Boulevard, Kenner, 504-469-7341; the **Candelight Inn,** 4801

Airline Highway, Metairie, 504-455-9300; or the **Holiday Inn,** 100 West-bank Expressway, Gretna, 504-366-2361. Occasionally space is rented at a local dance studio if more room is needed. For meals, they try different foods, ranging from Chinese to Japanese and even cajun. Folk dances are practiced if a local festival is looming on the calendar. As with other nationalities in New Orleans, the Taiwanese are always invited to partici-pate in the spring's Jazz & Heritage Festival. Usually at such events, both men and women present the traditional Moon Dance. A youth group of fourteen junior and senior high schoolers exhibit other traditional dances, such as the Three Sisters of the Ami.

"The young people are really excited to keep alive our traditions," exclaims Schon Shih. "By participating in activities with the Asia Pacific American Society and area festivals, our kids develop a strong sense of pride and identity. They are really contributing," he points out.

A majority of the Taiwanese retain a keen interest in the political situation in their homeland and on mainland China. Several times through-out the year, guest speakers are invited to discuss Asian affairs and how they pertain to Taiwan. The meetings are usually held in a church or local hall and traditional Taiwanese food is served, such as gumbolike soups, seafood and meat, rice cakes, and desserts.

For more information on the Taiwanese community, contact architect Li Schon Shih, 830 Roosevelt Place, New Orleans, LA 70119, 504-482-8404 (home); 482-523-6472 (work).

Churches

Evangelical Formosan Church, *services at the Kenner Presbyte-rian Church, 2939 Iowa, Kenner (504-889-1286).*   In 1994, the Tai-wanese congregation acquired a building of its own in New Orleans' old commercial area, with plans to convert the structure into a church.

Vietnamese

The Vietnamese make up the largest community of Asians in New Or-leans, numbering between fifteen and sixteen thousand individuals. The Vietnamese were drawn to the city because of the favorable climate; ready availability of a large fishing zone; familiar foods; such as rice and seafood; and the Catholic religious heritage.

Many of the Vietnamese in New Orleans were originally from near Haiphong, North Vietnam, when entire villages fled to the South after the signing of the Geneva Convention in 1954. The document divided French Indochina into North and South Vietnam. Most of those refugees were Catholic, remaining fiercely anti-Communist during the ensuing Vietnamese War, and many joined forces with troops to fight alongside the Americans. Subsequently, they had to escape again when the war ended. Since many were fishermen who had their own boats, they simply gathered up their families and pushed off from shore, heading out to sea, where they were picked up by American troop carriers. New Orleans Catholic Charities sponsored hundreds of the refugees by writing letters to Congress and the State Department, calling for relaxed immigration laws and promising to help the refugees become acclimatized in the United States.

One of the leaders of the community is Kiem Do, a former Vietnamese naval captain who organized the rescue sealift for thirty-five thousand Vietnamese when Saigon fell to the North. Do emigrated to the United States following several months in a refugee camp. Given the choice of moving to California or Louisiana, he decided on the port city of New Orleans because he thought he could find a naval job there. His move was sponsored by a friend's brother-in-law, a local judge. However, once he arrived, there were no permanent positions in his field, and his engineering degree from the French naval academy were not recognized in the United States. Do subsequently went back to UNO to get his business degree and worked from a clerk position at Louisiana Power & Light Company to his current status as a nuclear engineer. He currently is seeking an agent for a book he recently completed on his experiences, called *The Mulberry Field.*

One of the largest concentrations of Vietnamese is the Versaille Community along Alcee Fortier Street and Saigon Drive on the eastern outskirts of Orleans Parish, a complex where about six thousand Vietnamese live. To get there, drive east for about ten miles on Chef Menteur Highway from downtown New Orleans and turn off the highway when spotting bold yellow signs with Vietnamese spellings. The buildings in the development were originally a low-income housing project serving primarily African-Americans. The first Vietnamese were assigned there in the 1970s. The project began as a cluster of two- and four-story apartments encompassing some ten square blocks, with four to six buildings to a block. The first wave of Vietnamese who originally settled there have now purchased their own homes nearby.

Another fifteen hundred Vietnamese live in the suburb of Woodlawn, across the river from the French Quarter near Algiers in what they call the "St. Joseph Community," named after their patron saint.

The Vietnamese are very private. Some have admitted that they still don't see themselves as real members of the New Orleans community. It is as if they have been displaced from so many places that they prefer not to put down solid roots. If questioned, most older Vietnamese say they would like to return to their homeland once the political situation improves. However, others admit that returning would not be a good idea after twenty years of living abroad. Yet many Vietnamese high school and college students indicate they want to go back to Vietnam to perform social service work for a time or simply learn more about their native land. But for them, as with any second generation of most émigré groups, home has become the United States. The younger Vietnamese are bilingual, while their middle-aged parents typically cannot speak much English. The elders know very little English.

The larger of two shopping malls in the area, the Versaille Shopping Center on Alcee Fortier Boulevard near the housing complex, contains a Vietnamese bookstore, two or three Vietnamese video stores, and a pharmacy with an herbalist. Not many of the shopkeepers, except in the bookstore, speak English. An interesting sight is the *cho chom hom* (squatting market), where vegetable peddlers ply their trade. In the early 1990s, the market was moved inside a large building at the shopping center to protect shoppers and sellers from the weather outside. In a traditional Vietnamese market, the peddlers would sit on the ground and spread their wares in front of them rather than use stalls; hence the term *squatting market.* Smart shoppers arrive early Saturday and Sunday to get the best vegetables, rabbits, ducks, seafood, and pastries.

Plan on being there by 5 A.M. because by 8:30 A.M. almost everyone has headed home. Car parking is available at the shopping center. There is an apartment complex within a short walk over the levee with extensive gardens in back.

Religion still plays a major factor in the lives of many Vietnamese in New Orleans. In 1990, parishioners at **Mary, Queen of Vietnam, Catholic Church,** 14001 Dwyer Boulevard, built a large new church with a rectory behind the main structure. Alongside the church is a school from kindergarten through third grade. Many older Vietnamese children attend the best schools in the city because of their academic achievements. Other major Catholic parishes with many Vietnamese are St. Joseph's Church in Woodlawn and Tu Do (Freedom) Parish in Harvey.

Catholic churches with Vietnamese parishioners celebrate major Vietnamese holidays, such as *Tet,* the Vietnamese new year, which is usually held around Mardi Gras in early February. Fireworks, dancing, and traditional styles of gambling are part of the festivities. In one game of chance called *soc dia,* players shake a covered plate containing four coins and bet on how many of the coins will be even or odd, similar to a "heads or tails" coin flip. There is a certain skill in getting the right shake of the plate.

In addition to *Tet, Vu Lan,* a combination of Halloween and Mother's Day, is also celebrated in the spring. Buddha's birthday in June and the Harvest Festival, usually between August and September, provide opportunities for festivities. Timing for all these events is based on a lunar calendar, which means dates are never definite from year to year. Festivals are community-oriented, although the public is welcome. Sometimes news about a pending program is simply passed around by word of mouth, which makes it difficult for visitors to New Orleans to know exactly when to show up. In addition, the extent of a program depends on how many individuals are enthusiastic enough to set up a stage. Some years, activities are quite comprehensive, while in other years only a few carnival booths are set up in a churchyard.

Publications

Day Ngoc Lan (Here New Orleans), *Box 155, Gretna, LA 70054 (504-394-0218; FAX 504-391-9793).* Published biweekly, the free newspaper can be found at Vietnamese stores and restaurants. The editor is Vo Dong Chinh.

Ngoc Lan Thoi Boa (New Orleans Magazine), *Box 26877, New Orleans, LA 70186 (504-286-1867).* This free biweekly news and entertainment magazine is edited by Nhi Long. It can be found in most Vietnamese gathering places.

Nguoi Viet (Vietnamese People) This political monthly news magazine is published by the League of Democratic Vietnam. The editor is Le Hong Thanh.

Restaurants

There are a number of excellent Vietnamese eateries in the Greater New Orleans area, including **Bho Hoa Restaurant,** on Manhattan Boulevard; **Quan Kim Restaurant,** located on West Bank Expressway; and **The Vietnamese Restaurant,** 535 Holmes Boulevard, Gretna (504-362-5486). Here are some additional options.

Dong Phuong Resturant, *14207 Chef Menteur Highway (504-254-0296).* Located in east New Orleans, Dong Phong, which means

Easter Restaurant, offers traditional Vietnamese and Chinese foods. A bakery is attached to the building, offering traditional breads, cakes, and rolls (504-254-0214).

Pho Tau Bay Restaurant, *3709 Westbank Expressway, Gretna (504-368-9846). Daily 11 A.M. to 9 P.M.* Noted for its soups, Pho Tau Bay takes large fresh noodles and cooks them with beef and chicken. This is a very popular stop in the morning as workers head out to their jobs, pausing long enough for a bowl of the steaming noodle broth.

Kim Son Restaurant, *349 Whitney Ave., Gretna (504-366-2489).* Many of the local West Bank residents, mostly shipyard and government workers, business executives, and fishermen, visit Kim Son for its *cha gio* (egg roll) and *cua rang muoi* (fried crab).

Kim's Restaurant, *3709 Westbank Expressway, Harvey (504-340-0178). Monday through Friday, 9 A.M.–9 P.M.; Saturday and Sunday, 9 A.M.–10 P.M.* Located in a little shopping center off the West Bank Expressway, Kim's serves both Chinese and Vietnamese foods. Locals drop by for breakfast, usually noodles. The impeccable service at Kim's is under the watchful eye of manager Thy Bo. Major credit cards are accepted.

Churches

Vietnamese Baptist Mission, *100 Gretna Blvd., Gretna (504-362-0056).*

Mary, Queen of Vietnam Catholic Church, *14001 Dwyer Blvd. (504-254-5660). The pastor is Monsignor Mai Thanh Luong Dominic.*

Our Lady of Lavang Mission, *6054 Vermillion Blvd. (504-283-0559).* Named after a central Vietnamese town where an apparition of the Blessed Mother was believed to have occurred two hundred years ago, this is one of several outreach parishes for the Vietnamese community. Catechism and Sunday school are central activities for the two hundred fifty parish members who come from around New Orleans for church services.

The Immaculate Virgin Mary Mission Catholic Church, *6851 8th St., Marro (504-347-2572).*

Bo De Pagoda, *Algiers Rd. Celebration at 9 A.M. Sunday. Operated by the Vietnamese Buddhist Fellowship of New Orleans, Box 740157, New Orleans, LA 70174.*   The Woodlawn Vietnamese community's Buddhist temple is across the Mississippi River via the Crescent Connection bridge (which locals used to call the Gretna-New Orleans Bridge or just the GNO). Take the General DeGaulle Street exit and go to the end of the road, crossing the overpass on top of the West Bank Industrial Canal, and drive to English Turn; then exit right on the first ramp. The temple, which serves one thousand Vietnamese from the West Bank area and Jefferson Parish, can be seen from the exit ramp. Open to visitors each midday, a monk is on hand to show guests around the little building, which houses a gold-plated Buddha. The temple is near the Vietnamese community in Woodlawn.

chapter ten

Other Communities

Australian/New Zealand New Orleans

Vic's Kangaroo Cafe, *636 Tchoupitoulas St. (504-524-4329). Open daily, 11:30 A.M.–3:30 A.M. (or whenever the last patron leaves).* Yes, there are marsupial crossing signs in New Orleans. Just off the Central Business District (CBD) is Vic's Kangaroo Cafe, home away from home for any lost Aussie (Australian) or Kiwi (New Zealander) business executive, conventioneer, or backpacker. Manager/owner Vic Norman found his way to New Orleans from hometown Benigo, Victoria, in search of his fortune in the late 1980s. In 1990, he found an old warehouse in what was then a tattered section of the city and built 'is bar from scratch. The neighborhood has now swung around, having been "discovered." So Norman was in the right place at the "royt toyme."

Covering almost every inch of the cafe's dim, cool interior are "I Love Australia" bumper stickers, Australian flags, traditional curving boomerangs, and gaudy brewery signs. A long bar wraps its way along one wall, backed by a mirror and rows of liquor bottles. There is plenty of room to stand around and talk. A few tables are scattered about the place.

Vic's is one of the best places in which to hang out on a humid New Orleanian summer afternoon. The cool, dark interior; a bottle of Foster's ale; and a baseball game on the television or good chat with the bartender (who usually is an expatriate Aussie) set a relaxed tone for a visitor. There are plenty of newspapers, magazines, and battered old paperback books by the front entrance, along with board games for forgetting the spinning world outside. And this is the only place in town to get glasses of heady Australian wine, such as Rosemont Red, Brown Brothers, and Hardy's.

Norman celebrates Australia Day on January 26 by fixing a roast lamb dinner, vegetables, and pavalova for dessert. The latter is a delicious meringue covered with fresh cream. Two bands usually play, beginning at 4 P.M. and continuing until the sun rises over the Sydney opera house (or is it the Superdome?), which seems to be days later. He also figures ANZAC Day on April 25 is worth another party, with a barbecue and Australian biscuits (cookies).

Since his father was a hotel manager for thirty-five years, New Zealand-born Norman learned his hospitality trade early.

After an evening of talk and ale at the Kangaroo Cafe, just watch out for the 'roos–pink or otherwise.

══════════ Greek New Orleans ══════════

Several thousand New Orleanians trace their heritage to Greece; the first Greek traders were noted in New Orleans as early as 1850. Many of the early Greeks went into the cotton business and became successful merchants. But the real story of the Greeks is the story of their church, Holy Trinity.

As the community expanded to several hundred families, it sought a site to build an Orthodox church. In 1860, businessperson Nicholas Benachi, who doubled as Greek consul, led a committee seeking a religious home-base. After four years of unsuccessfully looking for a permanent site, Benachi donated one of his own buildings as a temporary place of worship. The establishment of this congregation, officiated over by Reverend Agapios Honcharenko until 1872, marked the foundation of the first Orthodox church in North America. However, it wasn't until 1866 that the community found its first real home, when Benachi sold the congregation a parcel of land at 1222 N. Dorgenois Street.

With Benachi's largesse and donations from the Demetrios and John Botassis families, the first Holy Trinity Church was erected. A parish house, a library, and a cemetery followed a few years later. The church was not limited only to Greeks, but enveloped Orthodox Serb, Russian, and Syrian faithful as well. In 1901, the church was chartered by Louisiana as the Eastern Orthodox Church of Holy Trinity. The facility was rechartered in 1920 by the state as the Hellenic Orthodox Church.

That first building was demolished as the congregation expanded, and another structure was built in 1950. Within ten years, the Biennial Clergy-Laity Congress, the legislative body for the Orthodox congregations in the South, authorized the consecration of Holy Trinity as a cathedral. The church remained on North Dorgenois Street until the property was sold in 1976. It was eventually relocated adjacent to Bayou St. John, at 1200 Robert E. Lee Boulevard (504-282-0259). The Hellenic Cultural Center was built there in 1980, followed by a new cathedral building in 1985. A rainbow of brilliantly colored tiles comprise the face of the church. The tiles, graceful white archway, and lofty bell tower make the church easily recognizable. Currently there are some four hundred fifty Orthodox families in Greater New Orleans, served by Reverend Nicholas W. Jonas.

Even today, almost all community activities still center around the cathedral. From 10 A.M. to 1:00 P.M. on Saturdays during the school year, language, religion, and Greek traditions are taught by parish members Steve Tsarellis and Dan Tadros in the congregation's Hellenic Cultural Center.

The church grounds are adequate for numerous parish programs, including the annual Greek Festival on Memorial Day weekend. At the fest, the teenage members of the Hellenic Dancers stage a musical program, and children from the cathedral's Greek school show off their language and craft skills. Pastries, roast lamb, and other delicacies are offered to hungry guests, both outdoors and indoors.

The lavish Greek Night, also sponsored by the cathedral, is usually held in autumn. A dinner of traditional Greek foods, followed by ballroom dancing at a local hotel, are the attractions. For details on times, dates, and locales, call church secretary Mary Kontas.

Restaurants

There are several popular Greek restaurants in New Orleans, ranging from quick service to fancy sitdown. For great gyros (flavorful sandwiches made with the traditional thin slices of ground, spiced, and minced lamb), **Mr. Gyros** has two locations: 819 Decatur Street (504-523-8792) and 3620 N. Causeway Boulevard, Metairie (504-833-9228). For a nightclub/restaurant setting, there is the **Athenian Room Greek Cuisine,** 127 Decatur (504-524-7091). John Skias' **Little Greek Restaurant,** 619 Pink Street, Metairie (504-831-9470), is also a hot spot for dining.

Other good Greek eateries include:

Zissis Restaurant, *2051 Metairie Rd., Metairie (504-837-7890). Open Monday through Friday for lunch 11 A.M.–2 P.M. Dinner Monday through Thursday is 5:30–10 P.M. and 5:30–11 P.M. on Friday* *and Saturday. The restaurant is closed Sundays. Reservations are required on weekends.* Mother and son—Ginny and Efthimios (Tim) Zissi—opened their new ninety-two-seat restaurant in 1993. But the Zissis' name has been well known in New Orleans for the past thirty-five years because Ginny's late husband George operated a restaurant. Chef Alison Zega specializes in New Orleans dishes, such as soft-shelled crab, shrimp, and crayfish with a Greek twist in seasonings and appearance. Traditional Greek dishes are also presented in fine style, such as lamb *souvlaki* and *kotopita* (chicken breast with feta and mushroom wrapped in thin-crusted phyllo dough). Prices range from $8 to $18.50. Paintings of the Greek islands by local artist Angela Angolo adorn the wall. Ginny's family, the Gianiotas, originated in northern Greece and from islands in the Ionian Sea, but immigrated to Cleveland. Her husband's family was also originally from northern Greece, settling in Massachusetts. George attended Tulane University in New Orleans and met Ginny at a Greek youth conference in Washington, D.C. They returned to New Orleans and eventually purchased the restaurant where George used to eat at while a student.

Mother's Restaurant, *131 Huey P. Long Ave., Gretna (504-368-8678). Open Monday through Friday, 6:30 A.M.–3 P.M.; dinners offered Thursday, 5–9 P.M. and Friday and Saturday, 5–10 P.M.* Mom could hardly do better at Mother's Restaurant, which serves *astanakotita,* a spinach pie shaped like an egg roll; *dolmades,* delicious stuffed grape leaves; or eggplant salad to start off a dinner of fried cod fish or *souvlaki,* beef tenderloin. The most popular dessert is *baklava,* a sweet honey and nut combo rolled together in a razor-thin phyllo dough. Prices range from $5.50 to $9. In 1971, restaurant owner George Tzavellan came to New Orleans from Greece, where he had worked as a chef. His wife Fotni (the "mother" of the place) joined him in 1973. Tzavellan worked in several other New Orleans restaurants before opening Mother's in 1976. The one hundred sixty-patron eatery is across the street from the Jefferson Parish Courthouse on the West Bank. Hungry jurors, judges, and lawyers fill the place from the wee hours on through the working day. A neighborhood crowd and Greek food fanciers from throughout the metro area pack the place for dinners.

══════════ Croatian New Orleans ══════════

Croatian seafarers visited New Orleans throughout the eighteenth and nineteenth centuries. Freighters from Austro-Hungarian ports, such as

Dubrovnik, were among the many docking at the city's quays, loaded with rich trade goods from Europe. The first recorded Croatians in New Orleans were sailors who left their vessels in the 1830s to take up residence along the docks. Another major influx from the Dalmatian Coast of old Yugoslavia came at the end of the nineteenth century, and many more came just before and immediately after World War I.

Since most were fishers in their home country, they turned toward the Gulf of Mexico and the deep Mississippi waters to continue their trade. Eventually most of the Louisiana oyster industry was taken over by the Croatians. Today they include fishers, dealers, and oyster-bar owners, such as Pete Vujnovich, whose **Captain Pete's Oyster House** is a popular drop-in place at 1731 N. Rampart Street. (504-947-2628). Plaquemine Parish is now a home for many Croatians, who celebrate their trade with an Oyster Festival each December.

After a horrendous hurricane about one hundred twenty years ago, the United Slovian Benevolent Association was organized to help bury the dead and take care of orphans and widows. Several hundred bodies were subsequently entombed in a magnificent granite burial site at St. Louis Cemetery on Esplanade Avenue near the Bayou St. John. Tour escorts often point out the tomb as one of the city's landmarks. In later years, many Croatian families built their own tombs in other cemeteries. But the main structure is still maintained by the benevolent association. Other large Croatian burial plots from that early era are in Buras, Empire, and Port Sulphur, Louisiana.

Typical of the Croatian community is Bilka Barisich, who came to the United States from Croatia fifty-five years ago with her immigrant parents. She belongs to the Louisiana Citizens for a Free Croatian Society, which has lists of Croatian children orphaned in the bloody Bosnian civil war. The organization also sends containers of food and clothes to families there.

St. Anthony's Day on June 12 provides an excuse for a Croatian festival at **St. Patrick's Church,** 724 Camp Street. (504-525-4413). Traditional dancing and singing are presented, as tables groan with homemade food to complete the celebration.

Restaurants

Drago's Seafood Restaurant, *3232 N. Arnult Rd., Metairie (504-888-9254). Open for lunch from 11 A.M.–2:30 P.M., Monday through Saturday; dinner 5–9:30 P.M., Monday through Thursday, and 5–10 P.M., Friday and Saturday. The restaurant is closed Sunday.* Drago's is one of New Orleans' prime seafood restaurants, offering some Croatian dishes as well. The menu includes *sarma* (stuffed cabbage) and *mousaka* (baked fried eggplant with ground veal) with prices in the $10 range. Grilled fish and monster charbroiled oysters on the half shell are also popular. The restaurant was opened in 1969 by Drago Cvitanovich, who came to New Orleans ten years before and had family in the city since the 1880s. For a time, he worked with his sister, Gloria Batinich, and her husband, also named Drago, at their Drago's Restaurant in Lake View. Consequently, the name Drago is well known around the Crescent City. Currently Tommy, Cvitanovich's son, is manager of the family-run restaurant. Clara, Cvitanovich's wife, also helps out. Cvitanovich is President of the two hundred-member United Slovian Benevolent Association.

===== Middle Eastern New Orleans =====

There is only a small, loosely knit number of New Orleanians of Middle Eastern ancestry: Iranians, Palestinians, Turks, and a few others. They are primarily upper-middle-class professionals in the medical, legal, and business fields. Typical of this small population is Egyptian-born Archie Casbarian, owner of the revered **Arnaud's Restaurant,** 813 Bienville Street (504-523-0611). Middle Easterners have blended well into the overall community and, as such, there is no distinct neighborhood of one nationality or the other. Serving the business and financial community is the **Arab USA Chamber of Commerce,** 2 Canal Street (504-588-1127).

Accommodating the religious needs of the community is the **Islamic Center of New Orleans,** 1911 St. Claude Avenue (504-944-3758). Daily prayer services are held at 1:30 P.M.

Shopping

The Bijou Gifts, *1015 Decatur St. (504-525-3054). Open daily from 10 A.M.–6 P.M.* Featuring clothing from Iran and other Middle Eastern countries, The Bijou Gifts also sells Mardi Gras masks and related New Orleans souvenirs. Opened in 1983, the shop was purchased shortly afterward by Rahim Rashkbar, a former Iranian journalist. Tired of spending time in jail cells because of his writings, Rashkbar fled to the United States and found his way to New Orleans while still in his early twenties. Especially proud of his hand-painted shirts, Rashkbar is always happy to show off his stock with its individualized explosion of intricately colored flowers, birds, and animals.

Suggested Reading

Brasseaux, Carl A. *The Founding of New Acadia: The Beginnings of Acadian Life In Louisiana, 1765–1803.* Baton Rouge, La.: Louisiana State University Press, 1987.

Calhoun, Milburn, ed. *Louisiana Almanac.* Gretna, La.: Pelican Publishing Inc., 1989.

Carter, Hodding, ed. *Past as Prelude: New Orleans 1718–1968.* New Orleans, La.: Tulane University Publications, 1968.

Comeaux, Malcolm L. *Atchafalaya Swamp Life: Settlement and Folk Occupation.* Baton Rouge, La.: Louisiana State University Press, 1972.

Dundee, Harold A. and Douglas A. Rossman. *The Amphibians and Reptiles of Louisiana.* Baton Rouge, La.: Louisiana State University Press, 1988.

Eakin, Sue, James Culbertson, and Marie Culbertson. *Louisiana: The Land and Its People.* Gretna, La.: Pelican Publishing Inc., 1986.

Garvey, Joan B. and Mary Lou Widmer. *Beautiful Crescent: A History of New Orleans.* New Orleans, La.: Garmer Press, 1984.

Griffin, Thomas K. *The Pelican Guide to New Orleans.* Gretna, La.: Pelican Publishing Inc., 1987.

Indians of Louisiana. Baton Rouge, La.: Governor's Commission on Indian Affairs, undated.

Knau, John S. *German People of New Orleans from 1850 to 1900.* Hattisburg, Miss.: Mississippi Southern College, 1989.

Kniffen, Fred B. *The Indians of Louisiana*. Gretna, La.: Pelican Publishing Inc., 1985.

Langtry, Walter D. *History of the Chinese Presbyterian Church in New Orleans, 1882–1982*. Presbyterian Church, 1982.

Leavitt, Mel. *A Short History of New Orleans*. San Francisco: Lexikos, 1982.

Lowery, George H. *Louisiana Birds*. Baton Rouge, La.: Louisiana State University Press, 1974.

Lowery, George H. *The Mammals of Louisiana and Its Adjacent Waters*. Baton Rouge, La.: Louisiana State University Press, 1974.

MacDonald, Robert, John R. Kemp, and Edward F. Haas, eds. *Louisiana's Black Heritage*. New Orleans: Louisiana State Museum, 1979.

Native Americans of Louisiana, Baton Rouge, La.: Governor's Commission on Indian Affairs, undated.

Rushton, William F. *The Cajuns: From Acadia to Louisiana*. New York: Farrar Straus Giroux, 1979.

Saxon, Lyle. *Lafitte the Pirate*. Gretna, La.: Pelican Publishing Inc., 1989.

Spitzer, Nicolas R., et al. "Mississippi Delta Ethnographic Overview." Unpublished study for Jean Lafitte National Historical Park and Preserve. New Orleans, 1979.

Sternberg, Mary Ann. *The Pelican Guide to Louisiana*. Gretna, La.: Pelican Publishing Inc., 1989.

Wilson, Samuel and Leonard V. Huber. *The St. Louis Cemeteries of New Orleans*. New Orleans, La.: St. Louis Cathedral Press, 1963.

Index

A

ABA Tours and Travel, 174
Acadians, 10, 49
Ace Camera Repair Service, 205
Adams, John Quincy, 134
Adeaux's Lounge & Nightclub, 148
Adriani, John, 105
AFRICAN-AMERICAN NEW ORLEANS, 123
  arts, 145–46, 153–54
  associations, 137
  broadcasting, 156
  catering, 143–44
  colleges, 138–39
  festivals, 148–51
  history and settlement, 123–34
  holiday offerings, 152
  music, 146–48, 151–52
  publications, 144–45
  restaurants, 139–43
  shopping, 138
  theater, 154–56
  tourism, 134, 136–37
African-American Voters League, 137
Agnelly, Bob, 106
Airboat tours, 29
Airline Lions Club, 107, 205
Airport Shuttle limo service, 15

Airport TravelLodge, 212
Alessandri, Franco, 107
Alexis, Russian Grand Duke, 34
Algiers Point Association, 29
Ali, Syed B., 209
Aliberti, Maria, 168
Almonester y Roxas, Don Andrés, 160
Amateur Athletic Association (AAU), 103
American Italian Museum and Research Library, 103, 105–6, 112
American Italian Renaissance Foundation, 100
American Revolution, 4–5
Amistad Research Center, 27, 36–37, 133–34, 145, 153
Amtrak, 17
Anacapri New Orleans Italian Bar & Grill, 110
Ancient Order of Hibernians, 73
Anti-Defamation League, 120
Antoine's Restaurant, 59
Anzelmo, Sal, 101
Aquí New Orleans, 171
Arab USA Chamber of Commerce, 224
Archdiocese of New Orleans Archives, 40
Armstrong, Louis, Jazz Club, 43
Armstrong, Louis (Satchmo), 40, 101, 126
Armstrong Park, 127–28

Arnaud's Restaurant, 59–60, 224
Arrive Magazine, 33
Arts
    African-American, 145–46, 153–54
    Hispanic/Caribbean, 167–68
Asia Marine and Supply Co., 205
Asia Market, 194, 209
Asian Food Store, 194
Asian Imports, 194
ASIAN NEW ORLEANS, 189–93
    history and settlement, 189–93
    nationalities, 194–218
    publications, 193
    restaurants, 196–98
    shopping, 193–94
Asian Pacific American Society
        (APAS), 190–92
Asian Pacific Society of America, 211
Asocación de Guatemala en Louisiana, 181
Association of Salvadorans Living in
        Louisiana, 180
Associations
    in African-American New Orleans, 137
    in German New Orleans, 90–92
    in Hispanic/Caribbean New Orleans,
        166–67
    in Irish New Orleans, 73–75
    in Italian New Orleans, 106–7
    in Jewish New Orleans, 119–21
Athenian Room Greek, 221
Audubon, John James (riverboat), 30
Audubon Park, 24, 190–91
Austin, Zenete, 131
**AUSTRALIAN/NEW ZEALAND NEW
        ORLEANS,** 219–20
    restaurants, 219–20

B
Babylonian All-Stars, 147
Balonos, Jack, 167
Bangkok Cuisine, 212
Bangkok Thai Restaurant, 212
Bangladesh, 194–95
    Consulate in, 194–95
Banking, 16–17, 44
Barataria Preserve Unit, 9
Bares, Basil J., 37
Barthelemy, Sidney, 129, 139
Bartholomew, Joseph, Memorial Park
        golf course, 134

Baudier, Roger, 40
Bayou Lafourche, 10
Bayou Plaza Hotel, 206
Bayou Steinverein, 90
Bazoon, Annie, 23
Bazoon, Otis, 43
Beaucoup Books, 172
Beauregard, P. G. T., 95
Beauregard House, 9
Beautiful Crescent, 84
Bechet, Sidney, 42, 126
Behrman, Martin, 86, 87, 117–18
Belton, Kevin, 22–23
Benachi, Nicholas, 220
Benjamin, Judah, 117
Bergen Gallery, 179
Bernard, Al, 40
Bernardo de Galvez, Don, 160–61
Beth Israel Congregation, 118
Bho Hoa Restaurant, 216
Bicycle tours, 29–30
Bienville, 114
Bienville monument, 7
Bijou Gifts, 224
Bilal Iban Rabah Islamic Center, 210
Black Arts National Diaspora, 146
Black Bridal Fair, 149–50
Black Code, 114, 124
Black Heritage Festival, 150
Black Theater Festival, 154–55
Black Tourism Summit, 135–36
Blanc, Antoine, 70
Blessed Melody Choir, 152
Boccacio 2000, 164
Bo De Pagoda, 218
Bolden, Buddy, 42
Bonaparte, Napoleon, 5, 162, 182
Bones Boutique, 138
Bonura, Henry ''Zeke,'' 106
Boswell Sisters, 40
Bottom Line, 148
Bracken, Karen, 164
Bray, Suzanne, 168
Broadcasting
    African-American, 156
    Hispanic/Caribbean, 169–70
Brocato, Angelo, Ice Cream &
        Confectionary, 108–9
Brossouard, Joseph, 49
Broussard, Al, 44

Brown, William G., 128
Brunius, Wendell, 43
Buddhist Fellowship of Louisiana, 193
Buses, 16, 17
Butler, Benjamin, 124

C
Cabildo, 11, 29, 132, 158
Cabin Restaurant, 136
Cabrini High School, 97
Cafe Baquet, 140
Cafe du Monde, 20, 61, 132
Cajun French Music Association, 57
Cajun Queen (riverboat), 30
CAJUNS, 10, 48–49, 51–52
    restaurants, 56–58
Calogero, Pascal F., Jr., 101
Calvary Korean Baptist Church of New
    Orleans, 208
Cámarade Comercio Hispana Louisiana,
    166–67
Canary Islanders, 11
Candelight Inn, 212–13
Canizaro, Joe, 102
Canzoneri, Tony, 103
Capra, Frank, 102
Captain Pete's Oyster House, 223
Carmine's Italian and Seafood
    Specialties, 109
Carnival Latino, 176–77
Car rental agencies, 16
Carriage tours, 30
Carrollton Street Festival, 149
Casa Garciá Mexican Restaurant, 186
Casa Tequila, 186
Casso, Evans J., 98
Castellón Discount Pharmacy, 172
Castillo's Mexican Restaurant, 185–86
Catering, African-American, 143–44
Catholic Youth Organization's
    (CYO), 103
Cavelier, Robert, sieur de La Salle, 2
C&C Club, 148
Celtic-American Heritage Society, 81
Celtic Folk, 76
Celtic Nations Festival of Louisiana, 80
Center for the Pacific Rim (CPM), 192
Central Business District (CBD), 19, 102
Central Grocery Co., 111
Centroamericana Mini Market, 173

Cervantes Foundation of Hispanic Art,
    167–68
Chabad House-Lubavitch, 118
Chabad of Metairie, 118
Chalmette Battlefield, 24
Chalmette National Historical Park, 9, 10
Chalmette Unit, 9
Charles IV, 162
Charlie B's, 148
Chàvarri, Ruperto, 165
Chesterfield's, 147
Chew, Beverly, 66
Chez Helene, 141
Children of Selma Theater Company, 155
China Doll, 196–97
CHINESE, 195–99
    associations, 195–96
    churches, 198
    festivals, 196
    publications, 199
    restaurants, 196–98
    shopping, 198–99
Chinese American Food Store, 199
Chinese Baptist Church, 198
Chinese Market, 199
Chinese Presbyterian Church, 198
Chinh, Vo Dong, 216
Chitimacha Cultural Center, 4, 10–11
Choctaw Club of Louisiana, 86–87
Chopsticks Restaurants, 197
Choudhury, Shameem, 191, 192
Christ Church, 114–15
Christian Unity Baptist Church, 146, 152
Christmas
    Creole, 60–62, 116
    tropical, 177
    Churches
    Chinese, 198
    Koreans, 207–8
Cipriano Espina, 199
City Hall Annex, 133
City magazines, 32–33
Civil War, 5
Clifton, Nat "Sweetwater," 139
Club Deportivo Ecuador (Ecuador Sporting
    Club), 177
Club Social Nicaraguense, 187
Club VIP, 148
Coastline/Mississippi Coast Limousine
    Service, 16

Cohen, Walter L., 131
Coleman, Thomas B., 194–95
College of Education, 192
Colleges, African-American, 138–39
Colón, Gustavo, 166
Columbus, Christopher, 182
Columns Hotel, 43
Commander's Palace, 88
Committee of Fifty, 99
Communal Hebrew School, 120
Community Book Store, 138
Compagno's, 107–11
Congo, Louis, 124
Congo Square, 126–27
Congregation Anshe Stard Synagogue, 118
Congregation Gates of Prayer, 118
Connemara marble cross, 72–73
Connick, Harry, Jr., 40
Connick, Harry, Sr., 43
Contemporary Art Center, 117, 154, 155
Cookin' Cajun Cooking School, 55–56
Corbett, Jim, 68
Cortina, Raquel, 168
Cosio, Ada, 171
Cosio, José R., 171
Costume shops, 36
Cotton Blossom (riverboat) 30–31
Country Flame, 186
Court of the Two Sisters, 60
Creative Artists Striving Together
    (C. A. S. T.), 155
CREOLE/CAJUN NEW ORLEANS, 48
    Cajun restaurants, 56–58
    Creole restaurants, 58–60
    festivals, 60–62
    food, 52
    history and settlement, 48–52
Creole Christmas, 60–62, 116
Creole Delicacies Gourmet Shop, 56
Creole Mansion Row, 50
Creole Queen (riverboat), 24, 30–31, 43
CREOLES, 48, 49–51
    restaurants, 58–60
Crescent City Brewhouse, 42–43
Crescent City Connection Bridge, 9
Crescent City Homebrewers, 90
Crescent Tours of New Orleans, 28
Crew, Tony, 130
Croatian New Orleans, 222–23
Cuban American Association, 178

Cuccia, Lucas T., & Son, 100
Culu, 145
Cusimano, Charles, 106

D

D'Abbadie, Jean-Jacques Blaise, 158–59
Dance studios, Hispanic/Caribbean, 168–69
Darby, William, 12
D'Arensbourg, Karl Freidrich, 82–83
Davis, A. L., 133
Davis, Arthur Q., Sr., 211
Davis, Frank, 22
Day Ngoc Lan (Here New Orleans), 216
de Bango, Guillermo, 167–68
Decatur House Restaurant, 60
Decatur Street Irish Club, 79
Dede, Sanite, 125
Dejean, Lois, 152
Delille, Henriette, 126
Dell, Katchia, 91
Delmonico Restaurant, 60
del Puerto, Paco, 169
de Marigny de Mandeville, Antoine
    Philippe, 50
de Marigny, Bernard, 50–51
de Marigny, Pierre Philippe, 50
Derom, Santiago (James Durham), 125
Derwent Company, 28–29
Des Allemands, 83
Destrehan Plantation, 25
De Tonti, Henri (Enrico), 94
De Ulloa, Don Antonio, 159
Deutsches-Haus, 90–91
DeVito, Matt, 103
d'Iberville, Sieur, 2, 33
Dillard University, 139
Dirty Dozen Brass Band, 42
Dirty Dozen-Treme Brass Festival, 149
Dispersed of Judah, 115
Do, Kiem, 190, 214
Dodds, Johnny, 42
Domenici, Heidi, 167
Dominican Republic, 179
Domino, Fats, 40
Dooky Chase Cookbook, 141
Dooky Chase Restaurant, 141
Doubletree Hotel New Orleans, 102
Douglas, Inez, 28
Doug's Steaks, 116, 193
Downtown Irish Club, 79

Drago's Seafood Restaurant, 223–24
Drag Queen Costume Contest, 36
Drinking, 45–46
Dryades YMCA, 133
Dukes of Dixieland, 43
Dunbar, Celestine, 142
Dunbar's Restaurant, 137, 142–43
Dundee, Angelo, 106
Durand, Charles, 51
Dutrey, Honore, 42

E

Eddie's Restaurant & Bar, 143
Elks Lodge, 42
Ellington, Duke, 126
El Palceno Grocery, 173
El Salvador, 179–81
Emmett, Dan, 85
Enlace, 171
Entellina, Contessa, Society, 102
Escuela de Danzas Españolas, 168–69
Espina, Cipriano, 190, 199
Espina, Marina, 190, 199
Ethnic Traders, 138
*Ethnographic Overview of the Mississippi
    Delta Region,* 28
Evangelical Formosan Church, 213

F

Fabacher, Peter Laurence, 86
Fahy's Irish Pub, 76
Fairmont Hotel, 92
FAME, 145
Fat Tuesday, 33
Faubourg Marigny, 51
Fest d'Italia, 106
Festivals
    African-American, 148–51
    Chinese, 196
    Creole/Cajun, 60–62
    Hispanic/Caribbean, 175
    Irish, 79–80
Filipino American Goodwill Society,
    199–200
Filipinos, 199–201
    Consulate, 199
Fine, Nora, 167
First Korean Baptist, 207
Fitzpatrick, John, 68, 86
Flabor's, 147

Folse, John, 48
Fong's Chinese & Cantonese Restaurant,
    197
Food, 20–23. *See also* Restaurants
Formento, Felix, 95
Forster, Roberto, 165
Foucher, Pierre, 71
Fountainbleau, Treaty of, 4
Fountain, Pete, Nightclub, 44
4th Edition, 147
Franklin, Carl, 43
French Market, 132
French Opera House, 38, 96
French Quarter, 3, 5, 7, 10, 13–14, 19
French Quarter Festival, 62, 116
Frey, Aston, 84
Friends of the Cabildo, 7, 29, 36–37

G

Gallier, James, 38, 65, 70, 75
Gallier House Museum, 65
Garden District, 25
Garvey, Joan B., 84
Gates of Loving Kindness, 114, 115
Gateway Reception Program, 15
Gayoso de Lemos, Manuel Luis, 161–62
Gay 90's Carriages, 30
Genghis Kahn, 206–7
German Heritage, Cultural and Genealogy
    Society, 90
German Heritage Festival Association, 91
German Heritage Museum, 89
GERMAN NEW ORLEANS, 82
    history and settlement, 82–89
    organizations, 90–92
    restaurants, 92–93
German Protestant Orphan Asylum, 91–92
German Seaman's Mission, 92
Giarrusso, Robin M., 101
Gigi Patout, 56
Gino's, 147
Good Government League, 87
Gray Line of New Orleans, 25
Greater New Orleans Archivists, 36–37
Greater New Orleans Black Tourism
    Network, 130–31, 134
Greater New Orleans Italian Cultural
    Society, 96
Greater New Orleans Tourist and
    Convention Commission, 7

Greater New Orleans Visitors and
    Convention Bureau, 34
Great Wall Chinese Restaurant, 197–98
GREEK NEW ORLEANS, 220–21
    restaurants, 221–22
Gregory, Angelo, 7
Guatemalan Consulate, 181
Guatemalans, 181
Guest Informant, 33
Gustavo's Authenic Mexican
    Restaurant, 186

H
Hadley, Charlie, 87
Haitians, 181–83
Hall, Abraham Oakley, 50
Hall, Edmond, 42
Hall, Maureen McTeggart, 75
Hampton, Lionel, 129
Hana Japanese Restaurant, 204
Han Kook Il Bo, 205, 209
Harrison, Benjamin, 99
Hasan's Restaurant, 142
Haughery, Margaret Gaffney, 71
Hearn, Lafcadio, 200
Heavenly Dishes, 143–44
Hector, Francisco Luis, 161
Hennessy, David, 68, 98–99
Henry's Soul Food, 142
Herman, Pete, 103
Hermann-Grima Historic House, 52, 117
Hillel Foundation, 118
**HISPANIC/CARIBBEAN NEW
    ORLEANS,** 157
    arts and entertainment, 167–69
    business and professional associations,
        166–67
    dance studios, 168–69
    festivals, 175
    history and settlement, 157–65
    media, 169–70
    nationalities, 177–88
    publications, 170–72
    restaurants, 178–79, 180–81,
        185–86, 188
    shopping, 172–74
    spiritualists, 175
    tour companies, 174–75
Hispanic Cultural Coalition of New
    Orleans, 167

Hispanic Festival, 180
Hispanidad, 168
Historical New Orleans Collection, 27,
    36–37, 38, 89
History and settlement, 1–7, 48–52
    African-Americans, 123–34
    Asians, 189–93
    Creole/Cajun, 48–52
    Germans, 82–89
    Hispanic/Caribbeans, 157–65
    Irish, 63–73
    Italians, 94–104
    Jewish, 113–14
Hodge, G. Jeannette, 146
Hogan, William Ransom, Jazz
    Archive, 37, 42
Holiday Inn, 213
Holiday offerings, African-American New
    Orleans, 152
Holy Trinity Church, 220
Honduran Association of Louisiana, 183
Honduran Consulate, 183
Honduran Festival, 183
Hondurans, 183
Horizons Club, 44
Hotel Inter-Continental, 43
Hot Ochra, 206
Howard-Tilton Memorial Library, 37
Hua Fong News, 199
Hudson, Julien, 126
Humphrey Brothers, 43
Hyatt Regency Hotel, 179

I
Ichiban Japanese Restaurant, 203–4
Ildefonso, Treaty of, 5
Immaculate Conception Church, 180, 185
Immaculate Virgin Mary Mission Catholic
    Church, 218
Indians, 202
Information Agencies, 13
Irish American Post, 80–81
Irish Cultural Society, 73–75
Irish Echo, 81
Irish Eyes, 81
IRISH NEW ORLEANS, 63–73
    festivals, 79–80
    history and settlement, 63–73
    newspapers, 80–81
    pubs, 76–79

shops, 75–76
social organizations, 73–75
Irish Shop of New Orleans, 75–76
Irish Voice, 81
Islamic Center of New Orleans, 224
Isleno Center, 11
Italian American Bocce Club, 106–7
Italian American Digest, 111–12
Italian-American Heritage and Culture
    Month, 103
Italian American Marching Club, 107
Italian American Sports Hall of Fame, 106
ITALIAN NEW ORLEANS
    attractions, 105–6
    history and settlement, 94–104
    organizations, 106–7
    publications, 111
    restaurants, 107
    stores, 111

J

Jackson, Andrew, 9, 24, 131
Jackson, Anthony, 126
Jackson, Mahalia, 40
Jackson Brewery, 86
Jackson Square, 131
Jaeger Seafood, 140, 147
Jahncke, Fritz, 85
James-Jones, Robin, 76
Japan Club, 203
Japanese, 203–4
Japan Society, 203
Jasime School of Dance, 169
Jazz Festival, 149
Jazz Museum, 130
Jefferson, Thomas, 5
Jefferson Transit, 16
Jelly Roll's, 147
Jewish Children's Regional Service, 120
Jewish Community Center, 119
Jewish Family Service Agency, 120
Jewish Federation of Greater
    New Orleans, 120
JEWISH NEW ORLEANS, 113
    associations, 119–21
    history and settlement, 113–14
    Kosher shopping, 121–22
    newspapers, 121
    synagogues and prayer facilities, 118–19
Jewish Voice, 121

Jewish Welfare Fund of New Orleans, 121
Joe's Cozy Corner, 148
Johnson, Emma, 130
Jung, Rodney, 74

K

K-Creole Kitchen Restaurant, 195
Kelly, Chris, 42
Keppard, Freddie, 42
Kerlerec, Governor, 114
Kerry Pub, 77
Keswani, Har, 202
Kids in the Act, 155
Kim, Quan, Restaurant, 216
Kim, Yup, 204
Kim Son Restaurant, 217
Kim's Restaurant, 217
King, Martin Luther, Jr., 133
King Oliver's Creole Jazz Band, 126
Kingsley House Community Center, 154
Knights of St. Peter Claver, 132
Kolb's Restaurant, 92
Korea House, 207
Korea Market, 208
Korean Association of Greater New
    Orleans, 204
Korean Catholic Church, 208
Korean Church of New Orleans, 208
Korean Culture and Language Academy of
    New Orleans, 206
Korean Presbyterian Church of New
    Orleans, 208
KOREANS, 204–9
    churches, 207–8
    consulate for, 206
    publications, 209
    restaurants, 206–7
    shopping, 208
Korean Travel Agency, 206
Korean United Methodist Church, 208
Kosher Cajun Deli & Grocery, 121–22
Kosher shopping, 121–22
Krewe of Comus, 34
Kumbuka, 145
Kung's Dynasty, 198
Kwanza holiday, 155

L

LaBranche Pharmacy, 132
La Côte des Allemands, 83

Ladies Hibernians, 73
Lafayette Acadian Cultural Center, 10
Lafitte, Jean, National Historic
     Park, 8–9, 11
Lafon, Thorny, 132
Laine, Jack, 42
Lake Pontchartrain, 1–2, 3
Landrieu, Maurice (Moon), 38, 162–63
Language Day, 194
LaRocca, James Nick, 42, 101
Laserie, Rolando, 172
La Societa Italiana di Beneficenza
     Contessa Entellina, 95
Latin American Restaurant, 188
Latin Tours, 174–75
Laveau, Marie, 125–26, 132, 133
Law, John, 3, 82, 83
Lazzerini, Edward, 192
Leavitt, Mel, 12, 48
Lee, Chang Kyu, 208
Lee, Henry, 207
Lee, Sun, 209
Legacy, 155
Lega dei Presidente, 95
Leidenheimer, George H., Baking Co.,
     Ltd., 84–85
Leigier's, Judy, Sacred Dance
     Ministry, 152
Le Meridien Hotel, 43
Le Moyne, Jean Baptiste, 2–3, 63, 94
Le Moyne, Pierre, 2–3, 23, 33
Le'ob's Tours and Transportation
     Service, 136
Les Mysterieuses, 35
Levell, "Steady Eddie," 15
Levi, Sam, 165
Liberty Theater, 10
Liborio's Cuban Restaurant, 178
Limo services, 15–16
Lipschitz, 117
Little Greek Restaurant, 221
Little Shop of Fantasy, 36
Liuzza, Ray, 102
Livingston, Abbot, 193
Livingston, Robert, 5
Long, Nhi, 216
Longfellow, Henry W., 49
Longoria, Salvador, 166, 178
Los Latinos Super Market, 173

Louise Day Care Nursery, 71
Louisiana Cruises, 31
Louisiana Landmarks Society, 7
Louisiana Nature and Science Center, 209
Louisiana Office of Tourism, 7–8
Louisiana Philharmonic Orchestra, 41
Louisiana Pizza Kitchen, 110
Louisiana Purchase, 5
Louisiana State Museum, 11–12, 29, 38
Louisiana Weekly, 144
Louis XIV, 2
Louis XV, 3, 158–59
L'Ouverture, Toussaint, 124, 182
Lowy, Maxime, 164
Loyola University, 38
Lula Elzy Dance Company, 145
Lupo, Tommy, 103

M

Macarty, Augustin, 65
MacCarthey-MacTaigs, Barthelmy, 63
MacCarthey-MacTaigs, Jean Jacques, 63
Maestri, Robert, 101
Magic Tour, 28
Maid of Orleans, 24
Maison Bourbon, 43
Mama Rosa's Slice of Italy, 109
Mandeville, 50
Maple Leaf Club, 148
Marcus Garvey Day, 151
Mardi Gras, 2–3, 33–40
Mardi Gras Indian Coalition, 145
Marie's Sugar Dumplings, 144
Marsalis, Wynton, 129
Martin, Benny, 21
Martin, Clovis, 21
Martina, Joseph, 106
Mary, Queen of Vietnam Catholic
     Church, 215, 217
Maselli, Joseph, 105, 112
Masjid Abu Bakr Al-Siddque, 210
Masjid Al-Rahmah, 211
Masjid Al-Shurabaa, 210
Masjid Al-Taubah, 210
Masjid-Ur-Rahim, 211
Masjid Yaseen, 210
Masonic Temple, 168
Maxwell, Jimmy, 43
Maxwell's Toulouse Cabaret, 43

Mayan Stall, 172–73
McCarty, Marie Celeste Elenore de, 161
McDonogh, John, 128
McGuire, Frank, 117
McShane, Andrew, 73, 87
McTeggart, Peg, 75
McTeggart School of Irish Dancing, 75
Medina, Emilio, 174–75
Melvin's, 147
Mensaje, 171–72
Metoyer, Rene C., 132
Mexican Consulate, 184
Mexicans, 184
Meyer the Hatter, 93
Michaul's, 56–57
Mick's Irish Pub, 79
MIDDLE EASTERN NEW
    ORLEANS, 224
    restaurants, 223–24
    shopping, 224
Miller Light Italian Fishing Rodeo, 103
Mintz, Donald, 116
Miró, Don Esteban Rodriguez, 161
Mississippi Bubble, 3
Mississippi River, 2, 8
Molly's at the Market, 78
Molly's Irish Pub and Restaurant, 77–78
Moncada, Alma, 168
Monsanto, Isaac, 113–14
Moore, Henry, 117
Moran, Diamond Jim (Jimmy Brocato), 105
Morgan, Sam, 126
Morial, Ernest N., 129
Morial, Marc, 129
Morrison, Chep, 102
Morton, Jelly Roll, 42, 130
Mosquitoes, 45
Mostly Mardi Gras, 36
Moten, Richard, 43
Mother Cabrini, 97
Mother's Restaurant, 222
Mudbugs Restaurant, 21
Muddy Water's, 147
Mulate's, 57
Mullon, James, 67, 70
Murphy, Alfonso, 163
Murphy, Cecil, 192
Murphy, Kiku, 192
Músia Latina, 172

Music, 8, 40–44
    African-American, 146–48, 151–52
Mutual of Omaha Business Service
    Center, 17
Myra Mier Escuela de Ballet, 169

N
Napoleon House, 20
Natchez (steamboat), 31
National Association for the Advancement
    of Colored People, 137
National Association of Asian Pacific
    Education, 190
National park service, 25–28
Native Americans, 1–2, 3–4, 10
Naylor, Honey, 40
Neighborhood Gallery, 153–54
Neitto, Rene, 43
Neuman, Heinz, 88
Neutral grounds, 50
Neville Brothers, 40, 44
New Basin Canal, 17, 66
Newcomb College Center for Research on
    Women, 37
New Flynn's Den, 147
New Orleans, Battle of, 9
New Orleans Canal and Banking
    Company, 66
New Orleans French Quarter Visitors
    Center, 25
New Orleans Friends of Ireland, 74
New Orleans Friends of Music, 41
New Orleans Hilton Riverside, 44
New Orleans Hispanic Heritage
    Festival, 176
New Orleans International Airport
    (NOIA), 14–17
New Orleans Islamic Center, 210
New Orleans Jazz Club Collection, 130
New Orleans Jazz & Heritage
    Festival, 42, 127, 146
New Orleans Jazz & Heritage
    Foundation, 148–49
New Orleans Notarial Archives, 38
New Orleans Public Library, 39
New Orleans School of Cooking, 22, 54–55
New Orleans School of Irish Dance, 75
New Orleans tours, 23–25
New Orleans Track Club, 196

New Orleans Tribune, 144–45
New Orleans Unit, 10
New Orleans University (NOU), 138
New Orlenas Masjid of Al-Islam, 210
Newspapers. *See* Publications
New Zion Baptist Church, 133
Ngoc Lan Thoi Boa (New Orleans Magazine), 216
Nguoi Viet (Vietnamese People), 216
Nicaraguan Consulate, 186–87
Nicaraguans, 186–88
Night clubs, Hispanic/Caribbean New Orleans, 169
Ninja, 204
N'Kfau, 145
Noguchi, 117
No-Joe Imports, 111
Noone, Jimmy, 40, 42
NSA Buddhist Church, 193
Nutcracker Swing, 152

O
Oak Alley, 25
Oasis Nightclub, 151
Offbeat, 32
O'Flaherty's Irish Channel Pub, 75, 76–77, 80
Oikawa, Katsu, 203
O'Keefe, Arthur, 73
Old Calcutta, 202
Old Dog New Trick Cafe, 31
Olde N'Awlins Cookery, 58
Oliver, Jean Baptiste, 115
Oliver, Joseph King, 40, 42
Olivier's Famous Creole Restaurant, 143
Olympia Brass Band, 43
Olympic bike rentals & tours, 29–30
Omar's Pies, 144
Operation Smile International, 187
O'Reilly, Alexandro, 4, 64, 159–60
Ormero, Robert, 201
Orpheum Theater, 41, 152
Ory, Kid, 42
Our Lady of Lavang Mission, 217

P
Pakenham, Edward, 9, 64–65
Pakistan Community Association (PCA) of Greater New Orleans, 209–10
Pakistanis, 209–11

Palm Court Jazz Cafe, 43
Palmers Restaurant, 143
Pampys Tight Squeeze Restaurant and Bar, 148
Panda Riverview Chinese Restaurant, 198
Pappalardo, Albert, 103
Parasol's Bar, 70
Parker, Harry, 130
Park Service Library, 27
Pastore's Restaurant, 109–10
Pastrano, Willie, 103
Paternostro, Joseph, 106
Patout, Alex, Louisiana Restaurant, 59
Patout, Gigi, 22, 55
Patout's Cajun Cabin, 56
Patout's Cajun Festival, 56
Patti, Adelina, 96
Pauger, Adrien de, 157
Pelican Club Restaurant & Bar, 58–59
Pena, Allison, 9
Percussion, Inc., 127
Perilli, Achille, 96
Perrin, Jimmy LaCava, 103
Peters, Samuel J., 49–50
Philharmonic Society, 41
Philippe, duc d'Orleans, 3
Philippine Independence Day, 201
Phillips, Bill, 130
Pho Tau Bay Restaurant, 217
Phuong, Dong Restaurant, 216–17
Piazza d'Italia, 106
Pieri, Sandro, 106
Pine Alley plantation, 51
Pineda Supermarket, 173
Plaza Tower, 102
Police, 13–14
Pollack, Oliver, 5, 64
Pollock, Joseph, 141
Pontalba Buildings, 131–32
Pontchartrain Center, 41
Pontchartrain Park, 134, 162
Post Office, 44–45
Prairie Acadian Cultural Center, 10
Praline Connection, 141–42
Praslin, Marcehal du Plessis, 22
Presbyter, 158
Preservation Hall, 43, 146–47
Prima, Joyce, 101
Prima, Louis, 40, 101
Progressive Food Company, 100

Publications, 32–33
    African-American, 144–45
    Asian, 193
    Chinese, 199
    Hispanic, 170–72
    Irish, 80–81
    Italian, 111
    Jewish, 121
    Korean, 209
Pubs. *See* Restaurants
Pupusería Divino Corazón de Jesús, 180–81

Q
¿Qué Pasa New Orleans?, 170–71

R
Rajun Cajun Airboat Tours, 29
Ramelli Janitorial Service, 205
Randolph, Bernard E., 139
Recile, Sam, 102
Reggae, 151–52
Reggae Fest, 150–51
Restaurant Garces, 178–79
Restaurants
    African-American, 139–43
    Asian, 196–98
    Australian/New Zealand, 219–20
    Chinese, 196–98
    Cajun, 56–58
    Creole, 58–60
    German, 92–93
    Greek, 221–22
    Hispanic, 178–79, 180–81, 185–86, 188
    Irish, 76–79
    Italian, 107
    Korean, 206–7
    Middle Eastern, 223–24
Reynolds, John, 67
Rillieux, Norbert, 126
Rita's Old French Quarter Restaurant, 141
Riverboat Hallelujah Hall, 181
Riverboat tours, 30–31
Riverside Cafe, 143
Riverside Hilton, 191
Riverwalk, 103
Riverwalk Festival Market, 56
Roots Heritage City Tour, 137
Ross, Walter, 156
Rousan, Wanda, 129
Ryan's Pub, 77

S
Sagona, Bob, 106
St. Alphonsus Church, 72, 88
St. Anthony's Day, 223
St. Bartelmo Apostolo (Bartholomew)
    Society, 95
St. Bernard Market, 132
St. Charles Avenue District, 6
St. Charles Streetcar Line, 18
St. John the Baptist Church, 70, 71
St. Joseph's Church, 96
St. Joseph's Day, 100, 103–4, 107
St. Louis Cathedral, 11, 50, 114, 116, 132,
    158
St. Louis Cemetery, 24, 132–33
St. Mary's Assumption Church, 88
St. Mary's Catholic Church, 100
St. Matthew United Church of Christ, 88
St. Patrick's Cathedral, 67, 70, 71
St. Patrick's Cemetery, 66–67
St. Patrick's Church, 50, 65, 223
St. Thomas Housing Project, 88
Salaam, Kalamu ya, 146, 154
Sala della Unione Italiana, 95
Salvadoran Club of New Orleans, 180
Salvadoran Consulate, 179–80
San Jacinto Dance Theater, 145
San Lorenzo, Treaty of, 5
Santana, Andrea, 170
Santería, 175
Savary, Joseph, 124
Sazerac Restaurant, 92
Scams, 46–47
Scanlon, Henry, 74
Schiavo, Giovanni, 96
Schiro, Victor H., 102
Schlaraffia, 90–91
Schwegmann, John, 85
Schweikert, Ernesto, III, 165, 169–70, 174
Seaplane tours, 31
Second Korean Presbyterian Church, 207
Semolina, 108
Seoul Restaurant & Club, 207
Serendipitous Masks, 36
Shaie Mei Temple, 199
Shakspeare, Joseph A., 86, 99
Shameem Choudhury, 191–92
Sheik, Kid, 43
Shepherd, Raizin, 115
Shih, Li Schon, 212

Ship Island, 2
Shogun Japanese Restaurant and Steak
    House, 204
Shopping
    African-American, 138
    Asian, 193–94
    Chinese, 198–99
    Hispanic, 172–74
    Irish, 75–76
    Jewish, 121–22
    Korean, 208
    Middle Eastern, 224
    tax-free, 45
Siegal, George, 117
Silver Palace, 164
Sisters of the Holy Family, 134
Slidell Masjid of Al-Islam, 211
Snug Harbor, 44
Social services, 13
Societa Italiana di Mutua Benefiza, 95
Socola, Angelo, 96
Somewhere Off Broadway, 155
Soong, Tina, 192, 193
Sounds of New Orleans, 43
Southern Region Bocce Tournament, 106
Southern Seaplane, 31
Southern University at New
    Orleans, 39, 139
Southwest Celtic Music Association, 81
Spanish Fort, 162
Spiritualists, Hispanic/Caribbean New
    Orleans, 175
Standard Fruit Company, 100
Star's, 148
Stillet, Jorge, 84
Story, Sydney, 129–30
Storyville, 129–30
Streetcars, 17–18
Street names, 19–20
Style, 144
Sullivan, John L., 68
Superdome, 7, 130
Super Luis, 170
Swaim, Mary Ann McGrath, 75
Synagogues and prayer facilities, 118–19

T
Taiwanese, 212–13
Taj Mahal Ethnic Eats, 202

Taj Mahal Indian Cuisine, 202
Tandoor Indian Cuisine, 202
Tax-free shopping, 45
Taxis, 15, 31
Tchoutchouma, 3
Telephones, 45
Temple Sinai Reform Congregation, 116,
    119
Thais, 211–12
Thanh, Le Hong, 216
Theater, African-American New
    Orleans, 154–56
Theater of the Performing Arts, 41
Theatre de la Rue St. Philippe, 41
Theatre d'Orleans, 41
Thomas, Richard, Gallery, 153
Thompson, Lydia, 34
Tidy Co., 205
Tikvat Shalom Congregation, 119
Times Picayune, 32, 172, 193
Tipitina's, 44, 151
Torres, Bella, 174
Tortilla el Sol, 173–74
Touceda, Julián, 167
Tour companies
    African-American, 136–37
    Hispanic, 174–75
Tourism, African-American, 134
Touro, Judah, 115, 120
Touro Congregation, 115, 117
Touro Infirmary, 39, 120
Tours, 23–31
Tours by Inex, 28
Transportation, 14
Treigle, Norman, 40
Treme Brass Band, 42
Treme Community Street Festival, 149
Treme Market, 132
Treme Music Hall, 147
Tricou House, 44
Trombone Shorty's, 148
Tropical Christmas, 177
True Brew Cafe, 43
Tujague Restaurant, 116
Tulane University, 37
Tunica-Biloxi Museum, 4, 11
Tureaud, A. P., 131
Tuxedo Brass Brand, 42
Two Sisters Kitchen, 140

U

Uddo, Guiseppe, 100
Union Station, 17
Union Supermarket, 173
United Dominican Club, 179
United Slovian Benevolent
    Association, 223
United States Mint, 130
United Supermarket, 173
University of New Orleans (UNO), 39
Unofficial Haitian Consulate, 181–83
Unzaga y Amezaga, Don Luis de, 160
Uptown Historic District, 12
Uptown Street fest, 149
Urban League of New Orleans, 137
Urhuru Dancers of St. Francis de Sales
    Choir, 152
Ursuline Convent, 158

V

Vahrenhorst, Hubert, Jr., 88
Vahrenhorst, Hubert, Sr., 88–89
Valenziano, Rose Serio, 106
Valenziano, Salvatore, 106
Valenziano, Zena, 105
Vázquez Supermarket, 173
Versailles Restaurant, 92
Vic's Kangaroo Cafe, 219
Vietnamese, 213–18
Vietnamese Baptist Mission, 217
Vietnamese Restaurant, 216
Vieux Carre Commission, 7
Vieux Carre Property Owners
    Association, 7
Villere, Joseph, 160
Vincent's Italian Cuisine, 110–11
Visual arts, African-American New
    Orleans, 153–54
Volksport, 91

Von Bargen, Karlheinzen, 91
Voodoo Museum, 125

W

WADU-AM, 170
Walking tours, 25–29
Walsh, Isabel, 200
Walsh, Patricio, 64
War of 1812, 5, 9
Weather, 45
This Week in New Orleans, 32
Werlein, Philip, 85
Wetland Acadian Cultural Center, 10
WGLA-AM, 169–70
Where Magazine, 32–33
*Where There's a Will/The Living
    Christmas Tree,* 152
Whisper's, 148, 152
White, Lulu, 130
White, Maunsell, 66
Whitney National Bank, 16
Widmer, Mary Lou, 84
Winnaha's Circle, 148
Woldenberg Village, 117, 120
World Trade Center (WTC), 23–24
WWL-TV, 156
WYLD-FM, 156

X

Xavier University, 39, 138–39

Y

Yolanda, Súarey, 172

Z

Zachary's, 140
Zen Buddhist, 193
Zissis Restaurant, 221–22

Notes

Notes

Notes

Notes

Notes

Notes

TRAVEL AND CULTURE BOOKS

"World at Its Best" Travel Series
Britain, France, Germany, Hawaii,
Holland, Hong Kong, Italy, Spain,
Switzerland, London, New York, Paris,
Washington, D.C., San Francisco

Passport's Travel Guides and References
IHT Guides to Business Travel in Asia &
Europe
Only in New York
Mystery Reader's Walking Guides:
London, England, New York, Chicago
Chicago's Best-Kept Secrets
London's Best-Kept Secrets
New York's Best-Kept Secrets
The Japan Encyclopedia
Japan Today!
Japan at Night
Japan Made Easy
Discovering Cultural Japan
Living in Mexico
The Hispanic Way
Guide to Ethnic Chicago
Guide to Ethnic London
Guide to Ethnic New York
Guide to Ethnic Montreal
Passport's Trip Planner & Travel Diary
Chinese Etiquette and Ethics in Business
Korean Etiquette and Ethics in Business
Japanese Etiquette and Ethics in Business
How to Do Business with the Japanese
Japanese Cultural Encounters
The Japanese

Passport's Regional Guides of France
Auvergne, Provence, Loire Valley,
Dordogne & Lot, Languedoc, Brittany, South
West France, Normandy & North West
France, Paris, Rhône Valley & Savoy,
France for the Gourmet Traveler

Passport's Regional Guides of Indonesia
New Guinea, Java, Borneo, Bali, East of
Bali, Sumatra, Spice Islands,
Sulawesi, Exploring the Islands of
Indonesia

Up-Close Guides
Paris, London, Manhattan, Amsterdam,
Rome

Passport's "Ticket To..." Series
Italy, Germany, France, Spain

**Passport's Guides: Asia, Africa, Latin
America, Europe, Middle East**
Japan, Korea, Malaysia, Singapore, Bali,
Burma, Australia, New Zealand, Egypt,
Kenya, Philippines, Portugal, Moscow,
St. Petersburg, The Georgian Republic,
Mexico, Vietnam, Iran, Berlin, Turkey

Passport's China Guides
All China, Beijing, Fujian, Guilin,
Hangzhou & Zhejiang, Hong Kong,
Macau, Nanjing & Jiangsu, Shanghai,
The Silk Road, Taiwan, Tibet, Xi'an,
The Yangzi River, Yunnan

Passport's India Guides
All India; Bombay & Goa; Dehli, Agra
& Jaipur; Burma; Pakistan;
Kathmandu Valley; Bhutan; Museums
of India; Hill Stations of India

Passport's Thai Guides
Bangkok, Phuket, Chiang Mai, Koh Sumi

On Your Own Series
Brazil, Israel

"Everything Under the Sun" Series
Spain, Barcelona, Toledo, Seville,
Marbella, Cordoba, Granada, Madrid,
Salamanca, Palma de Majorca

Passport's Travel Paks
Britain, France, Italy, Germany, Spain

Exploring Rural Europe Series
England & Wales, France, Greece,
Ireland, Italy, Spain, Austria,
Germany, Scotland, Ireland by Bicycle

Regional Guides of Italy
Florence & Tuscany, Naples & Campania,
Umbria, the Marches & San Marino

Passport Maps
Europe, Britain, France, Italy, Holland,
Belgium & Luxembourg, Scandinavia,
Spain & Portugal, Switzerland, Austria
& the Alps

Passport's Trip Planners & Guides
California, France, Greece, Italy

PASSPORT BOOKS
a division of NTC *Publishing Group*
Lincolnwood, Illinois USA